THE
SINNER'S GUIDE

By
Venerable Louis of Granada, O.P.

Translated by
a Dominican Father

"If you walk in my precepts, and keep my commandments, and do them, I will give you rain in due seasons. And the ground shall bring forth its increase, and the trees shall be filled with fruit: . . . And you shall eat your bread to the full, and dwell in your land without fear. I will give peace in your coasts: you shall sleep, and there shall be none to make you afraid. . . . I will set my tabernacle in the midst of you, and my soul shall not cast you off. I will walk among you, and will be your God, and you shall be my people."

—Leviticus 26:3-6, 11-12

TAN BOOKS AND PUBLISHERS, INC.
Rockford, Illinois 61105

Vidimus et Approbabimus: Fr. C. H. McKenna, O.P.
                            Fr. J. L. O'Neil, O.P.
                            Revisores Deputati
                            New York
                            November 15, 1883

Imprimi Potest: Fr. M. D. Lilly, O.P.
                            Prior Provincial
                            Province of St. Joseph
                            November 15, 1883

Imprimatur: ✝ John J. Williams, D.D.
                            Archbishop of Boston
                            By his Vicar General
                            November 22, 1883

Library of Congress Catalog Card No.: 84-51820

ISBN: 0-89555-254-X

Reset by TAN Books and Publishers, Inc. Typography is the property of TAN Books and Publishers, Inc., and may not be reproduced, in whole or in part, without written permission of the publisher.

The publisher gratefully acknowledges the kind permission of The Confraternity of the Precious Blood to reproduce the picture which appears on the cover.

Printed and bound in the United States of America.

TAN BOOKS AND PUBLISHERS, INC.
P.O. Box 424
Rockford, Illinois 61105

1985

"Be assured, ye who seek that true peace promised to a future life, that you may here enjoy it by anticipation, if you will but love and keep the commandments of Him who promises this reward; for you will soon find by experience that the fruits of justice are sweeter than those of iniquity. You will learn that the joys of virtue, even in the midst of trials and misfortunes, far exceed all the delights of pleasure and prosperity accompanied by the remorse of a bad conscience."

—*St. Augustine, quoted in*
The Sinner's Guide, p.130

Venerable Louis of Granada, O.P.
1504-1588
The Writer of the Spanish Empire

BRIEF OF OUR HOLY FATHER GREGORY XIII

*To our well-beloved Son, Louis of Granada,
of the Order of Friars Preachers*

GREGORY PP. XIII

Dearly Beloved Son, Health and Apostolic Benediction:

Your arduous and incessant labors, both for the conversion of sinners and for the guidance of souls to perfection, together with the valuable assistance you render those who are earnestly engaged in the work of the ministry, have always afforded us great consolation.

Your sermons and writings, filled with sublime doctrine and practical piety, are unceasingly drawing souls to God. This is particularly gratifying to us, for all who have profited by your teaching (and their number is very great) may be considered as so many souls gained to Christ. You have thus benefited your fellow creatures more than if you had given sight to the blind and raised the dead to life. For the knowledge of the Eternal Light and the enjoyment of the heavenly life, according as they are given to man on earth to know and enjoy, are far above the knowledge and enjoyment of the transitory goods of this world.

The charity with which you have devoted yourself to your great and important labor has gained for you many crowns.

Continue, then, to devote all your energies to the prosecution of your undertakings. Finish what you have

begun, for we understand that you have some works yet incomplete. Give them to the world for the health of the sick,
for the strength of the weak, for the delight of God's servants, and for the glory of the Church both militant and
triumphant.

> Given at Rome the 21st of July, 1582,
> in the eleventh year of our pontificate.

ANT. BUCCIPALULE

CONTENTS

CHAPTER 32

CHAPTER 33

CHAPTER 34

CHAPTER 35

CHAPTER 36

CHAPTER 37

CHAPTER 38

CHAPTER 39

CHAPTER 40

ABOUT THE AUTHOR

Venerable Louis of Granada
His Life and Work

The life of Venerable Louis of Granada (1504-1588) paralleled to a remarkable degree the greatest era of the Spanish Empire—that empire known as "the evangelizer of half the world, the hammer of heretics, and the light of the Council of Trent." Louis himself is known as "the writer of the Spanish empire." He was born only shortly after the famous year 1492, when Spain had, under King Ferdinand and Queen Isabella, defeated the Moors after eight centuries of Moorish occupation and oppression in Spain and financed Christopher Columbus' momentous voyage to America. These were the times of Spain's intense exploration and missionary activity in the New World, of the Council of Trent (1548-1563), and of the great Christian victory over the Turks at Lepanto (1571).

The end of this glorious era is marked by the great defeat in 1588 of the "invincible" Spanish Armada off the coast of England, an event which signalled the beginning of the end of Spain's brief but glorious reign as a world power. This was also the very year of Louis' death. But during the early and mid-16th century, Catholic Spain gave to the world many priceless gifts; not least of these were the books of her renowned son, Ven. Louis of Granada.

In the aftermath of the surrender of the Moors in 1492,

Ferdinand and Isabella were faced with the task of making Granada a Spanish city once again. In order to hasten the influx of Spanish influence into the city and the blending of the Moorish and the Spanish people, Ferdinand and Isabella granted free entrance to the city of Granada to any Spaniard from the provinces who wished to settle there. One young couple who took advantage of this opportunity was Francis Sarriá and his wife (whose name has been lost to history), a couple who in 1504 became the parents of a son named Louis, later to become famous as "Louis of Granada." Unfortunately, Francis died in 1509, and Louis and his mother were reduced to poverty, being supported by alms from the Dominican Monastery.

After a few years of destitution, there occurred an event whereby Louis de Sarriá's fortunes changed suddenly and dramatically. While engaged in a street fight with a boy who had insulted his mother, Louis was discovered by the Count de Tendilla, Mayor of the Alhambra, who was impressed with his courage. The Count took Louis under his patronage. Thereafter Louis spent many hours on the balconies of the Alhambra; thus, in addition to his other education, his soul was fed by the magnificent beauty of the surrounding countryside, fueling that deep love for the beauty of nature which was to be a hallmark of his thought and writing for the rest of his life.

When Louis de Sarriá reached young manhood, he turned his path toward the religious life. At the same Dominican Monastery where he had begged alms as an orphaned child, the Convent of the Holy Cross, he received the habit of a Friar Preacher on June 15, 1524, to the joyful tears of his beloved mother. A year later he made his religious profession.

At the Convent of the Holy Cross, Friar Louis, or *Fray* Louis, as he was called, undertook the rigorous Dominican *ratio studiorum:* a review of Latin and then three years of Philosophy and three years of Theology. The texts used were the grammar of Nebrija, the *Summae* of Peter the Spaniard, and the works of Aristotle and St. Thomas Aquinas. Louis de Sarriá was brilliant in scholastic disputations; he had no equal in mental capacity, application to study, and exact observance of the monastic life.

After some time, he was awarded a scholarship to the celebrated College of St. Gregory in Valladolid. Arriving there in 1529, he spent the designated eight days in preparation for taking the oath to uphold the statutes of the College; thus Louis de Sarriá became formally invested in the College of St. Gregory, taking on both the honors and the obligations thereof. In the mind of the young friar, his first duty was worthily to represent Holy Cross Convent of Granada. Grateful for the confidence placed in him by his fellow religious of Holy Cross, he changed his name from Fray Louis de Sarriá to Fray Louis of Granada. With such great seriousness did the Spanish ecclesiastical student of the 16th century hold his exalted position as a knight of Thomistic truth.

The students of St. Gregory studied logic, natural philosophy, moral philosophy, theology, exegesis, and cases of conscience. Latin only was spoken, except on vacation days, when Spanish was allowed.

The first fruit of Louis' pen to appear in print was a book he did not himself write; rather, he edited one written by the Regent of Studies, Astudillo, though he himself wrote and added to the book two encomiums of Astudillo. These small works by Louis portray their author as a man enamored of philosophy, and as an authentic man of the Renaissance.

But there was more than learning in Louis' heart and soul. By prayer and penance, as well as study, he was preparing for a future apostolate of preaching.

In the year 1534, at the age of 30, because of his ardent longings for the apostolate, Louis stepped forward and generously offered himself as a missionary to Mexico. Although he had not yet completed his eight-year course of studies, he was willing to abandon the lecture halls. He was all prepared to leave for the Americas; but when his departure was imminent, Fray Louis' superior commanded him to cancel his trip and let another go in his place.

This was a tremendous disappointment for Fray Louis. In fact, although he obediently accepted the sacrifice, the longing for the mission field remained a thorn in his soul all his life. This event ushered in a deepening in the soul of Louis of Granada. More and more he realized that prayer, rather than study, is the way to true spiritual knowledge of Christ. He saw more clearly that his goal should be to live the life of Christ within his own soul, and then to preach Christ to others. He even began to have a distaste for study. In this regard, the writings of the famous Master John of Avila also had a great influence in the changing of Fray Louis' attitude. At this time there also awakened in him his vocation as a spiritual writer. He desired that the riches of the spiritual treasure should be imparted to and shared by all, and the means by which he intended to diffuse them were preaching and writing.

In 1539, at the age of 35, he wrote a small tract on the method of prayer for a student at St. Gregory in Valladolid who had written to him for advice. The tone of this work is entirely different from the Renaissance humanist flavor of his prologue to the work of Astudillo; this little tract is spirituality pure and simple. It is the first lecture of Fray Louis from the chair of Spanish spirituality. This same tract was later to be transformed into a work that would make Fray Louis' name immortal: *The Book of Prayer and Meditation.*

In 1544 the Dominican Order gave Louis the title of

Preacher General. In 1546, he was granted the privilege of going anywhere in Spain to preach, in the company of a companion of his choosing, and no superior could prevent his preaching. During this period, Fray Louis spent much of his time travelling and preaching. He was in demand everywhere as a preacher and spiritual director—even among the royalty. He became widely known as a holy friar, a preacher, and a man of great administrative ability.

About the year 1552, Queen Catherine of Portugal, the sister of Charles V, selected him as her confessor and advisor. Practically the rest of his life was spent in Portugal, with occasional visits to Spain. Because of his great knowledge and his practical talents, Fray Louis was frequently called upon to help settle problems arising among the royalty—important problems upon which might hang the welfare of entire nations. But all such dealings with worldly affairs were painful to him, and appear to have constituted the greatest cross of his later life.

In addition, in 1556 he was elected Provincial of the Dominican Province of Portugal. A year later he turned down Queen Catherine's offer of the archbishopric of Braga, which would have made him Primate of Portugal. In the midst of such preoccupations, Fray Louis never forgot his apostolate of spiritual writing.

In 1554 *The Book of Prayer and Meditation* was published. Its success was a complete surprise, especially to Fray Louis, but it confirmed him in his vocation of spiritual writer. From that time forward he dedicated himself with a divine impatience to writing on spiritual themes for all.

Louis himself, because of his ascetical practices and the constant work of the pen and pulpit, came to appear older than his years. His cell was poor and his possessions few: a wooden bed, a crude table, a few books, reams of colored paper (so that the eyes would not tire as he wrote), and a collection of various penitential instruments. Fray Louis could have lived in the palace, but since childhood he was espoused of poverty and he disdained the delights and comforts of the world. He received many alms and he earned much money from his books, but all went to the convent or to the poor. He dressed in such poverty that he wore the same hat for forty years and his black cappa was worn and patched with twelve years of use. Although he was a frequent visitor in the royal palace, he paid no attention to the courtly atmosphere; his spirit rose above all the things that fascinate the worldly ones: gold, coaches, love, silk, and power. To subdue the rebellious flesh, he wore a penitential belt. He excelled in meekness, native and acquired humility, an exquisite distinction in his bearing, and good counsel for all who needed it.

Such is Granada's moral portrait. The physical portrait is given to us by one of his oldest biographers: "He was of large and majestic stature, with a well-distributed weight. He had a face of angelic affability and his flesh was delicate and of good color. His eyes were happy but modest; his forehead, wide and serene; his teeth, white and in good order; his nose, stately and aquiline and somewhat large; his mouth, of good proportion; his head, large and somewhat bald. Most cordial in conversation, he was a friend to all, although no one became too friendly with him. He had an indescribable gravity in his appearance, as if he were always absorbed in spiritual contemplation."

This affable and simple religious, entirely given to the things of God, was very active and even dynamic. He rose at four in the morning and spent two hours in prayer. At six o'clock he celebrated Mass with remarkable solemnity and devotion. In those days priests were not accustomed to celebrate Mass every day, but Fray Louis never omitted it, and stated that the best preparation for the celebration of

Mass was to celebrate daily. After Mass he devoted himself to a lengthy thanksgiving and then returned to his cell to begin the labors of the day.

The 16th century was a most turbulent time in the history of the Church, a time whose terrible legacy of heresy and apostasy is still with us today. (It was also a century of many, many great saints.) There was a crying need for true Catholic reform, but many heretics had arisen to feed the faithful with stones and scorpions instead of bread. An un-Christian humanism was spreading its contagion of rebellion against God; and in 1517, when Fray Louis was 12 years old, Martin Luther took the step that was to launch the tragic heresy of external justification, a doctrine which smothered the true supernatural life of the soul and thus led to the most man-centered form of humanism. Another error which was spreading at the time was a false form of spirituality which claimed that religion should be something completely interior. A fourth error was Quietism, which discounted the effort required for the Christian soul to grow in grace and virtue. A goodly number of spiritual writers of the time fell into one or another of these traps.

Louis of Granada, on the other hand, was a voice of true orthodox Catholic reform. Although, in the confusion, he was for a time accused of heresy, this false charge was disposed of at Trent and Rome. Louis presented life in Christ as the life proper to all Christians, and he showed the essential role which the virtues play in the growth of this life. He showed how grace is essential to life in Christ, and how the Christian must receive the Sacraments and pray in order to obtain the necessary grace of God. Thus, by reading Fray Louis' true picture of the Christian life, the 16th century Catholic—as well as the Catholic of today—is protected against many errors and given true and powerful spiritual food. His soul is protected against the error of man-centered humanism, against the error of external justification without an inner transformation into holiness in the soul, the error of religion as being something entirely interior and independent of laws and ceremonies, and the error that the Christian need not expend effort in order to live and grow in the life of grace. Fray Louis answers all these errors (which persist in one way or another yet today), even when he does not attack heresies as such; he preaches the true Christian doctrine with such clarity and beauty that the soul is attracted and enlightened and moved to embrace it. His talents and vocation as a spiritual writer were a gift of Divine Providence to the 16th century; they are likewise providential for the Catholics of today. St. Teresa of Avila, Louis' contemporary, called him "a man given to the world by God for the great and universal good of souls." St. Charles Borromeo, another contemporary, wrote: "Of all those who up to our time have written on spiritual matters ... it can be stated that no one has written books either in greater number or of greater selection and profit than Fray Louis of Granada ... In fact I do not know if in matters of this type there is today a man more beneficial to the Church than he is."

The teaching in Fray Louis' books is firmly orthodox, completely Catholic. These works are based on the Scriptures, the Fathers and Doctors of the Church, and on the principles of St. Thomas Aquinas; they also include many elements from the best of classical literature. Nevertheless, Fray Louis' writings are neither dry nor difficult; they breathe fire and life, touching the heart of the reader and motivating him to seek God's will as the only source of true happiness. Fray Louis was an astute observer of human nature, and his books are as notable for their solid common sense as for their sterling orthodoxy.

Louis of Granada also overcame the tendencies to separate asceticism and mysticism, which were started in his day. Both aspects of the mystical life were evaluated by him and he coordinated them in such a way that both the ascetics and the mystics can look to him as a master. Undoubtedly, he gives greater emphasis to ascetical matters, for the simple reason that he directs his words in a special way to the great number of simple faithful who need above all to become enamored of virtue and holiness of life so that they will eradicate evil inclinations and rise steadily to a higher life. Granada attempted to lead souls to the threshold of contemplation and the mystical life, and because he himself lived that life intensely, his soul frequently soared to the regions of intimate communion with God and at times seems to move entirely on the planes of the mystical life.

Yet Louis' writing on all subjects is so clear that he was accused of "writing for the wives of carpenters," and his zeal so apostolic that he was criticized for wanting "to make all Christians perfect." He quoted Scripture so often that he seems to have known it by heart. Louis of Granada is truly a "theologian of the people," who wrote for the simple and unlettered. Yet so sublime is his writing that he was read by princes and kings, saints and literary figures, pontiffs and ordinary laity, Protestants and pagans. No one knew as well as he did how to combine loftiness of doctrine with a clarity and transparency of style that is within the grasp of all.

In his 35 years of writing, Fray Louis produced 49 works. These can be classified into five categories: spiritual theology, apologetics, hagiography, sacred oratory, and translations. Four of his books are masterpieces of spiritual theology. These are *The Book of Prayer and Meditation,* a book that laments the miseries of life and manifests spiritual contempt for the world—this is the one of his books that Louis loved best, and one that has served as a manual of prayer for countless souls; *The Sinner's Guide* (first published in 1556), a masterwork of Aristotelian symmetry and the most scholastic work of Fray Louis, a book which covers from myriad angles the virtues of the Christian life, proving that this life is the only way to true happiness (even on earth); *Memorial of the Christian Life,* a book of a Platonic flavor, which reminds the Christian of his obligations and embodies such exquisite doctrine on love that St. Francis de Sales remarks that it is all that could be said or that one could wish to say; and *Introduction to the Creed,* a gigantic work written in Louis' old age, but which breathes the spirit of youth. This work shows Louis' preoccupation with the conversion of the Jews and Mohammedans; he knew the Oriental mind very well, and in this book he shows, among many other things, that only the Christian religion can give God due worship. This is undoubtedly his most admirable book, and modern critics never cease to be amazed at the genius that produced it.

Louis' books have been translated into 25 different languages, including Syrian, Arabic, and Japanese, in addition to the European languages (which often saw hundreds of editions in a single language). There have been some 6 thousand editions of Fray Louis' works. In fact, it is known from tales brought back by missionaries that the Japanese version of *The Sinner's Guide* was one of the bullwarks that sustained the faith of the Japanese Catholics during two centuries of terrible persecution, when both in Europe and Japan, Japanese Christianity was believed dead. In 1865, when missionaries were again allowed into Japan, missionary Father Bernard Petitjean was astonished to find in the hills around Nagasaki thousands of Japanese Catholics who had kept the Faith, hidden but vital, without priests, for over 200 years! Immense was the joy of these faithful ones at once again having a

Catholic priest among them. *The Sinner's Guide* had played a providential role in sustaining the Faith in their souls during that trying time.

The works of Fray Louis were included in the precious cargo brought to the New World by the Spanish missionaries; these missionaries even translated some of Granada's works into the native Indian languages. St. Rose of Lima, too, loved the books of Fray Louis; she had them always at hand. Her favorite was *The Book of Prayer and Meditation*. In one of her struggles with the devil, she protected herself by reading this book; the devil became furious, snatched the book from her, and threw it onto a rubbish heap. Rose remain unmoved, certain that the Lord would return it to her—as indeed He did.

Other famous Catholics who have read and loved the works of Venerable Louis include St. Vincent de Paul, St. Louise de Marillac, St. Francis de Sales, Cardinal Berulle and Bossuet (all French); St. Charles Borromeo (Italian), Louis of Leon (Spanish), and the Jesuit and Barnabite Orders. St. Teresa read Louis' books and commanded her nuns to do the same. She credited *The Sinner's Guide* with having converted over a million souls. In some religious rules and constitutions the works of Louis were mentioned as almost obligatory spiritual reading for the novices. There was no bishop in Spain in the 17th and 18th centuries who did not eulogize, recommend, and even grant indulgences for the reading of the works of Fray Louis. Regarding *The Book of Prayer and Meditation,* St. Peter of Alcantara wrote: "It is the best book that I have read in our language because it best expounds the practice and exercise of prayer. It contains good meditations and helpful counsels for beginners, the advanced, and the perfect." This book is also renowned for its literary beauty, so that Azorín could say of it that "the Spanish language has never reached such fierceness or such angelic suavity" as it does in this work. And it must be added that Fray Louis' books were read in England, as literature, long before the works of Cervantes were discovered there.

St. Francis de Sales urged a Bishop-elect of his acquaintance to read the works of Louis of Granada, and to treat them as a second breviary. He advised this man to read them *slowly,* beginning with *The Sinner's Guide,* then continuing with the *Memorial of the Christian Life,* then on to all the rest.

Granada's vast classical and ecclesiastical culture, his absorbing spirit, and the perfection of his literary style place him among the creators of Christian Spanish humanism. With good reason has he merited the title of "the Spanish Cicero." And the Spanish biographer, Nicholás Antonio, gave to Fray Louis this well-earned tribute: "Our nation has never had a greater or more useful man, and perhaps it will never again have one to equal Louis of Granada."

Yes, in his native Spain Fray Louis' influence was immense. He ushered in the golden age of spiritual literature in Spain, an age which was to become most famous for the magnificent works of St. Teresa of Avila and St. John of the Cross. Fray Louis was in some ways the creator, and in every sense the exponent, of Spanish devotion and piety; his is an extraordinary instance of one man's influence, and he contributed immeasurably to the Christian and theological formation of the Spanish people.

Even heretics and atheists were readers and admirers of Fray Louis. Most notable is the case of Marchena—an atheist, revolutionary, liberal, and the sworn enemy of all spiritual writings. This man carried *The Sinner's Guide* around with him for 20 years, and not a day passed but that he read part of it. To an amazed man who discovered him reading this book, tattered and worn in testimony of its constant use, Marchena exclaimed: "This book has a power over me that I cannot explain. I cannot read it nor can I stop reading it. I cannot read it because it convinces my understanding and moves my will in such a way that while I am reading it, I feel as much a Christian as you or any nun or as the missionaries who go to die for the Catholic faith in China or Japan. I cannot stop reading it because I know of no book more wonderful in our language."

Such is the power of Venerable Louis of Granada's writings. His books, filled with quotations from the Scriptures, and magnificently coordinated with Thomistic order, are yet written for all. Of their kind, nothing superior has been written since their author first gave them to the world four centuries ago. They speak to the heart, they convince, they persuade, they motivate. Anyone who becomes steeped in even one of Louis' masterpieces will thereby acquire a profound Catholic outlook on life and a powerful motivation to live that life. He will know clearly what he must do to gain eternity, the goal of every true Christian.

*   *   *   *   *

In Advent of 1588, when he was nearly 84 years old, Louis' health was unusually poor. Nevertheless he prayed more, fasted more, and took his discipline. In December he began to have attacks of nausea and vomiting which left him extremely weakened. By December 30 all hope for his recovery was abandoned. On December 31, 1588, in the bare and humble cell at Santo Domingo where monarchs of the world had visited him, it was obvious that Fray Louis' lamp of life was almost extinguished. With tears of joy he received the Last Sacraments. The novices knelt at the door to his cell for a last farewell. Fray Louis sensed the approach of death, and asked that they place him in his coffin. Then, at nine in the evening, he breathed his last and exchanged the counting of years for eternity.

His death was considered one of the greatest losses to Christianity. Lisbon became a city of mourning. Streams of people came to see him who in death seemed to be yet alive. It was only with difficulty that the funeral could be carried out, as people surged to the coffin to touch his clothing, to kiss his hands, and to touch his body with religious articles. As the body was carried out for burial, people tried to cut off pieces of his habit.

The General Chapter held in Rome in 1589 communicated to the entire Dominican Order the news of the death of Fray Louis of Granada, and the following terse comment serves well as his epitaph: *Vir doctrina et sanctitate insignis et in toto orbe celebris*—"A man signed with doctrine and sanctity, and celebrated throughout the entire world." Such was the earthly journey of Fray Louis of Granada, a journey filled with triumphs and crosses. He was truly, in the words of St. Teresa of Avila, "a man given to the world by God for the great and universal good of souls."

(This introduction to the life and work of Ven. Louis of Granada was taken largely from the work of Father Alvaro Huerga, O.P., Regent of Studies, Convent of the Holy Cross, Granada, Spain—with grateful acknowledgement.)

CHAPTER 1

The First Motive which obliges us to practice Virtue and to serve God: His Being in itself, and the excellence of His Perfections

Two things, Christian reader, particularly excite the will of man to good. A principle of justice is one, the other the profit we may derive therefrom. All wise men, therefore, agree that justice and profit are the two most powerful inducements to move our wills to any undertaking. Now, though men seek profit more frequently than justice, yet justice is in itself more powerful; for, as Aristotle teaches, no wordly advantage can equal the excellence of virtue, nor is any loss so great that a wise man should not suffer it rather than yield to vice. The design of this book being to win men to virtue, we shall begin by showing our obligation to practice virtue because of the duty we owe to God. God being essentially goodness and beauty, there is nothing more pleasing to Him than virtue, nothing He more earnestly requires. Let us first seriously consider upon what grounds God demands this tribute from us.

But as these are innumerable, we shall only treat of the six principal motives which claim for God all that man is or all that man can do. The first, the greatest, and the most inexplicable is the very essence of God, embracing His infinite majesty, goodness, mercy, justice, wisdom, omnipotence, excellence, beauty, fidelity, immutability, sweetness, truth, beatitude, and all the inexhaustible riches and perfec-

1

tions which are contained in the Divine Being.

All these are so great that if the whole world, according to St. Augustine, were full of books, if the sea were turned to ink, and every creature employed in writing, the books would be filled, the sea would be drained, and the writers would be exhausted before any one of His perfections could be adequately expressed. The same Doctor adds, "Were any man created with a heart as large and capacious as the hearts of all men together, and if he were enabled by an extraordinary light to apprehend one of the divine attributes, his joy and delight would be such that, unless supported by special assistance from God, he could not endure them."

This, then, is the first and chief reason which obliges us to love and serve God. It is a truth so universally acknowledged that even the Epicureans, who endeavored to destroy all philosophy by denying a Divine Providence and the immortality of the soul, nevertheless maintained religion, or the worship due to God.

One of these philosophers (Cicero, *De Natura Deorum*) proves the existence of God by strong and undeniable arguments. He proclaims the greatness and sovereignty of His admirable perfections, which oblige us to reverence and adore Him, and shows that for this reason alone, independently of any other title, God has a right to our love and service.

If we treat a king, even out of his own dominion, with respect and honor purely because of the dignity of his person, though we owe him nothing, with how much more justice should we render honor and service to this King and Lord, who, as St. John tells us, bears written "on his garment, and on his thigh: KING OF KINGS AND LORD OF LORDS"! (*Apoc.* 19:16). This is He who hath "poised with three fingers the bulk of the earth." (*Is.* 40:12).

All beings are in His power; He disposes of them as He wills. It is He who propels the heavenly bodies, commands the winds, changes the seasons, guides the elements, distributes the waters, controls the stars, creates all things; it is He, in fine, who, as King and Lord of the universe, maintains and nourishes all creatures.

Nor is His kingdom acquired or inherited. By His very nature it is for Him an inherent right. Just as man is above the ant, for example, so is the Divine Substance in an eminent degree above all created things, and the whole universe is no more than one of these little insects compared to Him. If this truth were so manifest to the Epicureans, otherwise unworthy of the name of philosophers, how much clearer ought it not be to us, who have been illumined by the light of true Christian philosophy! For this latter teaches us, in fact, that among the innumerable reasons which oblige us to serve God, this is the greatest; and though men were endowed with a thousand hearts and a thousand bodies, this reason alone should be sufficient to cause them to devote them all to His love and service.

Though of all motives this is the most powerful, yet it has the least influence on the imperfect. The reason for this is that, on the one hand, they are more moved by self-interest, self-love having deep root in their hearts; and on the other, being still ignorant, and novices in the ways of God, they are unable to appreciate His grandeur and beauty. Had they a better knowledge of His perfections, His beauty would enrapture their souls and cause them to love Him above all things. Therefore we shall furnish some considerations from the mystical theology of St. Denis which will help them to apprehend the perfections of the Master they serve.

To lead us to a knowledge of God, St. Denis teaches us first to turn our eyes from the qualities or perfections of creatures, lest we be tempted to measure by them the perfections of the Creator. Then, turning from the things of earth, he raises our souls to the contemplation of a Being above all beings, a Substance above all substances, a Light above all lights—or rather a Light before which all light is darkness—a Beauty above all beauties and before which all other beauty is but deformity. This is what we are taught by the cloud into which Moses entered to converse with God, and which shut out from his senses all that was not God. (*Ex.* 24:16, 18). And the action of Elias, covering his face with his cloak when he saw the glory of God passing before him, is a lively expression of the same sentiment. (*3 Kg.* 19:13). Therefore, to contemplate the glory of God, man must close his eyes to earthly things, which bear no proportion to this supreme Being.

We shall better understand this truth if we consider with more attention the vast difference between this uncreated Being and all other beings, between the Creator and His creatures. The latter without exception have had a beginning and may have an end, while this eternal Being is without beginning and without end. They all acknowledge a superior and depend upon another, while He has no superior and is the supreme Arbiter of all things. Creatures are composed of various substances, while He is a pure and simple Being; were He composed of diverse substances it would presuppose a being above and before Him to ordain the composition of these substances, which is altogether impossible. Creatures are subject to change; God is immutable. They all admit of greater perfection; they can increase in possessions, in knowledge. God cannot increase in perfection, containing within Himself all perfection; nor in possessions, for He is the source of all riches; nor in knowledge, for everything is present to His eternal omniscience. Therefore Aristotle calls Him a *pure act*—that is, Supreme Perfection, which admits of no increase. The needs of creatures subject them to movement and change; God, having no necessities, is fixed and immovable, and present in all places. We find in all creatures diversities which distinguish them one from another, but the purity of

God's Essence admits of no distinction; so that His Being is His Essence, His Essence is His Power, His Power is His Will, His Will is His Understanding, His Understanding is His Being, His Being is His Wisdom, His Wisdom is His Justice, His Justice is His Mercy. And though the last two attributes are differently manifested, the duty of mercy being to pardon, that of justice to punish, yet they are one and the same power.

The Divine Being thus comprises in its unity apparently opposite qualities and perfections which we can never sufficiently admire; for, as St. Augustine observes, "He is a profoundly hidden God, yet everywhere present; He is essentially strength and beauty; He is immutable and incomprehensible; He is beyond all space, yet fills all the universe; invisible, yet manifest to all creatures; producing all motion, yet is Himself immovable; always in action, yet ever at rest, He fills all things and is circumscribed by nothing; He provides for all things without the least solicitude; He is great without quantity, therefore He is immense; He is good without qualification, and therefore He is the Supreme Good." (*Meditations,* 19 and 20). Nay, "One is good, God." (*Matt.* 19:17).

Finally, all created things having a limited being, their power is likewise limited; the works they accomplish, the space they fill, their very names, are no less limited. Human words can define them; they can be assigned a certain character and reduced to a certain species. But the Divine Substance cannot be defined nor comprehended under any species, nor can It be confined to any place, nor can any name express It. Though nameless, therefore, as St. Denis says, It yet has all possible names, since It possesses in Itself all the perfections expressed by these names.

As limited beings, therefore, creatures can be comprehended; but the Divine Essence, being infinite, is beyond the reach of any created understanding. For that which is limitless, says Aristotle, can only be grasped by an infinite understanding. As a man on the shore beholds the sea, yet cannot measure its depth or vastness, so the blessed spirits and all the elect contemplate God, yet cannot fathom the abyss of His greatness nor measure the duration of His eternity. For this reason also God is represented "seated upon the cherubim" (*Dan.* 3:55 and *Ps.* 17:11), who, though filled with treasures of divine wisdom, continue beneath His majesty and power, which it is not given them to grasp or understand.

This is what David teaches when he tells us that God "made darkness His covert" (*Ps.* 17:12), or, as the Apostle more clearly expresses it, He "inhabiteth light inaccessible." (*1 Tim.* 6:16). The prophet calls this light darkness because it dazzles and blinds our human vision. Nothing is more resplendent and more visible than the sun, as a philosopher admirably remarks, yet because of its very splendor and the weakness of our vision there is nothing upon which we can gaze less. So also there is no being more intelligible in itself than God, and yet none we understand less in this present life.

Know, therefore, you who aspire to a knowledge of God, that He is a Being superior to anything you can conceive. The more sensible you are of your inability to comprehend Him, the more you will have advanced in a knowledge of His Being. Thus St. Gregory, commenting on these words of Job: "Who doth great things and unsearchable, and wonderful things without number" (*Job* 5:9), says, "We never more eloquently praise the works of the Almighty than when our tongue is mute in rapt wonder; silence is the only adequate praise when words are powerless to express the perfections we would extol."

St. Denis also tells us to honor with mute veneration, and a silence full of love and fear, the wonders and glory of God, before whom the most sublime intelligences are prostrate. The holy Doctor seems to allude here to the words of the prophet as translated by St. Jerome, "Praise is mute before thee, God of Sion," giving us to understand, doubtless, that the most adequate praise is a modest and respectful silence springing from the conviction of our inability to comprehend God. We thus confess the incomprehensible grandeur and sovereign majesty of Him whose being is above all being, whose power is above all power, whose glory is above all glory, whose substance is immeasurably raised above all other substances, visible or invisible. Upon this point St. Augustine has said with much beauty and force, "When I seek my God I seek not corporal grace, nor transient beauty, nor splendor, nor melodious sound, nor sweet fragrance of flowers, nor odorous essence, nor honeyed manna, nor grace of form, nor anything pleasing to the flesh. None of these things do I seek when I seek my God. But I seek a light exceeding all light, which the eyes cannot see; a voice sweeter than all sound, which the ear cannot hear; a sweetness above all sweetness, which the tongue cannot taste; a fragrance above all fragrance, which the senses cannot perceive; a mysterious and divine embrace, which the body cannot feel. For this light shines without radiance, this voice is heard without striking the air, this fragrance is perceived though the wind does not bear it, this taste inebriates with no palate to relish it, and this embrace is felt in the center of the soul." (*Conf.*, L. 10, 6; *Solil.*, c. 31).

If you would have further proof of the infinite power and greatness of God, contemplate the order and beauty of the world. Let us first bear in mind, as St. Denis tells us, that effects are proportioned to their cause, and then consider the admirable order, marvelous beauty, and incomprehensible grandeur of the universe. There are stars in heaven several hundred times larger than the earth and sea together. Consider also the infinite variety of creatures in all parts of the world, on the earth, in the air, and in the water, each with an organization so perfect that never has there been discovered in them anything superfluous or not suited to the end for which they are destined; and this truth is in no way weakened by the existence of monsters, which are but distortions of nature, due to the imperfection of created causes.

And this vast and majestic universe God created in a single instant, according to the opinion of St. Augustine and St. Clement of Alexandria; from nothing He drew being, without matter or element, instrument or model, unlimited by time or space. He created the whole world and all that is contained therein by a single act of His will. And He could as easily have created millions of worlds greater, more beautiful, and more populous than ours, and could as easily reduce them again to nothing.

Since, therefore, according to St. Denis, effects bear a proportion to their cause, what must be the power of a cause which has produced such effects? Yet all these great and perfect works are vastly inferior to their Divine Author. Who could not but be filled with admiration and astonishment in contemplating the greatness of such a Being? Though we cannot see it with our corporal eyes, yet the reflections we have just indicated must enable us in a measure to conceive the grandeur and incomprehensibility of His power.

St. Thomas, in his *Summa Theologica*, endeavors by the following argument to give us some idea of the immensity of God: We see, he tells us, that in material things that which excels in perfection also excels in quantity. Thus the water is greater than the earth, the air is greater than the water, and fire is greater than the air. The first heaven is more extensive than the element of fire, the second heaven is more extensive than the first, the third likewise exceeds the second, and so of the others till we come to the tenth sphere, or the empyreal heaven, to the grandeur and beauty of which nothing in the universe can be compared. Consequently the empyreal heavens, the finest and noblest of all the bodies which compose the universe, being incomparably greater than all the rest, we may infer, adds the Angelic Doctor, how far God, the first, the greatest, the most perfect of all beings, spiritual or corporal, and the Creator of all, exceeds them, not in material quantity—for He is a pure spirit—but in every possible perfection.

Thus we begin to understand, in some manner, what are the perfections of God, since they cannot but be in proportion to His being. For, as we read in Ecclesiasticus, "According to His greatness, so also is His mercy with Him." (*Ecclus.* 2:23). Nor are any of His other attributes less. Hence He is infinitely wise, infinitely merciful, infinitely just, infinitely good, and, therefore, infinitely worthy to be obeyed, feared, and reverenced by all creatures. Were the human heart capable of infinite homage, infinite love, it should offer them to this supreme Master. For if reverence and homage must be proportioned to the greatness and dignity of him to whom they are offered, then the homage we offer God should, if we were capable of it, be infinite also.

How great, then, is our obligation to love God, had He no other title to our love and service! What can he love who does not love such Goodness? What can he fear who does not fear this infinite Majesty? Whom will he serve who refuses to serve such a Master? And why was our will given to us, if not to embrace and love good? If, therefore, this great God be the Sovereign Good, why does not our will embrace it before all other goods? If it be a great evil not to love and reverence Him above all things, who can express the crime of those who love everything better than they love Him?

It is almost incredible that the malice and blindness of man can go so far; but yet, alas! How many there are who for a base pleasure, for an imaginary point of honor, for a vile and sordid interest, continually offend this Sovereign Goodness! There are others who go further and sin without any of these motives, through pure malice or habit. Oh! Incomprehensible blindness! Oh! More than brute stupidity! Oh! Rashness! Oh! Folly worthy of demons! What is the chastisement proportioned to the crime of those who thus despise their Maker? Surely none other than that which these senseless creatures will receive—the eternal fire of Hell.

Here, then, is the first motive which obliges us to love and serve God. This is an obligation so great that compared to it, all obligations to creatures, whatever their excellence or perfections, are only obligations in name. For as the perfections of creatures are mere imperfections compared with the perfections of God, so the obligations resulting therefrom cannot with justice be considered obligations when contrasted with those which we owe to God. Nor can our offences against the creature be regarded as offenses, except in name, when we remember the guilt we have incurred by our many sins against God.

For this reason David cried out, "Against thee only, O God, have I sinned" (*Ps.* 50:6), though he had sinned against Urias, whom he murdered; against the wife of Urias, whom he dishonored; and against his subjects, whom he scandalized. The penitent king knew that his offences against creatures, notwithstanding their different degrees of deformity, could not equal the enormity of his revolt against God. For God being infinite, our obligations towards Him and our offences against Him are, in a measure, infinite.

CHAPTER 2

*The Second Motive which obliges us to
practice virtue and to serve God: Gratitude
for our Creation*

We are obliged to practice virtue and keep God's commandments not only because of what God is in Himself, but
because of what He is to us, because of His innumerable
benefits to us.

The first of these benefits is *our creation,* which obliges
man to give himself wholly to the service of his Creator, for
in justice he stands indebted to Him for all he has received;
and since he has received his body with all its senses, and
his soul with all its faculties, he is obliged to employ them in
the service of his Creator, or incur the guilt of theft and ingratitude towards his gracious Benefactor. For if a man
builds a house, who should have the use and profit of it, if
not he who built it? To whom does the fruit of a vine
belong, if not to him who has planted it? Whom should
children serve, if not the father who gave them being?
Hence the law gives a father almost unlimited power over
his children, so natural does it seem that he should be
master of an existence of which he is the author.

What, then, should be the authority of God, the sovereign
Author of all being in Heaven and on earth? And if, as
Seneca remarks, those who receive benefits are obliged to
imitate good soil and return with interest what they have
received, what return can we make to God, when we have

nothing to offer Him but what we have received from His infinite goodness? What, therefore, must we think of those who not only make no return to their Creator, but use His benefits to offend Him? Aristotle tells us that man can never make adequate return to his parents or to the gods for the favors received from them. How, then, can we make a suitable return to the great God, the Father of us all, for the innumerable blessings bestowed upon us? If disobedience to parents be so grievous a crime, how heinous must it not be to rebel against this gracious God!

He Himself complains of this ingratitude by the mouth of His prophet: "The son honoreth the father, and the servant his master: if, then, I be a father, where is my honor? And if I be a master, where is my fear?" (*Mal.* 1:6). Another servant of God, filled with indignation at like ingratitude, exclaims, "Is this the return thou makest to the Lord, O foolish and senseless people? Is not he thy father, that hath possessed thee, and made thee, and created thee?" (*Deut.* 32:6). This reproach is addressed to those who never raise their eyes to Heaven to consider what God is, who never look upon themselves in order to know themselves. Knowing nothing, therefore, of their origin or the end for which they are created, they live as though they themselves were the authors of their being.

This was the crime of the unfortunate king of Egypt to whom God said, "Behold, I come against thee, Pharao, king of Egypt, thou great dragon that liest in the midst of thy rivers and sayest: The river is mine, and I made myself." (*Ezech.* 29:3). This is, at least practically, the language of those who act as though they were the principle of their own being, and who refuse to recognize any obligation to serve their Maker.

How different were the sentiments of St. Augustine, who by studying his origin was brought to the knowledge of Him from whom he had received his being! "I returned to myself," he says, "and entered into myself, saying: What art thou? And I answered: A rational and mortal man. And I began to examine what this was, and I said: O my Lord and my God, who has created so noble a creature as this? Who, O Lord, but Thou? Thou, O my God, hast made me! I have not made myself. What art Thou, Thou by whom I live and from whom all things receive being? Can anyone create himself or receive his being but from Thee? Art Thou not the source of all being, the fountain whence all life flows? For whatsoever has life lives by Thee, because nothing can live without Thee. It is Thou, O Lord, that hast made me, and without Thee nothing is made! Thou art my Creator, and I am Thy creature. I thank Thee, O my Creator, because Thy hands have made and fashioned me! I thank Thee, O my Light, for having enlightened me and brought me to the knowledge of what Thou art and what I myself am!"

This, then, the first of God's benefits, is the foundation of all the others, for all other benefits presuppose existence, which is given us at our creation. Let us now consider the acknowledgment God demands of us, for He is no less rigid in requiring our gratitude than He is magnificent in bestowing His benefits; and this is an additional proof of His love, for our gratitude results in no advantage to Him, but enables us to profit by the favors we have received, and thus merit other graces from His infinite goodness.

Thus we read in the Old Testament that whenever He bestowed a favor upon His people He immediately commanded them to keep it in remembrance. When He brought the Israelites out of Egypt He commanded them to commemorate by a solemn festival every year their happy deliverance from bondage. When He slew the firstborn of the Egyptians and spared the Israelites, He commanded that the latter, in return, should consecrate their firstborn to Him. When He sent them manna from Heaven to sustain them in the wilderness, He ordered that a portion of it should be put in a vessel and kept in the tabernacle as a memorial to generations of this extraordinary favor. After giving them victory over Amalec He told Moses to write it for a memorial in a book, and deliver it to Josue.

Since, therefore, God so rigidly requires a continual remembrance of the temporal favors He grants us, what return of gratitude will He not demand for this immortal benefit? Such we truly call the benefit of creation, because with it we receive from God the gift of an immortal soul. The patriarchs of old were deeply sensible of this obligation of gratitude, and therefore we read that whenever God bestowed upon them any special favor or blessing they evinced their gratitude by erecting altars to His name and by rearing other monuments to commemorate His mercies to them. Even the names they gave their children expressed the favors they had received, so desirous were they that their debt of gratitude to God should never be forgotten. St. Augustine, speaking on this subject in one of his soliloquies, says, "Man should think of God as often as he breathes; for as his being is continuous and immortal, he should continually return thanks to the Author of his being."

This obligation is so deeply graven in nature that even the philosophers and sages of this world earnestly inculcate gratitude to God. Hear the counsel of Epictetus: "Be not ungrateful, O man, to this sovereign Power, but return thanks for the faculties with which He has endowed thee, for thy life itself and for all the things which sustain it, for fruits, wine, oil, and whatever advantages of fortune thou hast received from Him; but praise Him particularly for thy reason, which teaches thee the proper use and the true worth of all these things." If a pagan philosopher teaches such gratitude for benefits common to all men, what should be the gratitude of a Christian, who has received the light of faith in addition to that of reason, as well as other gifts vastly superior to those we have just mentioned?

But perhaps you will urge that these benefits common to all seem the work of nature rather than graces emanating from God; and why, you ask, should I be grateful for the general order which reigns in the world, and because things follow their natural course? This objection is unworthy of a Christian, of a pagan, of any but an unreasonable animal. Hear how the same philosopher answers it: "You will say, perhaps, that you receive all these benefits from nature. Senseless man! In saying this you but change the name of God, your Benefactor. For what is nature but God Himself, the first and original nature? Therefore, it is no excuse, ungrateful man, to urge that you are indebted, not to God, but to nature; for without God there is no nature. Were you to receive a benefit from Lucius Seneca you would not dare to say that you were indebted to Lucius and not to Seneca. Such a subterfuge would change your benefactor's name, but would by no means cancel your obligation to him."

It is not only a motive of justice which obliges us to serve God, but our necessities force us to have recourse to Him if we would attain the perfection and happiness for which we were created.

In order to understand this more clearly, let us call to mind the general principle that creatures are not born with all their perfections. There remain many to be cultivated and developed, and only He who has begun the work can perfect it. Things instinctively go back to their first cause for their development and perfection. Plants unceasingly seek the sun, and sink their roots deep into the earth where they were formed. Fishes will not leave the element where they were engendered. Chickens seek vivifying warmth and shelter beneath their mother's wings. In like manner a lamb, until it has attained its strength, clings to the side of its ewe, distinguishing her among a thousand of the same color, arguing, doubtless, with blind instinct, that it must seek what it lacks at the source whence it has received all that it is.

This is apparent in all the works of nature, and if those of art could reason they would doubtless proceed in like manner. Were a painter to make a beautiful picture and omit the eyes, whither would the picture, were it sensible of its want, go to seek its completion? Not to the palaces of kings or princes, for all their power could not give it what it sought; no, it would seek its first cause, the master who designed it. And is not this thy position also, O rational creature? Thou art an unfinished work. Many things are lacking to the perfection of thy being. Thou hast naught of the beauty and luster which are yet to be thine. Hence thy restless, unsatisfied yearning; hence those unceasing aspirations for a higher, a better state, which arise from thy very necessities.

Yes, God let thee hunger, in order that, driven by necessity, thou mightest have recourse to Him. For this reason He did not give thee perfection at thy creation, but He withheld it only through love for thee. It was not to make thee poor, but to make thee humble; it was not to leave thee needy, but to compel thee to have recourse to Him.

If, then, thou art blind, poor, and in need, why dost thou not seek the Father who created thee, the Artist who designed thee, that He may satisfy thy wants and supply all that is lacking to thy perfection? Penetrated with this truth, David cried out, "Thy hands have made me and formed me: give me understanding, and I will learn thy commandments." (*Ps.* 118:73).

Thy hands have made me, the prophet would say, but the work is incomplete. The eyes of my soul are still imperfect; they see not what they ought to know. To whom shall I go in my necessities, if not to Him from whom I have received all that I possess? Enlighten, then, my eyes, O Lord, that they may know Thee, and that the work Thou hast begun in me may be perfected. Therefore, only God can perfect the understanding, the will, and all the faculties of the soul.

It is He alone who satisfies His creature and never fails him. With Him the creature is content in poverty, rich in destitution, happy in solitude, and though despoiled of all possessions, yet master of all things. Hence the wise man so justly says, "One is as it were rich, when he hath nothing: and another is as it were poor, when he hath great riches." (*Prov.* 13:7). Rich indeed is the poor man who, like St. Francis of Assisi, has God for his inheritance, though owning naught else; but poor would he be who knew not God, though he possessed the entire universe. What do their wealth and power avail the rich and great of this world when they are a prey to anxieties which they cannot calm, a victim to appetites which they cannot satisfy? For what comfort can costly raiment, luxurious viands, and overflowing coffers bring to a troubled mind? The rich man tosses restlessly on his soft couch, and his treasure is powerless to stifle the remorse which banishes sleep. Independently, therefore, of God's benefits to us, we are, from the necessities of our nature, obliged to serve Him, if we would attain our happiness and perfection.

CHAPTER 3

The Third Motive which obliges us to serve God: Gratitude for our Preservation and for the Government of His Providence

Another motive which obliges man to serve God is the benefit of *preservation*. God gave you being, and still preserves it to you, for you are as powerless to subsist without Him as you were incapable of coming into existence without Him. The benefit of preservation is not less than that of creation. It is even greater, for your creation was but a single act, while your preservation is a continuous manifestation of God's abiding love. If, then, your creation demands from you so great a return of gratitude, who can reckon the debt you owe for the gift of preservation? There is not a movement of your eye, there is not a step you take, which is not by His power. For if you do not believe that it is through Him that you live and act, you are no longer a Christian; and if, believing it, you continue deliberately to offend your Benefactor, how can I say what you are?

If a man on the top of a high tower held another suspended by a small cord over an abyss, do you think the latter would dare to address injurious words to him who held him thus suspended? How is it, then, that you, whose existence hangs by a thread which God can sever at any moment, dare excite the anger of this infinite Majesty by outraging Him with the very benefits He mercifully preserves to you?

The goodness of this sovereign Being is so great, says St. Denis, that while creatures are offending Him and madly rebelling against His will, He continues to give them the power and strength which they use to resist Him. How, then, can you be so rash, so ungrateful as to turn against God the blessings with which He has loaded you? Oh! Incredible blindness! Oh! Senseless rebellion—that the members would conspire against their Head, for which they ought to be ready to make any sacrifice!

But a time will come when God's outraged patience shall be avenged. You have conspired against God. It is just that He should arm the universe against you, that all creatures should rise up against you to avenge their Creator. They who closed their eyes to the sweet light of His mercy while it still shone upon them and allured them by so many benefits will justly behold it when, too late for amendment, they shall be groaning under the severity of His justice.

Consider in addition to this benefit the rich and delightful banquet of nature prepared for you by your Creator. Everything in this world is for man's use, directly or indirectly. Insects serve as food for birds, which in their turn serve as food for man. In like manner the grass of the fields supports the animals destined also for man's service. Cast your eye upon this vast world, and behold the abundance of your possessions, the magnificence of your inheritance. All that move upon the earth, or swim in the water, or fly in the air, or live under the sun are made for you.

Every creature is a benefit of God, the work of His Providence, a ray of His beauty, a token of His mercy, a spark of His love, a voice which proclaims His magnificence. These are the eloquent messengers of God continually reminding you of your obligations to Him. "Everything," says St. Augustine, "in Heaven and on earth calls upon me to love Thee, O Lord! And the universe unceasingly exhorts all men to love Thee, that none may exempt themselves from this sweet law."

Oh! That you had ears to hear the voice of creatures appealing to you to love God. Their expressive silence tells you that they were created to serve you, while yours is the sweet duty of praising your common Lord not only in your own name but in theirs also. I flood your days with light, the heavens declare, and your nights I illumine with the soft radiance of my stars. By my different influences all nature bears fruit in season for your necessities.

I sustain your breath, the air tells you; with gentle breezes I refresh you and temper your bodily heat. I maintain an almost infinite variety of birds to delight you with their beauty, to ravish you with their songs, and to feed you with their flesh. I maintain for your nourishment innumerable fishes, the water exclaims. I water your lands, that they may give you their fruit in due season. I afford you an easy passage to distant countries, that you may add their riches to those of your own.

But what says the earth, this common mother of all things, this vast storehouse of the treasures of nature? Surely she may tell you: Like a good mother I bear you in my arms; I prepare food for all your necessities; I procure the concurrence of the heavens and all the elements for your welfare. Never do I abandon you, for after supporting you during life, I receive you in death and in my own bosom give you a final resting place.

Thus can the whole universe with one voice cry out: Behold how my Master and Creator has loved you. He has created me for your happiness, that I might serve you, and that you in your turn might love and serve Him; for I have been made for you, and you have been made for God.

This is the voice of all creatures. Will you be deaf to it? Will you be insensible to so many benefits? You have been loaded with favors. Do not forget the debt you thence contract. Beware of the crime of ingratitude. Every creature, says Richard of St. Victor, addresses these three words to man: *Receive, give, beware.* Receive the benefit; give thanks for it; and beware of the punishment of ingratitude.

Epictetus, a pagan philosopher, fully appreciated this truth. He teaches us to behold the Creator in all His creatures, and to refer to Him all the blessings we receive from them. "When you are warned," he says, "of a change in the atmosphere by the redoubled cries of the crow, it is not the crow, but God who warns you. And if the voice of men gives you wise counsel and useful knowledge, it is also God who speaks. For He has given them this wisdom and knowledge, and, therefore, you must recognize His power in the instruments He wills to employ. But when He wishes to acquaint you with matters of greater moment He chooses more noble and worthy messengers."

The same philosopher adds, "When you will have finished reading my counsels, say to yourself: It is not Epictetus the philosopher who tells me all these things; it is God. For whence in fact has he received the power to give these counsels but from God? Is it not God Himself, therefore, who speaks to me through him?" Such are the sentiments of Epictetus. Should not a Christian blush to be less enlightened than a pagan philosopher? Surely it is shameful that they who are illumined by faith should not see what was so clear to them who had no other guide than the light of simple reason.

Since, then, every creature is a benefit from God, how can we live surrounded by these proofs of His love, and yet never think of Him? If, wearied and hungry, you seated yourself at the foot of a tower, and a beneficent creature from above sent you food and refreshment, could you forbear raising your eyes to your kind benefactor? Yet God continually sends down upon you blessings of every kind.

Find me, I pray you, but one thing which does not come from God, which does not happen by His special Providence. Why is it, then, that you never raise your eyes to this indefatigable and generous Benefactor? Ah! We have divested ourselves of our own nature, so to speak, and have fallen into worse than brute insensibility. I blush, in truth, to say what we resemble in this particular, but it is good for man to hear it. We are like a herd of swine feeding under an oak. While their keeper is showering down acorns, they greedily devour them, grunting and quarrelling with one another, yet never raising their eyes to the master who is feeding them. Oh! Brutelike ingratitude of the children of Adam! We have received the light of reason, and an upright form. Our head is directed to Heaven, not to earth, which ought to teach us to raise the eyes of our soul to the abode of our Benefactor.

Would that irrational creatures did not excel us in this duty! But the law of gratitude, so dear to God, is so deeply impressed on all creatures that we find this noble sentiment even in the most savage beasts. What nature is more savage than that of a lion? Yet Appian, a Greek author, tells us that a certain man took refuge in a cave, where he extracted a thorn from the foot of a lion. Grateful for the kindness, the noble animal ever after shared his prey with his benefactor while he remained in the cave. Some years later this man, having been charged with a crime, was condemned to be exposed to wild beasts in the amphitheater. When the time of execution arrived, a lion which had been lately captured was let loose on the prisoner. Instead of tearing his victim to pieces he gazed at him intently, and, recognizing his former benefactor, he gave evident signs of joy, leaping and fawning upon him as a dog would upon his master. Moved by this spectacle, the judges, on hearing his story, released both man and lion. Forgetful of his former wildness, the lion, until his death, continued to follow his master through the streets of Rome without offering the slightest injury to anyone.

A like instance of gratitude is related of another lion that was strangling in the coils of a serpent when a gentleman riding by came to his rescue and killed the serpent. The grateful animal, to show his devotion, took up his abode with his deliverer and followed him wherever he went, like a faithful dog. One day the gentleman set sail, leaving the lion behind him on the shore. Impatient to be with his master, the faithful animal plunged into the sea, and, being unable to reach the vessel, was drowned.

What instances could we not relate of the fidelity and gratitude of the horse! Pliny, in his *Natural History* (8,40), tells us that horses have been seen to shed tears at the death of their masters, and even to starve themselves to death for the same reason. Nor are the gratitude and fidelity of dogs less surprising. Of these the same author relates most marvelous things. He gives, among other examples, an instance which occurred in his own time at Rome. A man condemned to death was allowed in prison the companionship of his dog. The faithful animal never left him, and even after death remained by the lifeless body to testify to his grief. If food were given to him he immediately brought it to his master and laid it on his lifeless lips. Finally, when the remains were thrown into the Tiber, he plunged into the river, and, having placed himself beneath the body, struggled till the last to keep it from sinking. Could there be gratitude greater than this?

Now, if beasts, with no other guide than natural instinct, thus show their love and gratitude for their masters, how can man, possessing the superior guidance of reason, live in such forgetfulness of his Benefactor? Will he suffer the brute creation to give him lessons in fidelity, gratitude, and kindness? Moreover, will he forget that the benefits he receives from God are incomparably superior to those which animals receive from men? Will he forget that his Benefactor is so infinite in His excellence, so disinterested in His love, overwhelming His creatures with blessings which can in no way benefit Himself? This must ever be a subject of wonder and astonishment, and evidently proves that there are evil spirits who darken our understanding, weaken our memory, and harden our heart, in order to make us forget so bountiful a Benefactor.

If it be so great a crime to forget this Lord, what must it be to insult Him, and to convert His benefits into the instruments of our offences against Him? "The first degree of ingratitude," says Seneca, "is to neglect to repay the benefits we have received; the second is to forget them; the third is to requite the benefactor with evil." But what shall we say of that excess of ingratitude which goes so far as to outrage the benefactor with his own benefits? I doubt whether one man ever treated another as we dare to treat God. What man, having received a large sum of money from his sovereign, would be so ungrateful as immediately to employ it in raising an army against him? Yet you, unhappy creatures, never cease to make war upon God with the very benefits you have received from Him.

How infamous would be the conduct of a married woman who, having received a rich present from her husband, would bestow it upon the object of her unlawful love in order to secure his affections! The world would regard it as base, unparalleled treason; yet the offence is only between equals. But what proportions the crime assumes when the affront is from a creature to God! Yet is not this the crime of men who consume their health, and who waste, in the pursuit of vice, the means that God has given them? They pervert their strength to the gratification of their pride; their beauty but feeds their vanity; their wealth enables them to conceal their vices, to vie with the great, to pamper their flesh, to traffic in innocence, bargaining, even as the Jews did with Judas, for the Blood of Christ! What shall I say of their abuse of other benefits?

The sea serves but to satisfy their gluttony and their ambition; the beauty of creatures excites their gross sensuality; earthly possessions but feed their avarice; and talents, whether natural or acquired, only tend to increase their vanity and pride. Prosperity inflates them with folly, and adversity reduces them to despair. They choose the darkness of the night to hide their thefts, and the light of day to lay their snares, as we read in Job. In a word, they pervert all that God has created for His glory to the gratification of their inordinate passions.

What shall I say of their effeminate adornments, their costly fabrics, their extravagant perfumes, their sumptuous tables groaning under the weight of rare and luxurious viands? Nay, sensuality and luxury are so general that, to our shame, books are published to teach us how to sin in these respects. Men have perverted creatures from their lawful use, and instead of making God's benefits a help to virtue, they have turned them into instruments of vice. So great is the selfishness of the world that there is nothing which men do not sacrifice to the gratification of the flesh, wholly forgetful of the poor, whom God has so specially recommended to their care. Such persons never find that they are poor until they are asked for alms; at any other time there is no extravagant luxury their income cannot afford.

Beware lest this terrible accusation be made against you at the hour of death! The greater the benefits you have perverted, the more severe the account you will have to render. It is a great sign of reprobation for a man to continue to abuse the favors God has bestowed upon him. To have received much, and to have made but small return, is, in a manner, already to have judged oneself. If the Ninivites shall rise in judgment against the Jews for not having done penance at Our Saviour's teaching, let us see that the same Lord shall have no reason to condemn us upon the example of beasts that love their benefactors, while we manifest such gross ingratitude to the Supreme Benefactor of all.

CHAPTER 4

*The Fourth Motive which obliges us to
practice Virtue: Gratitude for the
Inestimable Benefit of our Redemption*

Let us now consider the supreme benefit of divine love,
the redemption of man. But I feel myself so unworthy, so
unfitted to spreak of such a mystery that I know not where
to begin or where to leave off, or whether it were not better
for me to be silent altogether. Did not man, in his lethargy,
need an incentive to virtue, better would it be to prostrate
ourselves in mute adoration before the incomprehensible
grandeur of this mystery than vainly essay to explain it in
imperfect human language. It is said that a famous painter
of antiquity, wishing to represent the death of a king's
daughter, painted her friends and relatives about her with
mournful countenances. In her mother's face grief was still
more strongly depicted. But before the face of the king he
painted a dark veil to signify that his grief was beyond the
power of art to express.

Now, if all that we have said so inadequately expresses
the single benefit of creation, how can we with any justice
represent the supreme benefit of Redemption? By a single
act of His will God created the whole universe, diminishing
thereby neither the treasures of His riches nor the power of
His almighty arm. But to redeem the world He labored for
thirty-three years by the sweat of His brow; He shed the last
drop of His Blood, and suffered pain and anguish in all His

senses and all His members. What mortal tongue can explain this ineffable mystery? Yet it is equally impossible for me to speak or to be silent. Silence seems ingratitude, and to speak seems rashness. Wherefore, I prostrate myself at Thy feet, O my God, beseeching Thee to supply for my insufficiency, and if my feeble tongue detract from Thy glory, while wishing to praise and magnify it, grant that Thy elect in Heaven may render to Thy mercy the worship which Thy creatures here below are incapable of offering Thee.

After God had created man and placed him in the delights of the terrestrial paradise, by the very favors which should have bound him to the service of his Creator he was emboldened to rebel against Him. For this he was driven into exile and condemned to the eternal pains of Hell. He had imitated the rebellion of Satan; therefore, it was just that he should share his punishment.

When Giezi, the servant of Eliseus, received presents from Naaman the leper, the prophet said to him: Since thou hast received Naaman's money, "the leprosy of Naaman shall also cleave to thee and to thy seed forever. And he went out from him a leper as white as snow." (*4 Kg.* 5:27). God pronounced a like sentence against man; Adam wished to share the riches of Lucifer, that is, his pride and his revolt, and, in consequence, the leprosy of Lucifer, that is, the punishment of his revolt, became his portion also. By sin, therefore, man becomes like Satan—he imitates him in his guilt, and shares in his punishment.

Having brought such misery upon himself, man became the object of the divine compassion, for God was more moved by the condition of His fallen creature than He was indignant at the outrage offered to His goodness. He resolved to restore man and reconcile him with Himself through the mediation of His only Son. But how was reconciliation effected? Again, what human tongue can express this mercy? Through our Mediator Christ such a friendship was established between God and man that the Creator not only pardoned His creature and restored him to His grace and love, but even became one with him. Man has become so one with God that in all creation there is no union that can be compared to this. It is not only a union of grace and love, but it is a union of person also. Who could have thought that such a breach would be so perfectly repaired? Who could have imagined that two beings so widely separated by nature and sin should one day be united, not only in the same house, at the same table, and in a union of grace, but in one and the same person [that is, in Christ]?

Can we think of two beings more widely separated than God and the sinner? Yet where will we find two beings more closely united? "There is nothing," says St. Bernard, "more elevated than God, and nothing more base than the clay of which man is formed. Yet God has with such great humility clothed Himself in this clay, and the clay has been so honorably raised to God, that we may ascribe to the clay all the actions of God, and to God all the sufferings of the clay." (*Super Cant. Hom.* 59 et 64).

When man stood naked and trembling before his Creator, who could have made him believe that one day his unhappy nature would be united to God in one and the same person? This union was so close that even the supreme moment of the cross could not sever it. Death dissolved the union between soul and body, but could not separate the divinity from the humanity, for what Christ had once taken upon Himself for love of us He never abandoned.

Thus was our peace established. Thus did God apply to us the remedy for our sovereign miseries. And we owe Him more gratitude, perhaps, for the manner of applying this remedy than for the remedy itself. Yes, Lord, I am infinitely indebted to Thee for redeeming me from Hell, for re-establishing me in Thy grace, and for restoring my liberty; but I should be still more grateful, were it possible, for the manner in which Thou hast wrought these wonders. All Thy works are admirable, O Lord! And when lost in wonder at a power that seems to have reached its limit, we have only to raise our eyes to behold still another marvel which eclipses all the rest. Nor is this any disparagement of Thy power, O Lord, but rather a manifestation of Thy glory!

But what, O Lord, is the remedy Thou didst choose for my deep misery? Innumerable were the ways in which Thou couldst have redeemed me without toil or suffering; but in Thy magnificence, and to testify to Thy great love for me, Thou didst will to endure such pain and sufferings that the very thought of them bathed Thee in a sweat of blood, and at the sight of them the rocks were rent asunder. May the heavens praise Thee, O Lord, and may the angels proclaim Thy mercies! What did our virtues avail Thee, or how wast Thou harmed by our sins? "If thou sin," says Eliu to Job, "what shalt thou hurt him! And if thy iniquities be multiplied, what shalt thou do against him? And if thou do justly, what shalt thou give him, or what shall he receive of thy hand?" (*Job* 35:6-7).

This great God, so rich and powerful, so free from all evils, whose wisdom and possessions can neither be increased nor lessened, who would be equally glorious in Himself whether men and angels praised Him forever in Heaven, or blasphemed Him forever in Hell; this great God, impelled by no necessity, but yielding to His love, came down from Heaven to this place of exile, clothed Himself with our nature when we were His enemies, took upon Himself our infirmities, and even death, and to heal our wounds endured torments more terrible than any that had ever before been borne, or that ever again will be undergone.

It was for me, O Lord, that Thou wast born in a stable, laid in a manger, and circumcised on the eighth day after

Thy birth! For me wast Thou driven from Thy country and exiled to Egypt. For my sake Thou didst fast and watch, shedding bitter tears, and sweating Blood from every pore. For me Thou wast seized as a malefactor, forsaken, sold, denied, betrayed, dragged from tribunal to tribunal, buffeted, spat upon, bruised with blows, and delivered to the gibes of an infamous rabble. For me Thou didst die upon a cross, in the sight of Thy most holy Mother, enduring poverty so great that even the consolation of a drop of water was denied to Thy burning lips. Thou wert abandoned by the world, and so great was Thy desolation that even Thy Father seemed to have forsaken Thee. At such a cost, O God, didst Thou restore to me my life!

Can we, without the deepest grief, behold this spectacle—God hanging as a malefactor upon an infamous gibbet? We could not withhold our compassion from a criminal who had brought such misfortune upon himself; and if our compassion be greater when the victim is innocent, and his excellence known to us, what must have been the astonishment and grief of the angels, with their knowledge of His perfection, when they saw Him overwhelmed with ignominy and condemned to die upon the cross?

The two cherubim, placed by God's command (*Ex.* 25:18) on each side of the ark, looking toward the mercy-seat in wonder and admiration, are an emblem of the awe with which the heavenly spirits were seized at the sight of God's supreme mercy in becoming the propitiation for the world on the sacred wood of His cross.

Who, then, can contain his astonishment or forbear to exclaim with Moses: "O Lord God, merciful and gracious, patient and of much compassion, and true!" (*Ex.* 34:6). Who would not, like Elias (*3 Kg.* 19:13), cover his eyes did he see God passing, not in the splendor of His majesty, but in the depths of His humiliation; not in the might of His power, moving mountains and rending rocks, but as a malefactor, delivered to the cruelties of a brutal multitude?

While, then, we confess our inability to understand this incomprehensible mystery, will we not open our hearts to the sweet influence of such boundless love, and make, as far as we are able, a corresponding return? Oh! Abyss of charity! Oh! Boundless mercy! Oh! Incomprehensible goodness! By Thy ignominy, O Lord, Thou hast purchased honor for me. By Thy Blood Thou hast washed away the stains of my sins. By Thy death Thou hast given me life. By Thy tears Thou has delivered me from eternal weeping. O best of Fathers! How tenderly Thou loved Thy children. O good Shepherd, who hast given Thyself as food to Thy flock! O faithful Guardian, who didst lay down Thy life for the creatures of Thy care! With what tears can I return Thy tears? With what life can I repay Thy life? What are the tears of a creature compared to the tears of his Creator, or what is the life of a man compared to that of his God?

Think not, O man, that thy debt is less because God suffered for all men as well as for thee. Each of His creatures was as present to His divine mind as if He died for him alone. His charity was so great, the holy Doctors tell us, that had but one man sinned He would have suffered to redeem him. Consider, therefore, what thou owest a Master who has done so much for thee and who would have done still more had thy welfare required it.

Tell me, O ye creatures, whether a greater benefit, a more generous favor, a more binding obligation can be conceived. Tell me, O ye celestial choirs, whether God has done for you what He has done for us? Who, then, will refuse to give himself without reserve to the service of such a Master? "I thrice owe Thee all that I am, O my God!" exclaims St. Anselm. "By my creation I owe Thee all that I am. Thou hast confirmed this debt by redeeming me; and by promising to be my eternal reward, Thou dost compel me to give myself wholly to Thee. Why, then, do I not give myself to One who has such a just claim to my service? Oh! Insupportable ingratitude! Oh! Invincible hardness of the human heart, which will not be softened by such benefits! Metals yield to fire; iron is made flexible in the forge; and diamonds are softened by the blood of certain animals. But oh! Heart more insensible than stone, harder than iron, more adamant than the diamond, wilt thou not be moved by the fire of Hell, or by the benefits of the tenderest of Fathers, or by the Blood of the spotless Lamb immolated for love of thee?"

Since Thy mercy and Thy love have been so powerfully manifested for us, O Lord, how is it that there are men who do not love Thee, who forget Thy benefits or use them to offend Thee? To whom will they give their love, if they refuse it to Thee? What can touch them, if they are insensible to Thy benefits? Ah! How can I refuse to serve a God who has so lovingly sought me and redeemed me? "And I," says Our Saviour, "if I be lifted up from the earth, will draw all things to myself." (*Jn.* 12:32). With what strength, Lord, with what chains? With the strength of My love, with the chains of My benefits, "I will draw them," says the Lord by His prophet, "with the cords of Adam, with the bands of love." (*Osee* 11:4). Ah! Who will resist these chains, who will refuse to yield to these mercies? If, then, it be so great a crime not to love this sovereign Lord, what must it be to offend Him, to break His commandments? How can you use your hands to offend Him whose hands are so full of benefits for you, whose hands were nailed to the cross for you?

When the unhappy wife of the Egyptian minister sought to lead Joseph into sin, the virtuous youth replied, "Behold, my master hath delivered all things to me, and knoweth not what he hath in his own house: Neither is there anything which is not in my power, or that he hath not delivered to me, but thee, who art his wife: how then can I do this

wicked thing, and sin against my God?" (*Gen.* 39:8-9).
Mark the words of Joseph. He does not say: "I should not,"
or "It is not just that I offend Him," but "How can I do this
wicked thing?" From this let us learn that great favors
should not only deprive us of the will, but, in a measure,
even of the power, to offend our benefactor.

If, therefore, the son of Jacob felt such gratitude for
perishable benefits, what should be ours for the immortal
blessings God has bestowed upon us? Joseph's master
entrusted him with all his possessions. God has given us not
only His possessions but Himself. What is there on earth
that He has not made for us? Earth, sky, sun, moon, stars,
tides, birds, beasts, fishes—in short, all things under
Heaven are ours, and even the riches of Heaven itself, the
glory and happiness of eternity. "All things are yours," says
the Apostle, "whether it be Paul, or Apollo, or Cephas, or
the world, or life, or death, or things present, or things to
come; for all are yours" (*1 Cor.* 3:22), for all these contribute to your salvation.

And we not only possess the riches of Heaven, but the
Lord of Heaven. He has given Himself to us in a thousand
ways: as our Father, our Teacher, our Saviour, our Master,
our Physician, our Example, our Food, our Reward. In
brief, the Father has given us the Son, and the Son has made
us worthy to receive the Holy Ghost, and the Holy Ghost
has united us to the Father and the Son, the Source of every
grace and blessing.

Again, since God has given you all the benefits you enjoy, how can you use these benefits to outrage so magnificent a Benefactor? If you are unmindful of the crime of
your ingratitude, you are more ungrateful than the savage
beasts, colder and more hardened than senseless objects. St.
Ambrose, after Pliny, relates the story of a dog that had witnessed the murder of his master. All night the faithful
animal remained by the body, howling most piteously, and

on the following day, when a concourse of people visited the scene, the dog noticed the murderer among them, and falling upon him with rage, thus led to the discovery of his crime. If poor animals testify so much love and fidelity for a morsel of bread, will you return offences for divine benefits? If a dog will manifest such indignation against his master's murderer, how can you look with indifference on the murderers of your sovereign Lord?

And who are these murderers? None other than your sins. Yes, your sins apprehended Him and bound Him with ignominious fetters, loaded Him with infamy, overwhelmed Him with outrages, bruised Him with blows, and nailed Him to the cross. His executioners could never have accomplished this without the fatal aid of your sins. Will you, then, feel no hatred for the barbarous enemies who put your Saviour to death? Can you look upon this Victim immolated for you, without feeling an increase of love for Him? All that He did and suffered upon earth was intended to produce in our hearts a horror and detestation of sin. His hands and feet were nailed to the cross in order to bind sin.

Will you render all His sufferings and labors fruitless to you? Will you remain in the slavery of sin when He purchased your freedom at the price of His Blood? Will you not tremble at the name of sin, which God has wrought such wonders to efface? What more could God have done to turn men from sin than to place Himself nailed to the cross between them and this terrible evil? What man would dare to offend God, were Heaven and Hell open before him? Yet a God nailed to a cross is a still more terrible and appalling sight. I know not what can move one who is insensible to such a spectacle.

CHAPTER 5

*The Fifth Motive which obliges us to practice
Virtue: Gratitude for our Justification*

What would the benefit of Redemption avail us, if it had not been followed by that of justification, through which the sovereign virtue of Redemption is applied to our souls? For as the most excellent remedies avail us nothing if not applied to our disorders, so the sovereign remedy of Redemption would be fruitless were it not applied to us through the benefit of justification. This is the work of the Holy Ghost, to whom the sanctification of man in a special manner belongs. It is He who attracts the sinner by His mercy, who calls him, who leads him in the ways of wisdom, who justifies him, who raises him to perfection, who imparts to him the gift of perseverance, to which, in the end, He will add the crown of everlasting glory. These are the different degrees of grace contained in the inestimable benefit of justification.

The first of these graces is our [baptismal] vocation. Man cannot throw off the yoke of sin; he cannot return from death to life, nor from a child of wrath can he become a child of God, without the assistance of divine grace. For Our Saviour has declared, "No man can come to me except the Father, who hath sent me, draw him." (*Jn.* 6:44).

St. Thomas thus explains these words: "As a stone, when other forces are removed, naturally falls to the ground, and cannot rise again without the application of some extraneous power, so man, corrupted by sin, ever tends downwards, attracted to earth by the love of perishable possessions, and cannot, without the intervention of divine grace, rise to heavenly things or a desire for supernatural perfection." This truth merits our consideration and our tears, for it shows us the depth of our misery, and the necessity, under which we labor, of incessantly imploring the divine assistance.

But to return to our subject: Who can express all the benefits brought to us by justification? It banishes from our souls sin, the source of all evils. It reconciles us to God and restores us to His friendship; for in truth the greatest evil which sin brings on us is that it makes us the objects of God's hatred. God, being infinite goodness, must sovereignly abhor all that is evil. "Thou hatest all the workers of iniquity," exclaims His prophet; "Thou wilt destroy all that speak a lie. The bloody and the deceitful man the Lord will abhor." (*Ps.* 5:7).

The enmity of God is evidently the greatest of evils for us, since it cuts us off from the friendship of God, the source of every blessing. From this misfortune justification delivers us, restoring us to God's grace, and uniting us to Him by the most intimate love, that of a father for a son. Hence the beloved disciple exclaims: "Behold what manner of charity the Father hath bestowed upon us, that we should be called, and should be the sons of God." (*1 Jn.* 3:1). The Apostle would have us understand that we wear not only the name, but are in truth the sons of God, in order that we may appreciate the liberality and magnificence of God's mercy to us.

If God's enmity be such a terrible misfortune, what an incomparable blessing His friendship must be! For it is an axiom in philosophy that according as a thing is evil, so is its opposite good; hence the opposite of that which is supremely evil must be supremely good. Now, man's supreme evil is the enmity of God; therefore, his supreme good must be the friendship of God. If men set such value upon the favor of their masters, their fathers, their princes, their kings, how highly should they esteem their sovereign Master, this most excellent Father, this King of kings, compared to whom all power and riches and principalities are as if they were not!

The benefit we are considering is largely enhanced by the liberality with which it is bestowed. For as man before his creation was unable to merit the gift of existence, so after his fall he could do nothing to merit his justification. No act of his could satisfy the Creator, in whose sight he was an object of hatred.

Another blessing flowing from justification is our deliverance from the eternal pains of Hell. Having driven God from him by sin, having despised His love, man in his turn is justly rejected by God. Inordinate love for creatures led him away from the Creator, and, therefore, it is but just that these same creatures should be the instruments of his punishment. Therefore, he was condemned to the eternal pains of Hell, compared to which the sufferings of this life are so light that they appear more imaginary than real. Add to these torments the undying worm which unceasingly gnaws the conscience of the sinner. What shall I say of his society, demons of perversity and reprobate men? Consider also the confusion and darkness of this terrible abode, where there is no rest, no joy, no peace, no hope, but eternal rage and blasphemies, perpetual weeping and ceaseless gnashing of teeth. Behold the torments from which God delivers those whom He justifies.

Another benefit of justification, more spiritual and therefore less apparent, is the regeneration of the interior man deformed by sin. For sin deprives the soul not only of God but of all her supernatural power, of the graces and gifts of the Holy Ghost, in which her beauty and strength consist. A soul thus stripped of the riches of grace is weakened and paralyzed in all her faculties. For man is essentially a rational creature, but sin is an act contrary to reason. Hence, as opposites destroy each other, it follows that the greater and the more numerous our sins are, the greater must be the ruin of the faculties of the soul, not in themselves, but in their power of doing good.

Thus sin renders the soul miserable, weak and torpid, inconstant in good, cowardly in resisting temptation, slothful in the observance of God's commandments. It deprives her of true liberty and of that sovereignty which she should never resign; it makes her a slave to the world, the flesh, and the devil; it subjects her to a harder and more wretched servitude than that of the unhappy Israelites in Egypt or Babylon. Sin so dulls and stupefies the spiritual senses of man that he is deaf to God's voice and inspirations; blind to the dreadful calamities which threaten him; insensible to the sweet odor of virtue and the example of the saints; incapable of tasting how sweet the Lord is, or feeling the touch of His benign hand in the benefits which should be a constant incitement to his greater love. Moreover, sin destroys the peace and joy of a good conscience, takes away the soul's fervor, and leaves her an object abominable in the eyes of God and His saints.

The grace of justification delivers us from all these miseries. For God, in His infinite mercy, is not content with effacing our sins and restoring us to His favor; He delivers us from the evils sin has brought upon us, and renews the interior man in his former strength and beauty. Thus He heals our wounds, breaks our bonds, moderates the violence of our passions, restores with true liberty the supernatural beauty of the soul, re-establishes us in the peace and joy of a good conscience, reanimates our interior senses, inspires us with ardor for good and a salutary hatred of sin, makes us strong and constant in resisting evil, and thus enriches us with an abundance of good works. In fine, He so perfectly renews the inner man with all his faculties that the Apostle calls those who are thus justified new men and new creatures. (Cf. *2 Cor.* 4:16 and *Gal.* 6:15).

This renewal of the inner man is so powerful, so true, that in Baptism it is called regeneration, in Penance, resurrection; not only because it restores the soul from the death of sin to the life of grace, but because it is an anticipation of the last glorious resurrection. No tongue can express the beauty of a justified soul; only the Holy Spirit, who is pleased to dwell therein, can tell the sweetness, loveliness, and strength with which He has enriched her. The beauty, the power, the riches of earth fade into insignificance before the unspeakable beauty of a soul in a state of grace. As far as Heaven is above earth, as far as mind is above matter, so far does the life of grace exceed that of nature, so far does the invisible beauty of a soul exceed the visible beauty of this world. God Himself is enamored with this divine beauty. He adorns such a soul with infused virtues and the seven gifts of the Holy Ghost, imparting, at the same time, renewed strength and splendor to all her powers.

Moreover, God, in His boundless liberality, sends us the Holy Ghost Himself, whilst the three Divine Persons take up their abode in a soul thus prepared, in order to teach her to make a noble use of the riches with which she is endowed. Like a good father, God not only leaves His inheritance to His children, but also sends them a prudent guardian to administer it. This guardian is no other than God Himself, for, as Christ has declared, "If any one love me, he will keep my word, and my Father will love him, and we will come to him, and will make our abode with him." (*John* 14:23).

From these words the Doctors of the Church and theologians conclude that the Holy Spirit resides in a special manner in the soul of a just man, and, distinguishing between the Holy Spirit and His gifts, they declare that the soul not only enjoys these gifts, but also the real presence of their Divine Author. Entering such a soul, God transforms her into a magnificent temple. He Himself purifies, sanctifies, and adorns her, making her a fitting habitation for her Supreme Guest. Contrast this glorious state with the miserable condition of a soul in sin, the abode of evil spirits and of every abomination. (Cf. *Matt.* 12:45).

Still another more marvelous benefit of justification is that it transforms the soul into a living member of Christ. This, again, is the source of new graces and privileges, for the Son of God, loving and cherishing us as His own members, infuses into us that virtue which is His life, and, as our Head, continually guides and directs us. How tenderly, too, does the Heavenly Father look upon such souls, as members of His Divine Son, united to Him by the participation of the same Holy Spirit! Their works, therefore, are pleasing to Him, and meritorious in His sight, since it is Jesus Christ, His only Son, who lives and acts in them. Hence, with what confidence they address God in prayer, because it is not so much for themselves as for His Divine Son that they pray, since to Him all the honor of their lives redounds. For as the members of the body can receive no benefit of which the Head does not partake, so neither can Christ, the Head of all the just, be separated from their virtues or merits. If it be true, as the Apostle tells us (Cf. *1 Cor.* 6:15), that they who sin against the members of Jesus Christ sin against Jesus Christ Himself, and that He regards a persecution directed against His members as directed against Himself (Cf. *Acts.* 9:4), is it astonishing that He regards the honor paid to His members as paid to Himself?

Pray, then, with confidence, remembering that your petitions ascend to the Eternal Father in the name of His Son, who is your Head. For His sake they will be heard, and will redound to His honor; for, as is generally admitted, when we ask a favor for the sake of another, it is granted not so much to the one who receives it, as to the one for whose sake it was asked. For this reason we are said to serve God when we serve the poor for His sake.

The final benefit of justification is the right which it gives to eternal life. God is infinitely merciful as well as infinitely just, and while He condemns impenitent sinners to eternal misery, He rewards the truly repentant with eternal happiness. God could have pardoned men and restored them to His favor without raising them to a share in His glory, yet in the excess of His mercy He adopts those whom He pardons, justifies those whom He has adopted, and makes them partakers of the riches and inheritance of His only-begotten Son. It is the hope of this incomparable inheritance which sustains and comforts the just in all their tribulations; for they feel even in the midst of the most cruel adversity that "that which is at present momentary and light of our tribulation, worketh for us above measure exceedingly an eternal weight of glory." (*2 Cor.* 4:17).

These are the graces comprehended in the inestimable benefit of justification, which St. Augustine justly ranks above that of creation. (*Super. Joan* 72, 9). For God created the world by a single act of His will, but to redeem it He shed the last drop of His Blood and expired under the most grievous torments. St. Thomas gives a like opinion in his *Summa Theologica.*

Though it is true that no man can be certain of his justification, yet there are signs by which we can form a favorable judgment. The principal of these is a change of life; as, for example, when a man who hitherto committed innumerable mortal sins without scruple would not now be guilty of a single grave offence against God even to gain the whole world.

Let him, then, who has attained these happy dispositions reflect upon what he owes the Author of his justification, who has delivered him from the multitude of evils which are the consequences of sin, and overwhelmed him with the benefits which we have attempted to explain. And as for him who has the misfortune to be still in a state of sin, I know nothing more efficacious to rouse him from his miserable condition than the consideration of the evils which sin brings in its train, and of the blessings which flow from the incomparable benefit of justification.

The effects produced in the soul by the Holy Ghost do not end here. This Divine Spirit, not content with causing us to enter the path of justice, maintains us therein, strengthening us against all obstacles until we arrive at the haven of salvation. His love will not permit Him to remain idle in a soul which He honors by His presence. He sanctifies her with His virtue, and effects in her and by her all that is necessary to win eternal life. He dwells in the soul as the father in the midst of a family, preserving order and peace by his prudent authority; as a master in the midst of his disciples, teaching lessons of Divine wisdom; as a gardener in a garden confided to his intelligent care; as a king in his kingdom, ruling and directing all; as the sun in the midst of the universe, enlightening and vivifying her, and directing all her movements.

Possessing, in an eminent degree, all the good that is in creatures, He produces, but in a far more perfect manner, all the effects of which these creatures are capable. As fire He vivifies our understanding, enkindles our will, and detaches us from earth to raise us to heavenly things; as a dove He renders us sweet, gentle, and compassionate to one another; as a cloud He shelters us from the burning sensuality of the flesh, and tempers the heat of our passions; as a violent wind He impels our wills to good and sweeps all evil affections from our hearts. Hence it is that just souls abhor the vices which they formerly loved, and embrace the virtues from which they formerly shrank. Witness David, who cries out, "I have hated and abhorred iniquity." "I have rejoiced in the way of thy testimonies as much as in all riches." (*Ps.* 118:104, 14).

It is to the Holy Ghost that we are indebted for all our progress in virtue. It is He who preserves us from evil and maintains us in good. It is He who is the principle of our perseverance, and who finally crowns us in Heaven. This it was which led St. Augustine to say that in rewarding our merits God but crowns His own gifts. (*Conf.* 1, 20).

The holy patriarch Joseph, not content with giving to his brethren the corn which they came to purchase, ordered also that the money which they paid for it should be secretly returned to them. God treats His elect with still greater liberality. He not only gives them eternal life, but furnishes them the grace and virtue to attain it. "We adore Him," says Eusebius Emissenus, "that He may be merciful to us, but He has already been merciful to us in giving us grace to adore Him."

Let each one, then, glance over his life and consider, as the same holy Doctor suggests, all the good he has been permitted to do, and all the sins of impurity, injustice, and sacrilege from which he has been preserved, and he will comprehend in some measure what he owes to God. On this point St. Augustine well observes that God shows no less mercy in preserving man from sin than in pardoning him after he has fallen. (*Conf.* 2, 7). Indeed, it is a greater proof of love. Therefore, the same saint, writing to a virgin, says: "Man should consider that God has pardoned him all the sins from which He has preserved him. Think not, therefore, that you may love this Master with a feeble love because He has pardoned you but a few sins. Your debt of love, on the contrary, is greater for His preventing grace which has saved you from committing many. For if a man must love a creditor who forgives him a debt, how much more reason has he to love a benefactor who gratuitously bestows upon him a like amount? For if a man live chastely all his life, it is God who preserves him; if he be converted from immorality to a pure life, it is God who reforms him; and if he continue in his disorders till the end, it is also God who justly forsakes him."

What, then, should our conclusion be but to unite our voices with the prophet, saying, "Let my mouth be filled with praise, that I may sing thy glory, thy greatness all the day long." (*Ps.* 70:8). St. Augustine, commenting upon these words of the prophet, asks, "What means *all the day long*"? And he answers, "Under all circumstances and without interruption. Yes, Lord, I will praise Thee in prosperity because Thou dost comfort me, and in adversity because Thou dost chastise me. For my whole being I will praise Thee, because Thou art its Author. In my repentance I will praise Thee, because Thou dost pardon me. In my perseverance I will praise Thee, because Thou wilt crown me. Thus, O Lord, my mouth will be filled with Thy praise, and I will sing Thy glory all the day long!"

It would be fitting to speak here of the Sacraments, the instruments of justification, particularly of Baptism, and the divine light and principle of faith which it imprints on our souls. But as this subject has been more fully treated in another work, we will confine ourselves, for the present, to the Eucharist, that Sacrament of sacraments, which gives to us—as our daily food and sovereign remedy—God Himself. He was offered once for us on the cross, but He is daily offered for us on the altar. "This is my body," Christ has declared; "do this for a commemoration of me." (*Lk.* 22:19).

Oh! Sacred Pledge of our salvation! Oh! Incomparable Sacrifice! Oh! Victim of love! Oh! Bread of life! Oh! Sweet and delicious Banquet! Oh! Food of kings! Oh! Manna containing all sweetness and delight! Who can fittingly praise Thee? Who can worthily receive Thee? Who can love and venerate Thee as Thou dost deserve? My soul faints at the thought of Thee; my lips are mute in Thy presence, for I cannot extol Thy marvels as I desire.

Had Our Lord reserved this favor for the pure and innocent, it would still be a mercy beyond our comprehension. But in His boundless love He does not refuse to descend into depraved hearts, nor to pass through the hands of unworthy ministers who are the slaves of Satan and the victims of their unruly passion. To reach the hearts of His friends and to bring them His divine consolations, He submits to innumerable outrages and profanations. He was sold once in His mortal life, but in this august Sacrament He is unceasingly betrayed. The scorn and ignominy of His Passion afflicted Him only once, but in this sacred Banquet His love and goodness are daily insulted and outraged. Once He was nailed to the cross between two thieves, but in this Sacrament of love His enemies crucify Him a thousand times.

What return, then, can we make to a Master who seeks our good in so many ways? If servants obey and serve their masters for a paltry support; if soldiers from a like motive brave fire and sword, what do we not owe God, who maintains us with this heavenly Food? If God in the Old Law exacted so much gratitude from the Israelites for the manna, which, with all its excellence, was only corruptible food, what gratitude will He not expect for this Divine Nourishment, incorruptible in Itself, and conferring the same blessing on all who worthily receive It? If we owe Him so much for the food which preserves our bodily life, what return must we not make Him for the Food which preserves in us the life of grace? And, finally, if our debt of gratitude be so great for being made children of Adam, what do we owe Him for making us children of God? For it cannot be denied, as Eusebius Emissenus observes, that "the day we are born to eternity is infinitely greater than the day which brings us forth to this world, with all its suffering and dangers."

Here, then, dear Christian, is another motive which should induce you to serve God, another link in that chain which should bind you irrevocably to your Creator.

CHAPTER 6

The Sixth Motive which obliges us to practice
Virtue: Gratitude for the Incomprehensible
Benefit of Election

To all the benefits which we have just enumerated we must add that of election, or predestination, which belongs to those whom God has chosen from all eternity to be partakers of His glory. The Apostle, in his Epistle to the Ephesians (*Eph.* 1:3-5), thus gives thanks, in his own name and that of the elect, for this inestimable benefit: "Blessed be the God and Father of our Lord Jesus Christ, who hath blessed us with spiritual blessings in heavenly places, in Christ; as he chose us in him before the foundation of the world, that we should be holy and unspotted in his sight, in charity; who hath predestinated us unto the adoption of children through Jesus Christ unto himself, according to the purpose of his will." The Royal Prophet thus extols this same benefit: "Blessed is he whom thou hast chosen and taken to thee: he shall dwell in thy courts." (*Ps.* 64:5).

Election, therefore, may be justly called the grace of graces, since God, in His boundless liberality, bestows it upon us before we have merited it; for, while giving to each one what is necessary for his salvation, He wills, as absolute Master of His gifts, to bestow them in greater abundance upon certain souls, without any injury, however, to others less favored. It is also the grace of graces not only because it is the greatest, but because it is the source of all the others

For in predestining man to glory, God determines to bestow upon him all the graces necessary to attain this happiness. This He has declared by the mouth of His prophet: "I have loved thee with an everlasting love, therefore have I drawn thee, taking pity on thee." (*Jer.* 31:3). This truth is still more clearly expressed by the Apostle: "For whom he foreknew, he also predestinated to be made conformable to the image of his Son; that he might be the firstborn amongst many brethren. And whom he predestinated, them he also justified. And whom he justified, them he also glorified." (*Rom.* 8:29-30). A father who destines his son for a special career in life prepares and educates him from his boyhood with a view to this career. In like manner, when God has predestined a soul to eternal happiness, He directs her in the path of justice, that she may attain the end for which He has chosen her.

All, therefore, who recognize in themselves any mark of election should bless God for this great and eternal benefit. Though it is a secret hidden from human eyes, yet there are certain signs of election, as there are of justification; and as the first mark of our justification is the conversion of our lives, so the surest mark of our predestination is our perseverance in the good thus begun. He who has lived for a number of years in the fear of God, carefully avoiding sin, may hope that God, in the words of the Apostle, "will confirm him unto the end without crime, in the day of the coming of our Lord Jesus Christ." (*1 Cor.* 1:8).

No man, however, can be certain of his perseverance or election. Did not Solomon, the wisest of kings, after having lived virtuously for many years, fall into iniquity in his old age? Yet his example is one of the exceptions to the rule, which he himself teaches in these words: "It is a proverb: A young man according to his way, even when he is old he will not depart from it" (*Prov.* 22:6); so that if his youth has been virtuous, his old age will likewise be honorable. From these and similar indications to be found in the lives of the saints a man may humbly hope that God has numbered him among the elect, that his name is written in the Book of Life.

How great, then, should be our gratitude for such a benefit! God Himself tells His Apostles, "Rejoice not in this, that spirits are subject unto you; but rejoice in this, that your names are written in heaven." (*Lk.* 10:20). What, in fact, can be a greater happiness than to have been from all eternity the object of God's love and choice; to have had a privileged place in His Heart throughout the eternal years; to have been chosen as the child of His adoption before the birth of His Son according to nature; and to have been always present to His Divine Mind, clothed in the splendor of the saints!

Weigh all the circumstances of this election, and you will find that each of them is an extraordinary favor, a new motive to love and serve God. Consider first the greatness of Him who has chosen you. It is God Himself, who, being infinitely rich and infinitely happy, had no need of you or any other creature. Next represent to yourself the profound unworthiness of the object of this election—a miserable creature exposed to all the infirmities of this life, and deserving by his sins the eternal torments of the future. Reflect, too, how glorious is this election, by which you are raised to the dignity of a child of God and heir to His kingdom. Consider, further, how generously and gratuitously this favor is bestowed. It preceded all merit on our part, and sprang solely from the good pleasure and mercy of God, and according to the Apostle, turns "unto the praise of the glory of his grace." (*Eph.* 1:6). Now, the more gratuitous a favor is, the greater the obligation it imposes.

The origin and the antiquity of this election also merit special consideration. It did not begin with this world; it preceded the existence of the universe; it was coeval with the very existence of God. From all eternity He loved His elect. They were ever present to Him, and His will to render them eternally happy was as fixed at His own Being.

Observe, finally, what a singular benefit this is. Among the many nations plunged in the darkness of paganism, among the many souls condemned to perdition, you have been selected to share the happy lot of the elect. Out of the mass of perdition He has raised you, and the leaven of corruption and death He has changed into the bread of angels and the wheat of the elect. The value of this benefit is still further increased when we reflect how small is the number of the elect and how great is the number of the lost. Solomon says that "the number of fools"—that is, the reprobate—"is infinite." (*Eccles.* 1:15).

But if none of these considerations moves you, be touched at least by the sight of all that it has cost God to confer this immortal benefit on you. He purchased it for you with the Life and Blood of His only Son; for He resolved from all eternity to send Him into this world to execute His loving and merciful decree. Who, then, would be so base as to wait until the end of his life to love God, who has loved him from eternity? "Forsake not an old friend," we are told in Scripture (*Ecclus.* 9:14), "for the new will not be like to him."

Who, then, will forsake this Friend whose love for us had no beginning, and whose claim to our love is likewise from eternity? Who will not give up all the goods of this world; who will not bear all the evils of this world, to share in this blessed friendship? How great would be our respect for the poorest beggar were we assured by divine revelation that he was predestined to share God's glory! Would we not kiss the ground upon which he trod? "O happy soul!" we would cry. "O enviable lot! Is it possible that thou art surely to behold God in all the splendor of His majesty? Art thou to rejoice with the angels forever? Will thy ears be ravished with sweet music for all eternity? Art thou to gaze upon the radiant beauty of Christ and His Blessed Mother? Oh! Happy day when thou wast born! But happier still the day of thy death, which will introduce thee to eternal life. Happy the bread thou eatest and the ground upon which thou dost tread! Happier still the pains and insults thou endurest, for they open to thee the way to eternal rest! For what clouds, what tribulations, can overcome the power and joy of such a hope as thine?"

We would doubtless break out into such transports as these did we behold and recognize a predestined soul. For if people run out to see a prince, the heir to a great kingdom, as he passes through the street, marveling at his good fortune, as the world esteems it, how much more reason have we to marvel at the happy lot of one who, without any previous merit on his part, has been elected from his birth, not to a temporal kingdom, but to reign eternally in Heaven!

You may thus understand, dear Christian, the gratitude the elect owe to God. And yet there is no one, provided he do what is necessary for salvation, who may not consider himself of this happy number. "Labor, therefore, the more," as St. Peter tells you, "that by good works you may make sure your calling and election." (*2 Pet.* 1:10). We should never lose sight, therefore, of our end, for God's grace is never wanting to us, and we can do all things in Him who strengthens us.

CHAPTER 7

The Seventh Motive for practicing Virtue:
The Thought of Death, the First of the Four
Last Things

Any one of the motives we have just enumerated should be sufficient to induce man to give himself wholly to the service of a Master to whom he is bound by so many ties of gratitude. But as the generality of men are more influenced by personal interest than by motives of justice, we will here make known the inestimable advantages of virtue in this life and the next.

We will first speak of the greatest among them: the glory which is the reward of virtue, and the terrible punishment from which it delivers us. These two are the principal oars which propel us in our voyage to eternity. For this reason St. Francis and our holy Father St. Dominic, both having been animated by the same spirit, commanded in their rules the preachers of their orders to make vice and virtue, reward and punishment, the only subjects of their sermons, in order to instruct men in the precepts of the Christian life and to inspire them with courage to put them into practice. Moreover, it is a common principle among philosophers that reward and punishment are the most powerful motives for good with the mass of mankind. Such, alas, is our misery, that we are not content with virtue alone; it must be accompanied with the fear of punishment or the hope of reward.

But as there is no reward or punishment so worthy of our consideration as those that never end, we will treat of eternal glory and eternal misery, together with death and judgment, which precede them. These are the most powerful incentives to love virtue and hate vice, for we are told in Scripture, "In all thy works remember thy last end, and thou shalt never sin." (*Ecclus.* 7:40).

The first of these is death. Let us, then, consider it, for it is a truth which of all others makes the most impression upon us, from the fact that it is so undisputed and so frequently brought before our minds. Especially do we realize this when we reflect on the particular judgment which each one must undergo as soon as his soul is separated from his body. The sentence then passed will be final; it will endure for all eternity. Since, then, death is such a powerful motive to turn us from sin, let us bring this terrible hour more vividly before us.

Bear in mind, therefore, that you are a man and a Christian. As man, you must die; as a Christian, you must, immediately after death, render an account of your life. The first truth is manifest in our daily experience, and the second our faith will not permit us to doubt. No one, whether king or pope, is exempt from this terrible law. A day will come of which you will not see the night, or a night which for you, will have no morning. A time will come, and you know not whether it be this present day or tomorrow, when you who are now reading my words, in perfect health and in full possession of all your faculties, will find yourself stretched upon a bed of death, a lighted taper in your hand, awaiting the sentence pronounced against mankind—a sentence which admits neither delay nor appeal.

Consider, also, how uncertain is the hour of death. It generally comes when man is most forgetful of eternal things, overturning his plans for an earthly future, and opening before him the appalling vision of eternity.

Therefore, the Holy Scriptures tell us that it comes as a thief in the night; that is, when men are plunged in sleep and least apprehensive of danger. The forerunner of death is usually a grave illness with its attendant weariness, sufferings, and pains, which weaken the powers of the body and give entrance to the king of terrors. Just as an enemy who wishes to take a citadel destroys the outer fortifications, so death with its vanguard of sickness breaks down the strength of the body, and, as it is about to fall before the repeated assaults of its enemy, the soul, no longer able to resist, takes its flight from the ruins.

Who can express the anguish of the moment when the severity of the sickness, or the declaration of the physician, undeceives us and robs us of all hope of life? The parting from all we hold dear then begins to rise before us. Wife, children, friends, relations, honors, riches are fast passing, with life, from our feeble grasp. Then follow the terrible symptoms which precede the awful hour. The coldness of death seizes our members; the countenance becomes deathly pale; the tongue refuses to perform its duty; all the senses, in fine, are in confusion and disorder in the precipitation of this supreme departure.

Strange resemblance between the beginning and the end of our pilgrimage! The mystery of suffering seems to unite them both. The terrified soul then beholds the approach of that agony which is to terminate its temporal existence. Before the distracted mind rise the horror and darkness of the grave, where the pampered body will become the prey of worms. But keener still is the suffering which the soul endures from the suspense and uncertainty of what her fate will be when she leaves her earthly habitation. You will imagine that you are in the presence of your Sovereign Judge, and that your sins rise up against you to accuse you and complete your condemnation. The heinousness of the evil you committed with so much indifference will then be manifest to you. You will curse a thousand times the day you sinned, and the shameful pleasure which was the cause of your ruin. You will be an object of astonishment and wonder to yourself. "How could I," you will ask, "for love of the foolish things upon which I set my heart, brave the torments which I now behold?" The guilty pleasures will have long since passed away, but their terrible and irrevocable punishment will continue to stare you in the face. Side by side with this appalling eternity of misery you will see the unspeakable and everlasting happiness which you have sacrificed for vanities, transitory and sinful pleasures.

Everything you will behold will be calculated to fill you with terror and remorse. Life will have been spent; there will be no time for repentance. Nor will the friends you have loved or the idols you have adored be able to help you. On the contrary, that which you have loved during life will be the cause of your most poignant anguish at the hour of death. What, then, will be your thoughts at this supreme hour? To whom will you have recourse? Whither will you turn? To go forward will be anguish. To go back impossible. To continue as you are will not be permitted.

"It shall come to pass in that day, saith the Lord God, that the sun shall go down at midday, and I will make the earth dark in the daylight." (*Amos.* 8:9). Terrible words! Yes, the sun shall go down at midday; for the sinner at the sight of his sins, and at the approach of God's justice, already believes himself abandoned by the Divine Mercy; and though life still remains, with its opportunities for penance and reconciliation, yet fear too often drives hope from the heart, and in this miserable state he breathes his last sigh in the darkness of despair.

Most powerful is this passion of fear. It magnifies trifles and makes remote evils appear as if present. Now, since this is true of a slight apprehension, what will be the effect of the terror inspired by a danger so great and imminent? The sinner, though still in life and surrounded by his friends, imagines himself already a prey to the torments of the reprobate. His soul is rent at the sight of the possessions he must leave, while he increases his misery by envying the lot of those from whom he is about to be separated. Yes, the sun sets for him at midday, for, turn his eyes where he will, all is darkness. No ray of light or hope illumines his horizon. If he thinks of God's mercy, he feels that he has no claim upon it. If he thinks of God's justice, it is only to tremble for its execution. He feels that his day is past and that God's time has come. If he looks back upon his life, a thousand accusing voices sound in his ears. If he turns to the present, he finds himself stretched upon a bed of death. If he looks to the future, he there beholds his Supreme Judge prepared to condemn him. How can he free himself from so many miseries and terrors?

If, then, the circumstances which precede our departure are so terrible, what will be those which follow? If such be the vigil of this great day, what will be the day itself? Man's eyes are no sooner closed in death than he appears before the judgment seat of God to render an account of every thought, every word, every action of his life.

If you would learn the severity and rigor of this judgment, ask not men who live according to the spirit of this world, for, like the Egyptians of old, they are plunged in darkness and are the sport of the most fatal errors. Seek, rather, those who are enlightened by the true Sun of Justice. Ask the saints, and they will tell you, more by their actions than by their words, how terrible is the account we are to render to God. David was a just man, yet his prayer was: "Enter not, O Lord, into judgment with thy servant, for in thy sight no man living shall be justified." (*Ps.* 142:2).

Arsenius was also a great saint, and yet at his death he was seized with such terror at the thought of God's judgment that his disciples, who knew the sanctity of his life, were much astonished, and said to him, "Father, why should you now fear?" To this he replied, "My children, this is no new fear which is upon me. It is one that I have known and felt during my whole life." It is said that St. Agatho at the hour of death experienced like terror, and having been asked why he, who had led such a perfect life, should fear, he simply answered, "The judgments of God are different from the judgments of men."

St. John Climachus gives a not less striking example of a holy monk, which is so remarkable that I shall give it as nearly as possible in the saint's own words: "A religious named Stephen, who lived in the same desert with us, had a great desire to embrace a more solitary life. He had already acquired a reputation for sanctity, having been favored with the gift of tears and fasting and other privileges attached to the most eminent virtues. Having obtained his superior's permission, he built a cell at the foot of Mount Horeb, where Elias was honored by his marvelous vision of God. Though his life here was one of great sanctity, yet, impelled by desire for still harder labors and greater perfection, he withdrew to a place called Siden, inhabited by holy anchorites who lived in the most complete solitude. Here he continued for some years in the practice of the severest penance, cut off from all human intercourse or comfort, for his hermitage was seventy miles from any human habitation. As his life approached its term he felt a desire to return to his first cell at the foot of Mount Horeb, where dwelt two disciples, natives of Palestine. Shortly after his arrival he was attacked by a fatal illness. The day before his death he fell into a state resembling ecstasy. He gazed first at one side of his bed, then at the other, and, as if engaged in conversation with invisible beings who were demanding an account of his life, was heard crying out in a loud voice. Sometimes he would say, 'It is true, I confess it; but I have fasted many years in expiation of that sin'; or, 'It is false;

that offence cannot be laid to my charge'; or again, 'Yes, but I have labored for the good of my neighbor so many years in atonement thereof.' To other accusations he was heard to say, 'Alas! I cannot deny it; I can only cast myself upon God's mercy.'

"Surely this was a thrilling spectacle," continues the saint. "I cannot describe the terror with which we assisted at this invisible judgment. O my God! What will be my fate, if this faithful servant, whose life was one long penance, knew not how to answer some of the accusations brought against him? If after forty years of retirement and solitude, if after having received the gift of tears, and such command over nature that, as I am credibly informed, he fed with his own hand a wild leopard which visited him, the saintly monk so trembled for judgment, and, dying, left us in uncertainty as to his fate, what have we not to fear who lead careless and indifferent lives?"

If you ask me the cause of this terror with which the saints are filled, I will let St. Gregory answer for me: "Men aspiring to perfection," says the holy Doctor, "constantly reflect upon the justice of the Sovereign Judge who is to pronounce sentence upon them in the dread hour which terminates their earthly career. They unceasingly examine themselves upon the account they are to render before this supreme tribunal. And if happily they find themselves innocent of sinful actions, they still ask with fear whether they are equally free from the guilt of sinful thoughts. For if it be comparatively easy to resist sinful actions, it is more difficult to conquer in the war which we must wage against evil thoughts. And though the fear of God's judgment is always before them, yet it is redoubled at the hour of death, when they are about to appear before His inflexible tribunal. At this moment the mind is freed from the disturbances of the flesh; earthly desires and delusive dreams fade from the imagination; the things of this world vanish at the portals of another life; and the dying man sees but God and himself. If he recalls no good which he has omitted, yet he feels that he cannot trust himself to give a correct and impartial judgment. Hence his fear and terror of the rigorous account to be exacted of him." (*Moral.*, 24:16, 17).

Do not these words of the great Doctor prove that this last hour and this supreme tribunal are more to be dreaded than worldly men imagine? If just men tremble at this hour, what must be the terror of those who make no preparation for it, whose lives are spent in the pursuit of vanities and in contempt of God's commandments? If the cedar of Lebanon be thus shaken, how can the reed of the wilderness stand? "And," as St. Peter tells us, "if the just man shall scarcely be saved, where shall the ungodly and the sinner appear?" (*1 Pet.* 4:18).

Reflect, then, on the sentiments that will be yours when you will stand before the tribunal of God, with no defenders but your good works, with no companion but your own conscience. And if then you will not be able to satisfy your Judge, who will give expression to the bitterness of your anguish? For the question at issue is not a fleeting temporal life, but an eternity of happiness or an eternity of misery. Whither will you turn? What protection will you seek? Your tears will be powerless to soften your Judge; the time for repentance will be past. Little will honors, dignities, and wealth avail you, for "Riches," says the Wise Man, "shall not profit in the day of vengeance, but justice shall deliver a man from death." (*Prov.* 11:4).

The unhappy soul can only exclaim with the prophet, "The sorrows of death have encompassed me, and the perils of hell have found me." (*Ps.* 114:3). Unhappy wretch! How swiftly this hour has come upon me! What does it now avail me that I had friends, or honors, or dignities or wealth? All that I can now claim is a few feet of earth and a winding-sheet. My wealth which I hoarded I must leave to be squandered by others, while the sins of injustice which I here committed will pursue me into the next world and there condemn me to eternal torments. Of all my guilty pleasures the sting of remorse alone remains. Why have I made no preparation for this hour? Why was I deaf to the salutary warnings I received? "Why have I hated instruction, and my heart consented not to reproofs, and have not heard the voice of them that taught me, and have not inclined my ear to my masters?" (*Prov.* 5:12-13).

To preserve you, my dear Christian, from these vain regrets, I beg you to gather from what has been said three considerations, and to keep them continually before your mind. The first is the terrible remorse which your sins will awaken in you at the hour of death; the second is how ardently, though how vainly, you will wish that you had faithfully served God during life; and the third is how willingly you would accept the most rigorous penance, were you given time for repentance.

Acting on this advice, you will now begin to regulate your life according as you will then wish to have done.

CHAPTER 8

The Eighth Motive for practicing Virtue:
The Thought of the Last Judgment, the
Second of the Four Last Things

Immediately after death follows the particular judgment, of which we have been treating. But there is a day of general judgment, when, in the words of the Apostle, "We must all be manifested before the judgment seat of Christ, that every one may receive the proper things of the body, according as he hath done, whether it be good or evil." (*2 Cor.* 5:10).

In considering this subject, what strikes us as most amazing, and what filled the holy soul of Job with awe, is that a frail creature like man, so prone to evil, should be subjected to such a rigorous judgment on the part of God, by whose command his every thought, word, and action are inscribed in the book of life. In his astonishment Job cries out, "Why hidest thou thy face, and thinkest me thy enemy? Against a leaf, that is carried away with the wind, thou showest thy power, and thou pursuest a dry straw. For thou writest bitter things against me, and wilt consume me for the sins of my youth. Thou hast put my feet in the stocks, and hast observed all my paths, and hast considered the steps of my feet: who am to be consumed as rottenness, and as a garment that is moth-eaten." (*Job* 13:24-28).

And returning to the same subject, he continues, "Man born of a woman, living for a short time, is filled with many miseries; who cometh forth like a flower and is destroyed, and fleeth as a shadow, and never continueth in the same state. And dost thou think it meet to open thy eyes upon such a one, and to bring him into judgment with thee? Who can make him clean that is born of unclean seed? Is it not thou who only art?" (*Job* 14:1-4).

Thus does holy Job express his astonishment at the severity of the Divine Justice towards frail man, so inclined to evil, who drinks up iniquity like water. That He should have exercised such severity towards the angels, who are spiritual and perfect beings, is not a matter of so much surprise. But it is truly amazing that not an idle word, not a wasted moment in man's life shall escape the rigor of God's justice. "But I say unto you that every idle word that men shall speak, they shall render an account of it in the day of judgment." (*Matt.* 12:36). If we must render an account of idle words which harm no one, how severe will be the account exacted of us for impure words, immodest actions, sinful glances, bloodstained hands, for all the time spent in sinful deeds? We could hardly credit the severity of this judgment, did not God Himself affirm it. Oh! Sublime religion, how great are the purity and perfection thou teachest!

What shame, then, and what confusion will overwhelm the sinner when all his impurities, all his excesses, all his iniquities, hidden in the secret recesses of his heart, will be exposed, in all their enormity, to the eyes of the world! Whose conscience is so clear that he does not blush, does not tremble, at this thought? If men find it so difficult to make known their sins in the secrecy of confession, if many prefer to groan under the weight of their iniquities rather than declare them to God's minister, how will they bear to see them revealed before the universe? In their shame and confusion "they shall say to the mountains: Cover us; and to the hills: Fall upon us." (*Osee* 10:8).

Consider also the terror of the sinner when this terrible sentence resounds in his ear: "Depart from me, ye cursed, into everlasting fire which was prepared for the devil and his angels." (*Matt.* 25:4). How will the reprobate hear these terrible words? "Seeing," says holy Job, "that we have heard scarce a little drop of his word, who shall be able to behold the thunder of his greatness?" (*Job* 26:14). When this dread sentence will have gone forth, the earth will open and swallow in its fiery depths all those whose lives have been spent in the pursuit of sinful pleasures.

St. John, in the Apocalypse, thus describes this awful moment: "I saw another angel come down from heaven, having great power: and the earth was enlightened with his glory. And he cried out with a strong voice, saying: Babylon the great is fallen, is fallen; and is become the habitation of devils, and the hold of every unclean spirit, and the hold of every unclean and hateful bird." (*Apoc.* 18:1-2). And the holy Evangelist adds, "And a mighty angel took up a stone, as it were a great millstone, and cast it into the sea, saying: With such violence as this shall Babylon, that great city, be thrown down, and shall be found no more at all." (*Apoc.* 18:21). In like manner shall the wicked, represented by Babylon, be cast into the sea of darkness and confusion.

What tongue can express the torments of this eternal prison? The body will burn with a raging fire which will never be extinguished; the soul will be tortured by the gnawing, undying worm of conscience. The darkness will resound with despairing cries, blasphemies, perpetual weeping and gnashing of teeth. The sinner, in his impotent rage, will tear his flesh and curse the inexorable justice which condemns him to these torments. He will curse the day of his birth, crying out in the words of Job, "Let the day perish wherein I was born, and the night in which it was said: A man child is conceived. Let that day be turned into darkness, let not God regard it from above, and let not the light shine upon it. Let darkness and the shadow of death cover it, let a mist overspread it, and let it be wrapped up in bitterness. Let a darksome whirlwind seize upon that night, let it not be counted in the days of the year, nor numbered in the months. Why did I not die in the womb, why did I not perish at once when I came out of the womb? Why was I placed upon the knees? Why was I suckled at the breasts?" (*Job* 3:3-6, 11-12).

Unhappy tongues which will henceforth utter only blasphemies! Unhappy ears to be forever filled with sighs and lamentations! Unhappy eyes which will never gaze upon anything but misery! Unhappy flesh consumed in eternal flames! Who can tell the bitter remorse of the sinner who has spent his life in pursuit of new pleasures and new amusements? Oh! How fleeting were the joys that brought such a series of woes! O senseless, unhappy man! What do your riches now avail you? The seven years of abundance are past, and the years of famine are upon you. Your wealth has been consumed in the twinkling of an eye, and no trace of it remains. Your glory has vanished; your happiness is swallowed up in an abyss of woe! So extreme is your misery that a drop of water is denied you to allay the parching thirst with which you are consumed. Not only is your former prosperity of no avail, but rather it increases the torture of your cruel sufferings. Thus shall the imprecation of Job be verified: "May worms be his sweetness" (*Job* 24:20), which St. Gregory thus explains: "The remembrance of their past pleasures will make their present sufferings more keen; and the contrast of their short-lived happiness with this endless misery will fill them with rage and despair." (*Moral.*, 15, 26; 16, 31).

They will recognize too late the snares of the evil one, and will exclaim in the words of the Book of Wisdom: "We have erred from the way of truth, and the light of justice hath not shone unto us, and the sun of understanding hath not risen upon us. We have wearied ourselves in the way of iniquity and destruction, and have walked through hard ways, but the way of the Lord we have not known." (*Wis.* 5:6-7). The contemplation of this terrible truth cannot but rouse us from our indifference and excite us to practice virtue.

St. John Chrysostom frequently uses this truth as a means to exhort his hearers to virtue. "If you would labor effectually," he says, "to make your soul the temple and the abode of the Divinity, never lose sight of the solemn and awful day when you are to appear before the tribunal of Christ to render an account of all your works. Represent to yourself the glory and majesty with which Christ will come to judge the living and the dead. Consider the irrevocable sentence which will then be pronounced upon mankind, and the terrible separation which will follow it. The just will enter into the possession of ineffable joy and happiness; the wicked will be precipitated into exterior darkness, where there will be perpetual weeping and gnashing of teeth. They will be gathered like weeds, and cast into the fire, where they will remain for all eternity." Ah! Then, before it is too late, let us save ourselves from this terrible misfortune by a humble and sincere confession of our sins—a favor that we will not receive on that day, for, as the Psalmist asks, "Who shall confess to thee in hell?" (*Ps.* 6:6).

Another thought which should here impress us is that God has given us two eyes, two ears, two hands, and two feet, so that if we lose one of these members we still have one left. But He has given us only one soul, and if we lose that we have no other with which to enjoy eternal happiness. Our first care, therefore, should be to save our soul, which is to share with the body either eternal happiness or eternal woe. It will avail no man at this supreme tribunal to urge, "I was dazzled by the glitter of wealth; I was deceived by the promises of the world." The inexorable Judge will answer, "I warned you against these. Did I not say, 'What doth it profit a man if he gain the whole world and suffer the loss of his own soul?'" (*Matt.* 16:26). Nor can you plead that the devil tempted you. He will remind you that Eve was not excused when she urged that the serpent had tempted her.

The vision of Jeremias teaches us what Our Lord's treatment of us will be. The prophet beheld first "a rod watching," and then "a caldron boiling." This is a figure of God's dealings with men. First He warns them, and if they do not heed, He punishes them; for he who will not submit to the correction of the rod will be cast into the caldron of fire. As you read of God's punishments in Scripture, have you ever observed that no one pleads for those whom God condemns? Father does not plead for son, nor brother for brother, nor friend for friend. Yes, even God's privileged servants, Noe, Daniel, Job, would seek in vain to alter the sentence of your Judge.

At the wedding feast no voice is raised to intercede for him who is driven from the banquet. No one pleads for the slothful servant who buried the talent entrusted to him by his Master. No one makes intercession with the Bridegroom for the five foolish virgins who, after despising the pleasures of the flesh and stifling in their hearts the fire of concupiscence, nay, after observing the great counsel of virginity, neglected the precept of humility and became inflated with pride on account of their virginity. You know the history of the avaricious man of the Gospel, and how vainly he pleaded with Abraham for a drop of water to quench his burning thirst.

Why, then, will we not help one another while we can? Why will we not render glory to God before the sun of His justice has set for us? Better let our tongues be parched with privation and fasting during the short space of this life, than by sinful indulgence expose ourselves to an eternal thirst. If we can hardly endure a few days of fever, how will we bear the parching thirst and burning torments of that fire which will never die? If we are so appalled at a sentence of death pronounced by an earthly judge, which, at most, deprives us of but forty or fifty years of life, with what feelings will we hear that sentence which deprives us of an immortal life and condemns us to an eternity of misery?

With what horror we read of the tortures inflicted by executioners upon malefactors; yet the most cruel are only shadows compared to the eternal torments of the life to come. The former end with this life; but in Hell the worm of conscience shall never die, the executioner shall never grow weary, the fire shall never be extinguished. What, then, will be the feelings of the wicked when suddenly transported from the midst of earthly happiness to this abyss of unspeakable miseries? In vain will they denounce their blindness and bewail the graces they refused. What can the pilot do when the ship is lost? Of what use is the physician when the patient is dead? Whither will we turn, on that terrible day, when the heavens and the earth, the sun, moon, and stars, when all creatures, will raise their voices against us to testify the evil we have committed? But even were these silent, our own consciences would still accuse us.

These reflections, dear Christian, we have gathered chiefly from the writings of St. John Chrysostom. Do they not prove the necessity of living with the fear of this supreme judgment constantly before us? This fear was never absent from the heart of St. Ambrose, notwithstanding the vigilant fervor of his life. "Woe is me," he exclaims in his commentary on St. Luke—"Woe is me if I weep not for my sins! Woe is me, O Lord, if I rise not in the night to confess and proclaim the glory of Thy name! Woe is me if I do not dissipate the errors of my brethren and cause the light of truth to burn before their eyes, for the axe is now laid to the root of the tree."

Let him, therefore, who is in a state of grace, bring forth fruits of justice and salvation. Let him who is in a state of sin bring forth fruits of penance, for the time approaches when the Lord will gather His fruit; and He will give eternal life to those who have labored courageously and profitably, and eternal death to those whose works are barren and useless.

CHAPTER 9

The Ninth Motive for practicing Virtue: The Thought of Heaven, the Third of the Four Last Things

A motive no less powerful than those we have enumerated is the thought of Heaven. This is the reward of virtue, and in it we must distinguish two things: the excellence and beauty of the abode promised us, which is no other than the empyreal heavens, and the perfection and beauty of the Sovereign King who reigns there with His elect.

But though no tongue can fully express the splendor and riches of the heavenly kingdom, we will endeavor to describe its beauty as well as our limited capacities will allow. Let us, therefore, first consider the grand end for which it was created, which will enable us to conceive some idea of its magnificence.

God created it to manifest His glory. Though "the Lord hath made all things for himself," (*Prov.* 16:4) yet this is particularly true of Heaven, for it is there that His glory and power are most resplendent. We are told in Scripture that Assuerus, whose kingdom included one hundred twenty-seven provinces, gave a great feast, which lasted one hundred eighty days, for the purpose of manifesting his splendor and power. So the Sovereign King of the universe is pleased to celebrate a magnificent feast, which continues, not for one hundred eighty days only, but for all eternity, to manifest the magnificence of His bounty, His power, His riches, His goodness.

It is of this feast that the prophet speaks when he tells us, "The Lord of hosts shall make unto all people in this mountain a feast of fat things, a feast of wine, of fat things full of marrow, of wine purified from the lees." (*Is.* 25:6). By this we are to understand that He will lavish upon His elect all the riches of the heavenly country and inebriate them with unutterable delights. Since this feast is prepared to manifest the greatness of God's glory, which is infinite, what must be the magnificence of this feast and the variety and splendor of the riches He displays to the eyes of His elect?

We will better appreciate the grandeur of Heaven if we consider the infinite power and boundless riches of God Himself. His power is so great that with a single word He created this vast universe, and with a single word He could again reduce it to its original nothingness. A single expression of His will would suffice to create millions of worlds as beautiful as ours, and to destroy them in one instant.

Moreover, His power is exercised without effort or exertion; it costs Him no more to create the most sublime seraphim than to create the smallest insect. With Him, to will is to accomplish. Therefore, if the power of the King who calls us to His kingdom be so great; if such be the glory of His holy Name; if His desire to manifest and communicate this glory be so great, what must be the splendor of the abode where He wills to display, in its fullness, His divine magnificence?

Nothing can be wanting to its perfection, for its Author is the Source of all riches, all power, and all wisdom. What must be the beauty of that creation in the formation of which are combined the almighty power of the Father, the infinite wisdom of the Son, the inexhaustible goodness of the Holy Spirit?

Another consideration no less striking is that God has prepared this magnificence not only for His glory, but for the glory of His elect. "Whosoever shall glorify me, him will I glorify." (*1 Kg.* 2:30). "Thou hast subjected all things under his feet," cries out the psalmist (*Ps.* 8:8); and this we see verified in the most striking manner among the saints. Witness Josue, whose word arrests the sun in its course, thus showing us, as the Scripture says, "God obeying the voice of man." (*Jos.* 10:14). Consider the prophet Isaias bidding King Ezechias choose whether he will have the sun go forward or backward in its course, for it was in the power of God's servant to cause either. (*4 Kg.* 20:9).

Behold Elias closing the heavens, so that there was no rain but at his will and prayer. And not only during life, but even after death, God continues to honor the mortal remains of His elect; for do we not read in Scripture that a dead body which was thrown by highwaymen into the tomb of Eliseus was brought to life by contact with the bones of the prophet? (*4 Kg.* 13:21). Did not God also honor in a marvelous manner the body of St. Clement? On the day that this generous defender of the Faith suffered, the sea was opened for a distance of three miles to allow the people to pass to the place of martyrdom to venerate the sacred remains. Is it not from a like motive that the Church has instituted a feast in honor of St. Peter's chains, to show us how God wills to honor the bodies of His servants, since we are to reverence their very chains?

A still more marvelous proof of this was the power of healing the sick communicated to the shadow of the same Apostle. Oh! Admirable goodness! God confers upon His Apostle a power which He Himself did not exercise. Of St. Peter alone is this related. But if God be pleased thus to honor the saints on earth, though it is but a place of toil and labor, who can tell the glory which He has reserved for them in His kingdom, where He wills to honor them, and through them to glorify Himself?

The Holy Scriptures teach us also with what liberality

God rewards the services we render Him. We are told that when Abraham was about to sacrifice his son in obedience to God's command, an angel of the Lord appeared to him and said, "By my own self have I sworn, saith the Lord: because thou hast done this thing, and hast not spared thy only begotten son for my sake, I will bless thee, and I will multiply thy seed as the stars of heaven and as the sand that is by the sea shore; thy seed shall possess the gates of their enemies. And in thy seed shall all the nations of the earth be blessed, because thou hast obeyed my voice." (*Gen.* 22:16-18). Was not this a reward befitting such a Master? God is sovereign in His rewards, as well as in His punishments.

We read also that David, reflecting one night that while he dwelt in a house of cedar, the Ark of the Covenant was kept in a poor tent, resolved to build it a more fitting habitation; and the next day the Lord sent the prophet Nathan to promise, in His name, the following magnificent reward: Because thou hast thought of building me a house, I swear to thee that I will build one for thee and thy posterity which shall have no end, nor will I ever remove my mercies from it. (Cf. *2 Kg.* 7). We see how faithfully His promise was fulfilled, for the kingdom of Israel was governed by the princes of the house of David until the coming of the Messias, who from that time has reigned, and shall reign for all eternity.

Heaven, then, is that superabundant reward which the faithful will receive for their good works. It is the manifestation of the Divine munificence, and of its greatness and glory we ought to have a lively appreciation. Another consideration which will help us to form some idea of the eternal beatitude promised us is the price which God, who is so liberal, required for it. After we had forfeited Heaven by sin, God, who is so rich and magnificent in His rewards, would restore it to us only at the price of the Blood of His Divine Son. The death of Christ, therefore, gave us life; His sorrows won for us eternal joy; and, that we might enter into the ranks of the celestial choirs, He bore the ignominy of crucifixion between two thieves.

Who, then, can sufficiently value that happiness to obtain which God shed the last drop of His Blood, was bound with ignominious fetters, overwhelmed with outrages, bruised with blows, and nailed to a cross? But besides all these, God asks on our part all that can be required of man. He tells us that we must take up our cross and follow Him; that if our right eye offend us we must pluck it out; that we must renounce father and mother, and every creature that is an obstacle to the Divine will. And after we have faithfully complied with His commands, the Sovereign Remunerator still tells us that the enjoyment of Heaven is a gratuitous gift. "I am Alpha and Omega; the beginning and the end," He says by the mouth of St. John (*Apoc.* 21:6); "to him that thirsteth, I will give of the fountain of the water of life freely."

Since God so liberally bestows His gifts upon the sinner as well as the just in this life, what must be the inexhaustible riches reserved for the just in the life to come? If He be so bountiful in His gratuitous gifts, how munificent will He be in His rewards?

It may further help us to conceive a faint image of this eternal glory to consider the nobility and grandeur of the empyreal Heaven, our future country. It is called in Scripture the land of the living, in contrast, doubtless, to our sad country, which may truly be called the land of the dying. But if, in this land of death inhabited by mortal beings, so much beauty and perfection are found, what must be the splendor and magnificence of that heavenly country whose inhabitants will live forever?

Cast your eyes over the world and behold the wonders and beauties with which it is filled. Observe the immensity of the blue vault of heaven; the dazzling splendor of the sun; the soft radiance of the moon and stars; the verdant beauty of the earth, with its treasures of precious metals and brilliant gems; the rich plumage of the birds; the grandeur of the mountains; the smiling beauty of the valleys; the limpid freshness of the streams; the majesty of the great rivers; the vastness of the sea, with all the wonders it contains; the beauty of the deep lakes, those eyes of the earth, reflecting on their placid bosoms the starry splendor of the heavens; the flower-enameled fields, which seem a counterpart of the starlit firmament above them. If in this land of exile we behold so much beauty to enrapture our soul, what must be the spectacle which awaits us in the haven of eternal rest?

Compare the inhabitants of the two countries, if you would have a still stronger proof of the superiority and infinite grandeur of the heavenly country. This earth is the land of death; Heaven is the land of immortality. Ours is the habitation of sinners, Heaven the habitation of the just. Ours is a place of penance, an arena of combat; Heaven is the land of triumph, the throne of the victor, the "city of God." "Glorious things are said of thee, O city of God." (*Ps.* 86:3). Immeasurable is thy greatness, incomparable the beauty of thy structure. Infinite thy price; most noble thy inhabitants, sublime thy employments; most rich art thou in all good, and no evil can penetrate thy sacred walls. Great is thy Author, high the end for which thou wast created, and most noble the blessed citizens who dwell in thee.

All that we have hitherto said relates only to the accidental glory of the saints. They possess another glory incomparably superior, which theologians call the essential glory. This is the vision and possession of God Himself. For St. Augustine tells us that the reward of virtue will be God Himself, the Author of all virtue, whom we will untiringly contemplate, love, and praise for all eternity. (*City of God,* 22, 30). What reward could be greater than this? It is not

Heaven, or earth, or any created perfection, but God, the Source of all beauty and all perfection. The blessed inhabitants of Heaven will enjoy in Him all good, each according to the degree of glory he has merited. For since God is the Author of every good that we behold in creatures, it follows that He possesses in Himself all perfection, all goodness, in an infinite degree. He possesses them, because otherwise He could not have bestowed them on creatures. He possesses them in an infinite degree, because as His Being is infinite, so also are His attributes and His perfections.

God, then, will be our sovereign beatitude and the fulfillment of all our desires. In Him we will find the perfections of all creatures exalted and transfigured. In Him we will enjoy the beauty of all the seasons—the balmy freshness of spring, the rich beauty of summer, the luxurious abundance of autumn, and the calm repose of winter. In a word, all that can delight the senses and enrapture the soul will be ours in Heaven. "In God," says St. Bernard, "our understandings will be filled with the plenitude of light; our wills with an abundance of peace; and our memories with the joys of eternity. In this abode of all perfection, the wisdom of Solomon will appear but ignorance; the beauty of Absolom deformity; the strength of Samson weakness; the longest life of man a brief mortality; the wealth of kings but indigence."

Why, then, O man, will you seek straws in Egypt? Why will you drink troubled waters from broken cisterns, when inexhaustible treasures, and the fountain of living water springing up into eternal life, await you in Heaven? Why will you seek vain and sensual satisfactions from creatures, when unalterable happiness may be yours? If your heart craves joy, raise it to the contemplation of that Good which contains in Itself all joys. If you are in love with this created life, consider the eternal life which awaits you above. If the beauty of creatures attracts you, live that you may one day possess the Source of all beauty, in whom are life, and strength, and glory, and immortality, and the fullness of all our desires. If you find happiness in friendship and the society of generous hearts, consider the noble beings with whom you will be united by the tenderest ties for all eternity. If your ambition seeks wealth and honors, make the treasures and the glory of Heaven the end of all your efforts. Finally, if you desire freedom from all evil and rest from all labor, in Heaven alone can your desires be gratified.

God, in the Old Law, ordained that children should be circumcised on the eighth day after birth, teaching us thereby that, on the day of the general resurrection which will follow the short space of this life, He will cut off the miseries and sufferings of those who, for love of Him, have circumcised their hearts by cutting off all the sinful affections and pleasures of this world. Now, who can conceive a happier existence than this, which is exempt from every sorrow and every infirmity?

"In Heaven," says St. Augustine, "we shall cease to feel the trials of want or sickness. Pride or envy will never enter there. The necessity of eating or drinking will there be unknown. The desire for honors will never disturb our calm repose. Death will no longer reach body or soul, united as they will be with the Source of all life, which they will enjoy throughout a blessed immortality." (*Soliloq.*, 35). Consider, moreover, the glory and happiness of living in the company of the angels, contemplating the beauty of these sublime spirits; admiring the resplendent virtue of the saints, and the rewards with which the obedience of the patriarchs and the hope of the prophets have been crowned; the brilliant diadems of the martyrs, dyed with their own blood; and the dazzling whiteness of the robes with which the virgins are adorned.

But what tongue can describe the beauty and the majesty of the Sovereign Monarch who reigns in their midst? "If by daily enduring fresh torments," says St. Augustine

(*Manual.*, 15), "and even suffering for a time the pains of Hell, we were permitted for one day to contemplate this King in all His glory and enjoy the society of His elect, surely it would be a happiness cheaply purchased."

What, then, can we say of the happiness of possessing these joys for all eternity? Conceive, if you can, the ravishing harmony of the celestial voices chanting the words heard by St. John: "Benediction, and glory, and wisdom, and thanksgiving, honor, and power, and strength to our God for ever and ever. Amen." (*Apoc.* 7:12). If the harmony of these voices will cause us such happiness, how we will rejoice at the unity that we will behold between soul and body! And this concord will be still more marked between angels and men, whilst between God and men the union will be so close that we can form no adequate idea of it. What glory, then, will it be for the creature to find himself seated at the banquet of the King of kings, partaking of His table—that is, of His honor and His glory! Oh! Enduring peace of Heaven! Oh! Unalterable joy! Oh! Entrancing harmonies! Oh! Torrents of celestial delight, why are ye not ever present to the minds of those who labor and combat on earth?

If such be the happiness which faith tells us is the reward of the just, how great is your blindness if you are not moved thereby to practice virtue!

CHAPTER 10

*The Tenth Motive for practicing Virtue: The
Thought of Hell, the Fourth of the Four Last
Things*

The least part of the happiness we have endeavored to portray should be sufficient to inflame our hearts with a love of virtue. Nevertheless, we shall also consider the terrible alternative of misery reserved for the reprobate. The sinner cannot comfort himself by saying, "After all, the only result of my depraved life will be that I shall never see God. Further than this I shall have neither reward nor punishment." Oh, no; we are all destined to one or the other—either to reign eternally with God in Heaven or to burn forever with the devils in Hell!

This happiness and misery, either of which must inevitably be our portion, are represented by the two baskets of figs which Jeremias saw in the vision, one containing "very good figs, like the figs of the first season, and the other basket very bad figs, which could not be eaten." (*Jer.* 24:1-2). God willed thus to represent to His prophet the two classes of souls, one of which forms the object of His mercy, and the other of His justice. The happiness of the first is unequaled, and the misery of the second is also incomparable; for the just enjoy the perpetual vision of God, which is the greatest of all blessings, while the wicked are forever deprived of this vision, and thereby suffer the greatest of all evils.

If men who sin so rashly would weigh this truth, they would know the terrible burden that they lay upon themselves. Those who earn their living by carrying burdens first estimate the weight they are to bear, that they may know whether it is beyond their strength. Why, then, O rash man, will you—for a passing pleasure—so lightly assume the terrible burden of sin, without considering your strength to bear it? Will you not reflect on the heavy weight you thus condemn yourself to bear for all eternity? To help you do this I shall offer you a few considerations which will enable you to realize in some measure the greatness of the punishment reserved for sin.

Let us first reflect on the almighty power of God, whose justice will chastise the sinner. God's greatness is apparent in all His works. He is God, not only in Heaven, earth, and sea, but in Hell and in every other place. He is God in His wrath and in the justice with which He avenges the outrages offered to His divine majesty. Therefore, He Himself exclaims by the mouth of His prophet, "Will you not then fear me, and will you not repent at my presence? I have set the sand a bound for the sea, an everlasting ordinance, which it shall not pass over; and the waves thereof shall toss themselves, and shall not prevail: they shall swell, and shall not pass over it." (*Jer.* 5:22).

In other words, will you not fear the almighty power of that Arm which controls the elements, which sustains the universe, and which no power can resist? If the works of His mercy excite us to love and praise Him, we have no less reason to fear the greatness of His justice. Hence the prophet Jeremias, though innocent, and even sanctified in his mother's womb, was deeply penetrated with this salutary fear. "Who," he cries out, "shall not fear thee, O king of nations?" (*Jer.* 10:7). And again: "I sat alone, because thou hast filled me with threats." (*Jer.* 15:17). Doubtless the prophet knew that these threats were not uttered against him; yet they filled him with terror. The pillars of Heaven, we are told, tremble before the majesty of God, and the powers and principalities prostrate themselves in awe before His throne. If these pure spirits, confirmed in bliss, and in no manner doubting of their happiness, but only through admiration of the Divine Perfections, tremble before His power, what should be the terror of the sinner who has made himself the object of His wrath? It is the power of our Sovereign Judge which is most appalling in the punishment of sin. Speaking of God's punishments, St. John says, "Babylon's plagues shall come in one day, death, and mourning, and famine, and she shall be burnt with fire, because God is strong, who shall judge her." (*Apoc.* 18:8). The great Apostle, filled with awe of this power, exclaims, "It is a fearful thing to fall into the hands of the living God." (*Heb.* 10:31).

We have not such reason to fear the hands of men, from whom we can escape, and who at least cannot thrust the soul into Hell. Hence Our Saviour tells His disciples, "And fear ye not them that kill the body and are not able to kill the soul. But rather fear him who can destroy both soul and body in Hell." (*Matt.* 10:28). The author of Ecclesiasticus, impressed with the might of this power, thus warns us: "Unless we do penance we shall fall into the hands of the Lord, and not into the hands of men." (*Ecclus.* 2:22). This united testimony proves, as we have said, that as God is great in His mercy and rewards, so will He be great in His justice and punishments.

This truth is still more apparent in the terrible chastisements inflicted by God which are related in Scripture. Witness the punishment of Dathan and Abiron, who, with all their accomplices, were swallowed alive into the earth and thrust into the depths of Hell for rebelling against their superiors. Who can read unmoved the threats against transgressors recorded in Deuteronomy? Among others equally terrible, here is one which the sacred writer puts into the mouth of God: "Thou shalt serve thy enemy, whom the Lord will send upon thee, in hunger, and thirst, and nakedness, and in want of all things: and he shall put an iron yoke upon thy neck till he consume thee . . . And thou shalt eat the fruit of thy womb, and the flesh of thy sons and of thy daughters, which the Lord thy God shall give thee, in the distress and extremity wherewith thy enemy shall oppress thee." (*Deut.* 28:48, 53).

We can scarcely imagine punishments more dreadful than these; yet they, as well as all the sufferings of this life, are but a shadow when compared to the terrible torments of the life to come. If His justice be so rigorous in this world, though always tempered by His love, what will it be in eternity when exercised without mercy? For the sinner who has despised God's mercies in this life will feel only the effects of His justice in the life to come.

Another consideration which may help us to appreciate the rigor of these sufferings is the greatness of the mercy which the sinner has despised. What is there more astonishing than that mercy which caused God to clothe Himself in human flesh, to endure innumerable sufferings and humiliations, to take upon Himself the transgressions of the world, and for these transgressions to expire as a malefactor on an infamous gibbet? God is infinite in all His attributes; and, therefore, the justice with which He will punish man will equal the boundless mercy with which He redeemed him.

When God first came upon earth there was nothing in us to excite His mercy; but at His second coming our every sin will be an additional reason for Him to exercise His justice. Judge, therefore, how terrible it will be. "At His second coming," says St. Bernard, "God will be as inflexible and as rigorous in punishing as at His first coming He was patient and merciful in forgiving. There is now no sinner living who is cut off from His reconciliation; but in the day of His justice none will be received." These words of St. Bernard are confirmed by the royal prophet, who tells us, "Our God is the God of salvation: and of the Lord, of the Lord are the issues from death. But God shall break the heads of his enemies: the hairy crown of them that walk on in their sins." (*Ps.* 67:21-22). Behold, then, how great is God's mercy to those who are converted to Him, and how great is the rigor with which He punishes obdurate sinners.

The same truth is manifested by God's patience with the world, and with the vices and disorders of every sinner in particular. How many there are who, from the age of reason to the end of their lives, continually offend Him and despise His law, regardless of His promises, His benefits, His warnings, or His menaces! Yet God does not cut them off, but continues to bear with them, unceasingly exhorting them to repentance. But when the term of His patience will come, and His wrath, which has been accumulating in the bosom of His justice, will burst its bounds, with what terrible violence it will be poured out upon them! "Knowest thou not," says the Apostle, "that the benignity of God leadeth thee to penance? But according to thy hardness and impenitent heart, thou treasurest up to thyself wrath, against the day of wrath, and revelation of the just judgment of God, who will render to every man according to his works." (*Rom.* 2:4-6).

The meaning of these words is not difficult. A *treasure of wrath* is a terrible figure. Just as the miser adds coin to coin, riches to riches, so the wrath of God is daily and even hourly increased by the transgressions of the sinner. Were a man to let no day or hour pass without adding to his material fortune, consider what an immense amount he would have accumulated at the end of fifty or sixty years. Alas, then, for thee, unhappy sinner, for there is hardly an hour in which thou dost not add to the treasures of God's wrath which thy sins are accumulating against thee. Thy immodest glances, the evil desires of thy corrupt heart, and thy scandalous words and blasphemies would alone suffice to fill a world. If to these are added the many other grievous crimes of which thou hast been guilty, consider the treasure of vengeance and wrath which a long life of sin will heap up against thee.

If to the considerations already given we add a brief reflection on the gratitude of men, it will help us realize, in some measure, the severity of the punishment inflicted upon the sinner. Contemplate God's goodness to men; the benefits He has heaped upon them; the means He has given them to practice virtue; the iniquities He has forgiven them; the evils from which He has delivered them. Consider, moreover, the ingratitude of men for all these blessings; their many treasons and rebellions against God; their contempt of His laws, which they trample underfoot for a paltry interest, and often through malice or mere caprice. What, then, can he expect who has thus outraged God's mercy, who, in the words of the Apostle, has "trodden under foot the Son of God, and hath esteemed the blood of the testament unclean, by which he was sanctified?" (*Heb.* 10:29). God is a just Judge, and their punishment will be proportioned to their crimes. Remember the majesty of Him who has been offended, and consider the sufferings of that body and soul which must offer satisfaction for such an outrage. If the Blood of Christ were needed to make reparation for man's offences, the dignity of the Victim supplying what was lacking in the severity of His sufferings, how terrible will be those sufferings which sinners must endure, and which must supply by their vigor what is wanting in the merit of the victim!

If the thought of the Judge impress us so deeply, what ought to be our feelings when we consider who it is that will be the executioner! The executioner will be the devil.

What, then, may we not expect from the malice of such an enemy? If we would form some idea of his cruelty, consider his treatment of the holy man Job, whom God delivered into his hands. He destroyed his flocks; laid waste his lands; overthrew his houses; carried off his children by death; made his body a mass of ulcers, and left him no other refuge but a dunghill and a potsherd to scrape his sores. In addition to his suffering he left him a scolding wife and cruel friends, who reviled him with words which tortured him more keenly than the worms which preyed upon his flesh. Thus was Job afflicted by Satan, but it is impossible to describe in human language Satan's treatment of our Blessed Saviour during the night in which He was the victim of the powers of darkness.

Seeing, then, how cruel are the devil and his angels, will you not tremble with horror at the thought of being delivered into their hands? They will have power to execute upon you the most terrible inventions of their malice, not for a day, or a night, or a year only, but for all eternity. Read the appalling picture of these evil spirits given by St. John: "I saw a star," says the Apostle, "fall from heaven upon the earth, and there was given to him the key of the bottomless pit. And he opened the bottomless pit; and the smoke of the pit arose as the smoke of a great furnace; and the sun and the air were darkened with the smoke of the pit. And from the smoke of the pit there came out locusts upon the earth. And power was given to them, as the scorpions of the earth have power. And it was commanded them that they should not hurt the grass of the earth, nor any green thing, nor any tree, but only the men who have not the seal of God on their foreheads. And it was given to them that they should not kill them, but that they should torment them five months: and their torment was as the torment of a scorpion when he striketh a man. And in those days men shall seek death, and shall not find it; and they shall desire to die, and death shall fly from them. And the shapes of the locusts were like unto horses prepared unto battle; and on their heads were, as it were, crowns like gold; and their faces were as the faces of men. And they had hair as the hair of women, and their teeth were as the teeth of lions; and they had breastplates as breastplates of iron, and the noise of their wings was as the sound of chariots of many horses running to battle. And they had tails like to scorpions, and there were stings in their tails." (*Apoc.* 9:1-10).

Does not the Holy Ghost design to teach us by these terrible figures the fearful effects of God's justice, the awful instruments of His wrath, and the appalling tortures of the reprobate? Does He not wish that the fear of these evils should save us from the lot of the sinner? What is that star which fell from Heaven, and received the key of the bottomless pit, but that bright angel who was precipitated from Heaven to reign forever in Hell? Do not the locusts, so well equipped for battle, represent the ministers of Satan? And are not the green things which they were commanded to spare, the just who flourish under the dew of God's grace and bring forth fruits of eternal life? Who are they who have not the seal of God upon their foreheads but men who have not His Spirit, which is the mark and seal of His faithful servants? It is against these unhappy souls that the ministers of God's vengeance will work.

Yes, they will be tormented in this life and in the next by the devils whom they willed to serve, just as the Egyptians were tormented by the various living creatures which they had adored. What terrible pictures are given us in Scripture of the monsters of this eternal abyss! What can be conceived more horrible than the behemoth, "that setteth up his tail like a cedar, whose bones are like pipes of brass, who drinketh up rivers and devoureth mountains?" (*Job* 40:10-19).

The considerations already given are certainly sufficient

to inspire us with a horror of sin; but to strengthen this salutary fear let us reflect upon the duration of these terrible torments. Try to realize what a comfort it would be to the damned if at the end of millions of years they could look forward to any term or alleviation of their sufferings. But no; their suffering shall be eternal; they shall continue as long as God shall be God. If one of these unhappy souls, says a Doctor of the Church, were to shed one tear every thousand years, and if these tears accumulated to such a flood as to inundate the world, he would still be as far as ever from the end of his sufferings. Eternity would only be at its beginning. Is there anything worthy of our fears but this terrible fate? Truly, were the pain of Hell no more than the prick of a pin, yet if it must continue forever there is no suffering in this world which man should not endure to avoid it.

Oh! That this eternity, this terrible *forever,* were deeply graven in our hearts! We are told that a worldly man, giving himself to serious reflection upon eternity, made use of this simple reasoning: There is no sensible man who would accept the empire of the world at the expense of thirty or forty years spent upon a bed, even were it a bed of roses. How great, then, is the folly of him who, for much smaller interests, incurs the risk of being condemned to lie upon a bed of fire for all eternity! This thought wrought such a change in his life that he became a great saint and most worthy prelate of the Church.

What consideration will be given to this by the soft and effeminate, who complain so much if the buzzing of a mosquito disturbs their night's repose? What will they say when they will find themselves stretched upon a bed of fire, surrounded by sulphurous flames, not for one short summer night, but for all eternity? To such the prophet addresses himself when he says, "Which of you can dwell with devouring fire? Which of you shall dwell with everlasting burnings?" (*Is.* 33:14). O senseless man! Will you continue to allow yourself to be deceived by the arch-enemy of your soul? How can you be so diligent in providing for your temporal welfare, and yet be so careless of your eternal interests?

If you were penetrated with these reflections, what obstacle could turn you from the practice of virtue? Difficult as it may appear, is there any sacrifice you would refuse to escape these eternal torments? Were God to allow a man to choose whether he would be tormented while on earth with a gout or toothache which would never allow him a moment's repose, or embrace the life of a Carthusian or a Carmelite, do you think there is anyone who would not, purely from a motive of self-love, choose the state of a religious rather than endure this continual suffering? Yet there is no pain in this life which can be compared to the pains of Hell, either in intensity or in duration. Why, then, will we not accept the labor God asks of us, which is so much less than the austerities of a Carthusian or a Carmelite? Why will we refuse the restraint of His law, which will save us from such suffering?

What will add most keenly to the sufferings of the damned will be the knowledge that by a short penance and self-denial upon earth they might have averted these terrible pains which they must fruitlessly endure for all eternity. We see a figure of this awful truth in the furnace which Nabuchodonosor caused to be built in Babylon (*Dan.* 3), the flames of which mounted forty-nine cubits, but could never reach fifty, the number of the year of jubilee, or general pardon. In like manner the eternal flame of this Babylon, though it burns so fiercely, filling its unhappy victims with pain and anguish, will never reach the point of mercy, will never obtain for them the grace of pardon of the heavenly jubilee.

Oh! Unprofitable pains! Oh! Fruitless tears! Oh!

Rigorous and hopeless penance! If borne in this life, the smallest portion of them might have saved the sinner from everlasting misery. Mindful of all these, send forth your tears and sighs, remembering the prophet who "lamented and howled, who went stripped and naked, making a wailing like the dragons, and a mourning like the ostriches, because her wound was desperate." (*Micheas* 1:8-9).

If men were ignorant of these truths, if they had not received them as infallible, their negligence and indifference would not be so astonishing. But have we not reason to wonder, since men have received them on the word of Him who has said, "Heaven and earth shall pass away, but my words shall not pass away"? (*Lk.* 21:33). Yet behold in what forgetfulness of their duty and their God they continue to live.

Tell me, blind soul, what pleasure you find in the riches and honors of this world which is a compensation for the eternal fire of Hell. "If you possessed the wisdom of Solomon," says St. Jerome, "the beauty of Absalom, the strength of Samson, the longevity of Henoch, the riches of Croesus, the power of Caesar, what will all these avail you at death, if your body becomes the prey of worms, and your soul, like the rich glutton's, the sport of demons for all eternity?"

CHAPTER 11

The Eleventh Motive for practicing Virtue:
The Inestimable Advantages promised it
even in this Life

With such powerful reasons for embracing virtue, I know not what excuse men can make for refusing to practice it. That pagans, who are ignorant of its value, do not prize it is not astonishing. A peasant digging in the earth and finding a precious stone will probably throw it away, because he does not know its worth. But that Christians, who have been taught the value and beauty of virtue, continue to live in forgetfulness of God and wedded to the things of this world, as if there were no such thing as death or judgment, or Heaven or Hell, is a continual subject of sorrowful wonder. Whence this blindness, whence this folly?

It has several causes, the principal of which is the mistaken opinion of the generality of men, who believe that no advantages are to be reaped from virtue in this life, that its rewards are reserved for the life to come.

Men are so powerfully moved by self-interest, and present objects make such an impression upon them, that they think very little of future rewards and seek only their immediate satisfaction. The same was true even in the days of the prophets; for when Ezechiel made any promise or uttered any threat in the name of the Lord, people laughed at him and said to one another, "The vision that this man seeth is for many days to come; and this man prophesieth of times afar off." (*Ezech.* 12:27). In like manner did they ridicule the prophet Isaias: "Command, command again, command, command again; expect, expect again, expect, expect again." (*Is.* 28:10). Solomon teaches us the same when he says, "Because sentence is not speedily pronounced against the evil, the children of men commit evils without any fear . . . Because all things equally happen to the just and the wicked . . . to him that offereth victims and to him that despiseth sacrifices . . . the hearts of the children of men are filled with evil, and with contempt while they live, and afterwards they shall be brought down to hell." (*Eccles.* 8:11; 9:2-3).

Yes, because the wicked seem to prosper in the world they conclude that they are safe, and that the labor of virtue is all in vain. This they openly confess by the mouth of the prophet Malachias, saying, "He laboreth in vain that serveth God; and what profit is it that we have kept His ordinances, and that we have walked sorrowful before the Lord of hosts? Wherefore now we call the proud people happy, for they that work wickedness are built up, and they have tempted God and are preserved." (*Mal.* 3:14-15). This is the language of the reprobate, and is the most powerful motive which impels them to continue in sin; for, in the words of St. Ambrose, "They find it too difficult to buy hopes at the cost of dangers, to sacrifice present pleasures to future blessings." To destroy this serious error I know nothing better than the touching words of Our Saviour weeping over Jerusalem: "If thou also hadst known, and that in this thy day, the things that are for thy peace; but now they are hidden from thy eyes." (*Lk.* 19:42).

Our Divine Lord considered the advantages which this people had received from Him; the happiness He had reserved for them; and the ingratitude with which they rejected Him when He came to them in meekness and humility. For this they were to lose not only the treasures and graces of His coming, but even their temporal power and freedom. This it was which caused Him to shed such bitter tears and to foretell the unhappy fate that was in store for His people. His words apply with great force to our present subject.

Consider the inestimable riches, the abundant graces, which accompany virtue; yet it is a stranger, a wanderer on earth. Men seem to be blind to these divine blessings. Have we not, therefore, reason to weep and to cry out, *O man, if thou also hadst known?* If thou hadst known the peace, the light, the strength, the sweetness, and the riches of virtue, thou wouldst have opened thy heart to it, thou wouldst have spared no sacrifice to win it. But these blessings are hidden from worldlings, who regard only the humble exterior of virtue, and, having never experienced its unutterable sweetness, they conclude that it contains nothing but what is sad and repulsive.

They know not that Christian philosophy is like its Divine Founder, who, though exteriorly the humblest of men, was nevertheless God and sovereign Lord of all things. Hence the Apostle tells the faithful that they are dead to the world, that their "life is hid with Christ in God." (*Col.* 3:3). Just as the glory of Christ was hidden by the veil of His humanity, so should the glory of His faithful followers be concealed in this world. We read that the ancients made certain images, called Silenes, which were rough and coarse exteriorly, but most curiously and ingeniously wrought within. The ignorant stopped at the exterior and saw nothing to prize, but those who understood their construction looked within and were captivated by the beauty they there beheld. Such have been the lives of the prophets, the Apostles, and all true Christians, for such was the life of their Divine Model.

If you still tell me that the path of virtue is rugged, that its duties are difficult, I beg you to consider the abundant and powerful aids which God gives you. Such are the infused virtues, interior graces, the gifts of the Holy Ghost, the sacraments of the New Law, with other divine favors, which are to us like sails to a ship, or wings to a bird, to help us on our voyage to eternity. Reflect upon the very name and nature of virtue. It is a noble habit, which, like all other habits, ought to make us act with facility and pleasure. Remember also that Christ has promised His followers not only the riches of glory, but those of grace: the former for the life to come, the latter for this present life. "The Lord," says the prophet, "will give grace and glory." (*Ps.* 83:12). The treasures of grace are for this life, and the riches of glory are for the next.

Consider further with what care God provides for the necessities of all creatures. How generously He supplies even the smallest creatures with all that is necessary to the end for which they were created! Is it not unreasonable, then, to think that He will disregard the necessities of man, the most important of which is virtue, and leave him a prey to his weak will, his darkened understanding, and his corrupt nature? The world and the prince of darkness are most assiduous in procuring vain pleasures and joys for those who serve them. Can you doubt, then, that God will grant refreshment, light, and peace to His faithful in the midst of the labors performed for Him? What did God wish to teach us by the words of the prophet: "You shall return, and shall see the difference between the just and the wicked, and between him that serveth God and him that serveth him not." (*Mal.* 3:18). Was it not that if we would be converted we would see and know, even in this life, the rewards of the good, "the difference between the just and the wicked"? We would behold the contrast between the true riches of the just and the poverty of the wicked; between the joy of the former and the misery of the latter; between the peace of the one and the conflicts of the other; between the light with which the good are surrounded and the darkness by which the wicked are enveloped. Experience will show you the real value of virtue and how far it exceeds your former anticipations.

Upon another occasion God replied in like manner to men who, having been deceived by appearances, ridiculed the virtuous, saying, "Let the Lord be glorified, and we shall see in your joy." (*Is.* 66:5). After depicting the torments which God's justice prepares for the wicked, Isaias thus describes the happiness reserved for the just: "Rejoice with Jerusalem, and be glad with her, all ye that love her. Rejoice for joy with her, all you that mourn for her. That you may suck, and be filled with the breasts of her consolation; that you may milk out, and flow with delights, from the abundance of her glory. For thus saith the Lord: Behold I will bring upon her as it were a river of peace, and as an overflowing torrent, the glory of the Gentiles, which you shall suck; you shall be carried at the breasts, and upon the knees they shall caress you. As one whom the mother caresseth, so will I comfort you, and you shall be comforted in Jerusalem. And you shall see, and your heart shall rejoice, and your bones shall flourish like an herb, and the hand of the Lord shall be known to his servants . . ." (*Is.* 66:10-14). Yes, "the hand of the Lord shall be known to his servants"; for as men by the beauties and wonders of the universe judge of the infinite beauty and omnipotence of God, so shall the just recognize the infinite love and goodness of God in the incomparable joys and favors which He will bestow upon them.

As a further proof of what has been said, I will add the remarkable words uttered by Our Saviour when St. Peter asked what reward they would have for leaving all things for love of Him: "Amen I say to you, there is no man who hath left house, or brethren, or sisters, or father, or mother, or children, or lands for my sake and for the gospel, who shall not receive a hundred times as much, now in this time . . . and in the world to come life everlasting." (*Mk.* 10:29-30). Mark how explicitly the rewards of this life and the next are distinguished. Nor can we doubt these words, for they are those of Him who has said, "Heaven and earth shall pass away, but my words shall not pass away."

And what is this hundredfold which the just receive in this life? Honors, riches, titles, and dignities are not their portion; the greater number of the just lead hidden, obscure lives, forgotten by the world and overwhelmed with infirmities. How, then, does God fulfill His infallible promise to give them a hundredfold even in this life? Ah! It is not with the perishable goods of this world that He will reward His servants.

Joy and peace and happiness are the spiritual treasures with which the liberality of our God enriches those who love Him. These are the blessings which the world does not know, and which the wealth of the world can never buy. And how fitting this is; for as man does not live by bread alone, so the craving of his soul cannot be satisfied by anything short of spiritual blessings.

Study the lives of the saints, and you will see that they have received the hundredfold promised in this life. In exchange for the false riches which they forsook, they received true riches which they can bear with them to eternity. For the turmoil and conflicts of the world, they received that "peace which surpasseth all understanding." Their tears, their fasting, and their prayers brought them more joy and consolation than they could ever hope to obtain from the fleeting pleasures of this life.

If, then, you have forsaken an earthly father for love of God, your Heavenly Father will receive you as His child, and make you His heir to an everlasting inheritance. If you have despised earthly pleasures for love of Him, He will fill you with the incomparable sweetness of heavenly consolations. The eyes of your soul will be opened, and you will love and cherish what formerly frightened you. What was formerly bitter will become sweet; and, enlightened by grace, you will see the emptiness of worldly joys, and you will learn to relish the delights of God's love. Thus does He manifest His merciful goodness; thus does He fulfill His promise to us.

The annals of the Cistercian Order mention an incident which, in connection with our subject, is worth recording. Arnulph, a man of prominence in Flanders, who was strongly wedded to the things of this world, was converted by the preaching of St. Bernard. He was so touched by grace that he became a Cistercian monk. On a certain occasion he fell dangerously sick and remained unconscious for some time. The monks, believing him to be dying, administered Extreme Unction. But soon after, his consciousness returned, and he broke out into transports of praise, frequently repeating, "How true are Thy words, O merciful Jesus!" To the questions of his brethren he continued to repeat, "How true are Thy words, O merciful Jesus!" Some of them remarked that pain had made him delirious. "No, my brethren," he exclaimed; "I am conscious, I am in full possession of my senses, and again I assure you that all the words Jesus has uttered are true."

"But we do not doubt this," said the monks; "why do you repeat it so often?"

"God tells us in the Gospel," he answered, "that he who forsakes earthly affections for love of Him shall receive a hundredfold in this world, and in the world to come, life everlasting, and I have already experienced the truth of His promise. Great as my present pains are, I would not exchange them, with the anticipation of heavenly sweetness which they have procured me, for a hundred or a thousand fold of the pleasures I forsook in the world. If a guilty sinner like me receives such sweetness and consolation in the midst of his pains, what must be the joys of perfect souls?" The monks marveled to hear a man of no learning speak so wisely, but recognized in his words the inspiration of the Holy Spirit.

Therefore, we must conclude that the just, though deprived of earthly blessings, enjoy the rewards promised to virtue in this life. To convince you more fully of this we shall treat in the following chapters of the twelve privileges attached to virtue in this world. Taken as a whole, they are the twelfth motive for practicing virtue. We shall treat of each, however, in a separate chapter. Though some experience in the practice of virtue is necessary to comprehend what we are about to say, yet the want of it may be supplied by our faith in the Holy Scriptures, which firmly establish the doctrine we are teaching.

CHAPTER 12

The First Privilege of Virtue: God's fatherly Care of the Just

The greatest privilege attached to virtue is the care which God exercises over those who serve Him. From this, as from a fountainhead, flow all other favors. Though God's providence is extended to all His creatures, yet He manifests a special care for His faithful servants. To appreciate the greatness and goodness of God's providence we must have experienced it, or attentively studied the Holy Scriptures, which, from the beginning to the end, treat either directly or indirectly of God's care for His creatures.

Throughout the Bible we behold two characteristic features: on the one hand God commanding man to obey Him, and on the other promising him, in return for this obedience, inestimable rewards. To those who disobey, He threatens the severest torments. This doctrine is so distributed through the Bible that all the moral books contain God's commands and promises and threats, while the historical books record the fulfillment of the same, manifesting how differently God deals with the just and with the wicked. All that God commands us is to love and obey Him, and in return He offers us inestimable blessings for this life and the next.

The most important of these blessings is the fatherly love and care with which He watches over His children. His solicitude for them exceeds that of any earthly father. What man ever reserved for his children an inheritance comparable to that of eternal glory? What man ever suffered for his children the torments endured by Our Saviour? At no less a price than the last drop of His Blood He purchased the Kingdom of Heaven. What can equal His constant care for us? We are ever present to His mind, and He constantly helps and supports us in all the labors of life. "Thou hast upheld me by reason of my innocence," says David, "and hast established me in thy sight forever." (*Ps.* 40:13). And again: "The eyes of the Lord are upon the just, and his ears unto their prayers. But the countenance of the Lord is against them that do evil things: to cut off the remembrance of them from the earth." (*Ps.* 33:16-17).

As the greatest reward of the Christian in this life is God's fatherly care, and as our joy and confidence must increase in proportion to our faith in this providence, we shall add here a few passages from Scripture in proof of this doctrine. In Ecclesiasticus we read, "The eyes of the Lord are upon them that fear him; he is their powerful protector, and strong stay, a defence from the heat, and a cover from the sun at noon; a preservation from stumbling, and a help from falling; he raiseth up the soul, and enlighteneth the eyes, and giveth health, life, and blessing." (*Ecclus.* 34:19-20).

"With the Lord," says the prophet, "shall the steps of a man be directed, and he shall like well his way. When he shall fall he shall not be bruised, for the Lord putteth his hand under him." (*Ps.* 36:23-24). And he says again: "Many are the afflictions of the just, but out of them all will the Lord deliver them. The Lord keepeth all their bones; not one of them shall be broken." (*Ps.* 33:20-21). This providence is still more strongly set forth in the Gospel, where Our Saviour affirms that not a hair of the just shall perish. (Cf. *Lk.* 21:18). Even stronger is His assurance expressed by the mouth of His prophet: "He that toucheth you toucheth the apple of my eye." (*Zach.* 2:8).

Besides this care which He Himself has for us, "He hath given his angels charge over thee, to keep thee in all thy ways. In their hands they shall bear thee up, lest thou dash thy foot against a stone." (*Ps.* 90:11-12). Thus the mission of these pure spirits is to help the just, who are their younger brethren, to walk in the way of piety. Nor does their ministry cease at death, for we read in St. Luke that the holy beggar Lazarus was carried by angels into Abraham's bosom. (Cf. *Lk.* 16:22). The royal prophet tells us that "the angel of the Lord shall encamp round about them that fear him, and shall deliver them." (*Ps.* 33:8).

We find another illustration of God's guardianship and defence of the just in the Fourth Book of Kings (*4 Kg.* 6), where we are told that when the servant of Eliseus feared for his master, against whom the King of Syria with all his army advanced, the prophet begged the Lord to open the eyes of his servant, to show him that there were as many for Eliseus as there were coming against him. The prophet's prayer was heard, and the servants beheld the mountain full of horses and chariots of fire, and in the midst of them Eliseus. Does not the Holy Spirit will to teach us by these symbols the care with which God surrounds the just?

This protection not only delivers the just from evil and leads them to good, but turns to their profit the sins into which they are sometimes permitted to fall. For after a fall they acquire greater prudence, greater humility, and love God more tenderly for pardoning their offences and delivering them from their evils. Hence the Apostle tells us, "All things work together unto good" to them that love God. (*Rom.* 8:28).

And this protection God extends to the children of the just and to all their posterity, as He Himself assures us, saying, "I am the Lord thy God, mighty, jealous, visiting the iniquity of the fathers upon the children, unto the third and fourth generation of them that hate me; and showing mercy unto thousands to them that love me and keep my commandments." (*Ex.* 20:5-6). His words are verified in His treatment of the house of David, for whose sake He would not destroy his posterity, though they several times merited it by their crimes.

No less striking was His mercy to the children of Abraham, for whose sake He repeatedly pardoned them. He even promised that Ismael, Abraham's son, though born of a bondwoman, should "increase and multiply exceedingly," and grow into a great nation. (*Gen.* 17:20). He protected even the holy patriarch's servant, whom He guided in his journey and instructed in the means he should adopt to procure a wife for Isaac. He is not only merciful to servants for the sake of a good master, but He even blesses wicked masters because of just servants, as we see in the history of Joseph, whose master God visited with prosperity because of the virtuous youth who abode in his house. Who, then, would not be devoted to so generous, so grateful a Master, who watches so carefully over the interest of His servants?

Numerous are the titles which the Holy Scriptures use to express God's providence. The one most frequently recurring is the sweet name of Father, which we find not only in the Gospel but also throughout the Old Testament. Thus the Psalmist says, "As a father hath compassion on his children, so hath the Lord compassion on them that fear him; for he knoweth our frame, he remembereth that we are dust." (*Ps.* 102:13-14).

But because the love of a mother is deeper and more tender than that of a father, God makes use of it to express His care and solicitude for the just. "Can a woman," He says by the mouth of His prophet, "forget her infant, so as not to have pity on the son of her womb? And if she should forget, yet will not I forget thee. Behold, I have graven thee in my hands; thy walls are always before my eyes." (*Is.* 49:15-16). What sweeter or more tender assurances of love could God express?

And shall we continue blind to so many proofs of His tenderness? And not content with illustrating His love for us by that of a mother, He compares His watchfulness to that of the eagle, a creature noted for its devotion to its young, saying by Moses, "As the eagle enticing her young to fly, and hovering over them, he spread his wings, and hath taken him and carried him on his shoulders." (*Deut.* 32:11). Even more forcibly did Moses express the paternal goodness of God when he told the Israelites, "The Lord thy God hath carried thee, as a man is wont to carry his little son, all the way that you have come, until you came to this place." (*Deut.* 1:31).

As our Father, God does not disdain to call us His children, His cherished children, as the prophet Jeremias attests when, speaking in the name of God, he says, "Surely Ephraim is an honorable son to me, surely he is a tender child; for since I spoke of him, I will still remember him. Therefore are my bowels troubled for him; pitying I will pity him." (*Jer.* 31:20). Let us ponder these words, which are uttered by God Himself, that they may inflame our hearts and move us to make some return for His affectionate tenderness to us.

It is an illustration of this same providence that God assumes the title of Shepherd. "I am the good shepherd," He tells us; "and I know mine, and mine know me." (*Jn.* 10:14). How dost Thou know them, O Lord? "As the Father knoweth me, and I know the Father." (*Jn.* 10:15). Oh! Blessed care! Oh! Sovereign providence! What happiness is comparable to this?

Hear the prophet Ezechiel, speaking in the person of God, and beautifully describing His loving watchfulness over us: "Behold I myself will seek my sheep, and will visit them. As the shepherd visiteth his flock in the day when he shall be in the midst of his sheep that were scattered, so will I visit my sheep, and will deliver them out of all places where they have been scattered in the cloudy and dark day. And I will bring them out from the peoples, and will gather them out of the countries, and will bring them to their own land; and I will feed them in the mountains of Israel, by the rivers, and in all the habitations of the land. I will feed them in the most fruitful pastures, and their pastures shall be in the high mountains of Israel. There shall they rest on the green grass, and be fed in fat pastures upon the mountains of Israel. I will feed my sheep; and I will cause them to lie down, saith the Lord God. I will seek that which was lost, and that which was driven away I will bring again; and I will bind up that which was broken, and I will strengthen that which was weak, and that which was fat and strong I will preserve; and I will feed them in judgment" (*Ezech.* 34:11-17)—that is, with great care and tenderness.

"I will make a covenant of peace with them," the prophet continues, "and will cause the evil beasts to cease out of the land; and they that dwell in the wilderness shall sleep secure in the forests. And I will make them a blessing round about my hill; and I will send down the rain in its season. There shall be showers of blessing." (*Ezech.* 34:25-26). In what stronger terms could God express the tenderness of His love? It is needless to say that the flock mentioned represents the just, and the fat lands and pastures the spiritual riches and treasures with which God surrounds them. The Holy Spirit makes use of the same touching figure again in the Twenty-second Psalm, where the different offices of a shepherd are portrayed.

God is our Shepherd, because He guides us; He is also our King, because He protects us; our Master, because He instructs us; our Physician, because He heals us; and our Guardian, because He watches over us. Holy Scripture is full of these names. But the tenderest of all, the one which best expresses His love, is that of Spouse, which occurs most frequently in the Canticles of Canticles, though mentioned many times in other parts of the Scriptures. With this name would He have even sinners invoke Him: "From this time call to me: Thou art my father, the guide of my virginity." (*Jer.* 3:4).

But why seek in Scripture various names? Cannot every name expressive of good be applied to Our Saviour? Does not he who seeks and loves Him find in Him the fulfillment of all his desires? Hence, St. Ambrose says, "We possess all things in Christ, or rather Christ is all things to us. If you would be healed of your wounds, He is a Physician; if you thirst, He is a living Fountain; if you fear death, He is your Life; if you are weary of the burden of sin, He is your Justification; if you hate darkness, He is uncreated Light; if you would reach Heaven, He is the Way; if you hunger, He is your Food." (*De Virg.* L. 3). Behold how numerous are the titles which represent this one and indivisible God, who is all things to us for the healing of our innumerable infirmities.

We have selected a few of the passages of Scripture bearing on our subject, to comfort the just and to win and encourage souls who have not yet begun to serve God. These consoling truths will support them in labor; will reassure them in danger; will comfort them in tribulation; will inflame them with love for so good a Master, and impel them to give themselves wholly to the service of Him who gives Himself so completely to them. Thus we see that the principal foundation of the Christian life is the practical knowledge of this truth.

What are all the promises of the world compared to the assurance and hopes contained in these blessed titles? How much reason have they to rejoice who are the objects of the love of which the Scriptures speak in such beautiful terms!

"Be glad in the Lord," says the prophet, "and rejoice, ye just; and glory, all ye right of heart." (*Ps.* 31:11). Yes, let others rejoice in honors, in riches, or in dignities; but you who possess God for your portion enjoy an inheritance which exceeds all other blessings as far as God exceeds all created things. "They have called the people happy," says the psalmist, "that hath these things; but happy is that people whose God is the Lord." (*Ps.* 143:15).

Why, O prophet? Because in possessing God all things are possessed. Therefore, though I am a king and the ruler of a great nation, I will glory only in the Lord. How, then, can men refuse to serve Him who is the Source of all blessings? "What iniquity have your fathers found in me," God asks by the mouth of His prophet, "that they are gone far from me, and have walked after vanity, and are become vain? Am I become a wilderness to Israel, or a lateward springing land?" (*Jer.* 2:5, 31). If God complains so bitterly of the ingratitude of a people who had received from Him but temporal favors, how much more reason has He to reproach us, upon whom He has lavished so many spiritual and divine blessings!

If unmoved by the loving providence of God towards the just, at least be not insensible to the rigor with which He punishes the wicked, to whom His justice is meted out according to their own measure. For if they forget their Creator, He will forget them. If they despise Him, He will despise them. How miserable will their condition then be! They will be as a school without a master, a ship without a rudder, a flock without a shepherd. "I will not feed you," God says; "that which dieth, let it die; and that which is cut off, let it be cut off. Let the rest devour every one the flesh of his neighbor." (*Zach.* 11:9). "I will hide my face from them, and will consider what their last end shall be." (*Deut.* 32:20).

The just punishment inflicted by God on the wicked is

still more plainly declared in Isaias. The prophet speaks of his people under the figure of a vine which has been carefully pruned and dressed, but has failed to bear fruit. God, therefore, pronounces sentence against it: "I will show you what I will do to my vineyard. I will take away the hedge thereof, and it shall be wasted. I will break down the wall thereof, and it shall be trodden down. And I will make it desolate; it shall not be pruned, and it shall not be digged; but briers and thorns shall come up; and I will command the clouds to rain no rain upon it." (*Is.* 5:5-6). That is, God will take from man all the efficacious help and protection which he ungratefully refused, and will leave him to inevitable ruin and destruction.

What greater misfortune can befall a man than to be thus deprived of God's care in a world beset with dangers? With what arms will a creature so frail, helpless, and blind resist the attacks of the numerous enemies that assail him? Where will he find strength to resist them? Who will enlighten him, to enable him to avoid their snares? Without the divine assistance, how can he avoid destruction?

But the punishment of the wicked does not end here. God not only abandons them to their weakness, but scourges them with His justice, so that the eyes which hitherto watched for their happiness now look unmoved upon their ruin. This God Himself tells us by the mouth of the prophet: "I will set my eyes upon them for evil, and not for good" (*Amos* 9:4)—that is, the providence which hitherto watched for their defence will now work for vengeance on their crimes and disorders.

Even more expressive is the language of Osee: "I will be like a moth to Ephraim, and like rottenness to the house of Juda. I will be like a lioness to Ephraim, and like a lion's whelp to the house of Juda: I, I will catch, and go; I will take away, and there is none that can rescue." (*Osee* 5:12, 14). Here also the prophet Amos, who, after telling us that

God will put the wicked to the sword for their sins of covetousness, thus continues: "They shall flee, and he that shall flee of them shall not be delivered. Though they go down even to hell, thence shall my hand bring them out; and though they climb up to heaven, thence will I bring them down. And though they be hid in the top of Carmel, I will search and take them away from there; and though they hide themselves in the depth of the sea, there will I command the serpent, and he shall bite them. And if they go into captivity before their enemies, there will I command the sword, and it shall kill them. And I will set my eyes upon them for evil, and not for good." (*Amos* 9:1-4).

Who can read these words, remembering that they are uttered by God, and not tremble at the misfortune of having an enemy so powerful and so relentless in seeking his destruction? What rest or peace can he enjoy who knows that God's eyes are upon him with wrath and indignation? If it be so great a calamity to lose God's love, what must it be to have His providence armed against you; to have turned against you that sword which was formerly drawn in your defence; to have your destruction now viewed without emotion by those eyes which formerly watched so solicitously for your welfare; to have that arm which hitherto sustained you now stretched forth to annihilate you; to have that Heart which in the time of your goodness breathed but love and peace for you now filled with projects for your abasement; to have your shield and defence changed into a moth to consume you, a roaring lion to devour you? Who can sleep securely, knowing that God is over him like the rod of Jeremias to chastise him? Who can thwart the designs of God? What power can resist His arm? "Who hath resisted him," says Job, "and hath had peace?" (*Job* 9:4).

Numerous are the passages in Scripture in which God threatened the withdrawal of His providence as one of the most terrible punishments which He could inflict upon the sinner. "My people heard not my voice," He says, "and Israel hearkened not to me. So I let them go according to the desires of their heart. They shall walk in their own inventions." (*Ps.* 80:12-13). Abandoned to the desires of their corrupt hearts, they will proceed from disorder to disorder until their ruin is accomplished. What, then, is man without God, but a garden without a gardener, a ship without a pilot, a state without a ruler, an army without a general, a body without a soul?

Behold, dear Christian, how God's providence encompasses you. If you are not incited to fidelity through gratitude for His paternal care, at least the fear of abandonment by Him should impel you to serve Him. For many are moved by threats and the fear of punishment, while they remain utterly insensible to the hope of favor or reward.

CHAPTER 13

*The Second Privilege of Virtue: The Grace
with which the Holy Spirit fills Devout Souls*

God's fatherly providence, of which we have just been treating, is the source of all the favors and privileges which He bestows upon those who serve Him. For it belongs to this providence to furnish man with all the means necessary for his perfection and happiness.

The most important of these means is the grace of the Holy Ghost, which in its turn is the source of all other heavenly gifts. This is the garment with which the good father in the parable ordered the prodigal to be clothed. But, that we may have a clearer idea of it, let us see how theologians define it. Divine grace, they tell us, is a participation of the divine nature, that is, of God's sanctity, purity, and greatness, by virtue of which man is despoiled of the baseness and corruption of his nature and is clothed with the beauty and nobility of Jesus Christ.

Holy writers illustrate this by a familiar example. A piece of iron, when taken out of the fire, though it still continues to be iron, resembles the fire on account of its heat and brightness. Grace acts in like manner. As a divine quality it is infused into the soul, and so transforms man into God that, without ceasing to be man, he assumes the virtues and purity of God. This was the change wrought in St. Paul when he said, "I live, now not I, but Christ liveth in me." (*Gal.* 2:20).

Grace may also be called a supernatural and divine form, by means of which man lives as becomes his origin, which is also supernatural and divine.

Grace is, moreover, a spiritual dress, a chaste ornament of the soul, which renders her so beautiful in the eyes of God that He adopts her as His child, or rather accepts her as His spouse. It was this adornment which made the prophet rejoice when he said, "I will greatly rejoice in the Lord, and my soul shall be joyful in my God. For he hath clothed me with the garments of salvation; and with the robe of justice he hath covered me, as a bridegroom decked with a crown, and as a bride adorned with her jewels." (*Is.* 61:10). Such are the gifts with which the Holy Spirit enriches and adorns the soul. This is the garment of various colors in which the king's daughter was gloriously arrayed. (*Ps.* 44:14). For from grace proceeds that glorious variety of virtues which forms the power and beauty of the soul.

From what has been said we can judge of the effects of grace in a soul. It renders her so beautiful, as we have said, that God, who is captivated with her loveliness, chooses her for His spouse, His temple, and His dwelling.

Another effect of grace is the strength which it imparts to the soul. This beauty and this strength are extolled in the Canticle of Canticles, in which the angels exclaim, "Who is she that cometh forth as the morning rising, fair as the moon, bright as the sun, terrible as an army set in array?" (*Cant.* 6:9).

Grace, then, is like an invulnerable armor. So strong does it render man that, according to St. Thomas, the least degree of grace suffices to triumph over all sin. (*S.T.* III, Q. 62, a. 6).

A third effect of grace is to render man so pleasing to God that every good action performed by him contributes to merit for him eternal life. By good we here mean not only acts of virtue, but all those which arise from the necessities of nature, such as eating, drinking, and sleeping, which, by an upright intention, become pleasing to God and meritorious in His sight. In addition to all this, grace makes man the adopted child of God and heir to His kingdom.

Our Saviour showed the greatness of this privilege when, seeing His Apostles rejoicing that evil spirits obeyed them in His name, He said, "Rejoice not in this, that spirits are subject unto you; but rejoice in this, that your names are written in heaven." (*Lk.* 10:20).

Grace, finally, qualifies man for all good, smooths the way to Heaven, makes the yoke of Christ sweet and light, cures man of his infirmities and lightens his burdens, so that he is enabled to run in the path of virtue. Moreover, it strengthens all the faculties of the soul, enlightens the understanding, inflames the heart, moderates the appetites of the flesh, and constantly stimulates us, so that we may not relax in the pursuit of virtue. And as all the passions which reside in the inferior part of the soul are so many breaches in the fortification of virtue, through which the enemy effects an entrance, grace guards these avenues of sin with sentinels. These are the infused virtues, each of which is the opposite of the passion or vice which imperils the peace of the soul. Thus, temperance resists gluttony, chastity combats impurity, humility overcomes pride.

But the crowning effect of grace is that it brings God into our souls, in order to govern us, protect us, and lead us to Heaven. There God is pleased to abide, like a king in his kingdom, a father in the bosom of his family, a master with beloved disciples, a shepherd in the midst of his flock. Since, then, this inestimable pearl, the pledge of so many other blessings, is the unfailing lot of the virtuous, who will hesitate to imitate the wisdom of that merchant who sold all he had to purchase this pearl? (Cf. *Matt.* 13:45-46).

CHAPTER 14

*The Third Privilege of Virtue: The
Supernatural Light and Knowledge granted
to Virtuous Souls*

The heavenly light and wisdom with which God
enlightens the just form the third reward of virtue. And
this blessing, as well as all the others, is the effect of that
grace which not only rules our appetites and strengthens
our will, but removes the darkness of sin from our understanding and enables us to know and fulfill our duty.

St. Gregory tells us that ignorance of our duty, as well
as inability to do our duty, are alike punishments of sin.
(*Moral.* L. 25, c. 9.). Hence, David so frequently repeats,
"The Lord is my light" against ignorance, "the Lord is my
salvation" against weakness. (*Ps.* 26:1). On the one side
He teaches us what we should desire, and on the other He
strengthens us to execute our desires. And both of these
favors are bestowed on us through grace. For in addition
to a habit of faith and infused wisdom which teach us
what we are to believe and practice, grace imparts to us
the gifts of the Holy Ghost.

Four of these gifts relate particularly to the understanding: wisdom, which instructs us in spiritual and sublime
things; knowledge, which informs us of the things of earth
and time; understanding, which helps us appreciate the
beauty and harmony of the divine mysteries; and counsel,
which guides and directs us amidst the difficulties which

we encounter in the path of virtue.

These gifts are so many rays of light which proceed from the divine center of grace, and in Scripture are called an unction or anointing. "But you have the unction from the Holy One, and know all things." (*1 Jn.* 2:20). Oil has the double virtue of giving light and healing, and fitly represents the divine unction which enlightens the darkness of our understanding and heals the wounds of our will. This is the oil which exceeds in value the purest balsam, and for which David rejoiced when he said: Thou, O Lord, hast anointed my head with oil. (Cf. *Ps.* 22:5). It is evident that the royal prophet did not speak here of a material oil, and that by the head, he designated, according to the interpretation of Didymus, the noblest part of the soul, or the understanding, which is illumined and supported by the unction of the Holy Spirit.

Since it is the property and function of grace to make us virtuous, we must love virtue and abhor sin, which we cannot do if the understanding be not divinely enlightened to discern the malice of sin and the beauty of virtue. For the will, according to philosophers and theologians, is a blind faculty, incapable of acting without the guidance of the intellect, which points out the good it should choose and love, and the evil it should reject and hate. The same is true of fear, of hope, and of hatred for sin. We can never acquire these sentiments without a just knowledge of the goodness of God and the malice of sin.

Grace, as you have already learned, causes God to dwell in our souls; and as God, in the words of St. John, is "the true light, which enlighteneth every man that cometh into this world" (*Jn.* 1:9), the purer a soul is, the brighter will this Light shine in her—just as glass, according as it is clearer, reflects more strongly the rays of the sun. Hence, St. Augustine calls God the "wisdom of a purified soul" (*De Lib. Arbit.*, L. 2), because He fills her with His light, which enables her to apprehend all that is necessary for salvation.

Nor should this surprise us when we consider with what care God provides even the brute creation with all that is necessary for the maintenance of life. For whence is that natural instinct which teaches the sheep to distinguish among plants those which are poisonous and those which are wholesome? Who has taught them to run from the wolf and to follow the dog? Was it not God, the Author of nature? Since, then, God endows the brute creation with the discernment necessary for the preservation of animal life, have we not much more reason to feel that He will communicate to the just the knowledge necessary for the maintenance of their spiritual life?

This example teaches us not only that such a knowledge really exists, but also marks the character of this knowledge. It is not a mere theory or speculation; it is eminently practical. Hence the difference between knowledge divinely communicated and that which is acquired in the schools. The latter only illumines the intellect, but the former, the inspirations of the Holy Ghost, communicates itself to the will, strengthens it for good, governs and stimulates it. By its efficacious virtue this divine knowledge penetrates into the depths of the soul, transforms our passions, and remodels us upon the likeness of Christ. Hence, the Apostle tells us, "The word of God is living and effectual, and more piercing than any two edged sword, and reaching unto the division of the soul and spirit" (*Heb.* 4:12)—that is, separating the spiritual man from the animal man.

This, then, is one of the principal effects of grace, and one of the most beautiful rewards of virtue in this life. But to prove this truth more clearly to carnal men, who reluctantly accept it, we will confirm it by undeniable passages from both the Old and the New Testament. In the New

Testament, Our Saviour tells us, "The Holy Ghost, whom the Father will send in my name, he will teach you all things, and bring all things to your mind, whatsoever I shall have said to you." (*Jn.* 14:26). And again, "It is written in the prophets: *And they shall all be taught of God.* Every one that hath heard of the Father, and hath learned, cometh to me." (*Jn.* 6:45).

Numerous are the passages in the Old Testament which promise this wisdom to the just. "I am the Lord thy God, that teach thee profitable things, that govern thee in the way that thou walkest." (*Is.* 48:17). "The mouth of the just," says David, "shall meditate wisdom, and his tongue shall speak judgment." (*Ps.* 36:30). Throughout the one hundred and eighteenth Psalm, how frequent is his prayer for this divine wisdom! "Blessed art thou, O Lord: teach me thy justifications. Open thou my eyes, and I will consider the wondrous things of thy law. Give me understanding, and I will search thy law; and I will keep it with my whole heart."

Shall we not, therefore, appreciate the happiness and honor of possessing such a Master, from whom we may learn sublime lessons of immortal wisdom? "If Apollonius," says St. Jerome, "traversed the greater part of the world to behold Hipparchus seated upon a golden throne in the midst of his disciples, and explaining to them the movements of the heavenly bodies, what should not men do to hear God, from the throne of their hearts, instructing them, not upon the motions of the heavenly bodies, but how they may advance to the heavenly kingdom?"

If you would appreciate the value of this doctrine, hear how it is extolled by the prophet in the psalm from which we have already quoted: "I have understood more than all my teachers," he exclaims, "because thy testimonies are my meditation. I have had understanding above ancients, because I have sought thy commandments." (*Ps.* 118:99-100). More expressive still are the words in which Isaias enumerates the blessings promised to God's servants: "The Lord will give thee rest continually, and will fill thy soul with brightness, and deliver thy bones, and thou shalt be like a watered garden, and like a fountain of water whose waters shall not fail." (*Is.* 58:11).

What is this brightness—with which God fills the soul of the just—but that clear knowledge of all that is necessary for salvation? He shows them the beauty of virtue and the deformity of vice. He reveals to them the vanity of this world, the treasures of grace, the greatness of eternal glory, and the sweetness of the consolations of the Holy Spirit. He teaches them to apprehend the goodness of God, the malice of the evil one, the shortness of life, and the fatal error of those whose hopes are centered in this world alone. Hence the equanimity of the just. They are neither puffed up by prosperity nor cast down by adversity. "A holy man," says Solomon, "continueth in wisdom as the sun, but a fool is changed as the moon." (*Ecclus.* 27:12). Unmoved by the winds of false doctrine, the just man continues steadfast in Christ, immovable in charity, unswerving in faith.

Be not astonished at the effect of this wisdom, for it is not earthly, but divine. Is there anything of earth to be compared with it? "The finest gold shall not purchase it, neither shall silver be weighed in exchange for it. It cannot be compared with the . . . most precious stone sardonyx, or the sapphire. The fear of the Lord is wisdom, and to depart from evil is understanding." (*Job* 28:15-16, 28).

And this wisdom increases in the just, for Solomon tells us, "The path of the just, as a shining light, goeth forwards and increaseth even to perfect day" (*Prov.* 4:18), the beginning of a blessed eternity, when God's wisdom and beauty will be revealed to us in all their brightness and power.

This great gift is the portion of the just only, for the wicked are plunged in an ignorance so intense that it was well symbolized by the darkness which covered the land of Egypt. The wicked themselves confess their blindness, "We looked for light, and behold darkness; brightness, and we have walked in the dark. We have groped for the wall, like the blind, and we have groped as if we had no eyes; we have stumbled at noonday as in darkness; we are in dark places as dead men." (*Is.* 59:9-10).

What can equal the blindness of him who sells eternal happiness for the fleeting and *bitter* pleasures of this world? How incomprehensible is the igorance of him who neither fears Hell nor strives for Heaven; who feels no horror for sin; who disregards the menaces as well as the promises of God; who makes no preparation for death, which hourly seizes its victims; who does not see that momentary joys here are laying up for him eternal torments hereafter! "They have not known or understood; they walk on in the darkness" (*Ps.* 81:5) of sin through this life, and will pass from it to the eternal darkness of the life to come.

Before concluding this chapter we would make the following suggestion: Notwithstanding the power and efficacy of this wisdom with which God fills the souls of the just, no man, however great the light he has received, should refuse to submit his judgment to his lawful superiors, especially the authorized teachers and doctors of the Church. Who ever received greater light than St. Paul, who was raised to the third heaven; or than Moses, who spoke face to face with God? Yet St. Paul went to Jerusalem to confer with the Apostles upon the Gospel which he had received from Christ Himself; and Moses did not disdain to accept the advice of his father-in-law, Jethro, who was a Gentile.

For the interior aids of grace do not exclude the exterior succors of the Church. Divine Providence has willed to make them both an aid to our salvation. As the natural heat of our body is stimulated by that of the sun, and the healing powers of nature are aided by exterior remedies, so the light of grace is strengthened by the teaching and direction of the Church. Whoever refuses, therefore, to humble himself and submit to her authority will render himself unworthy of any favor from God.

CHAPTER 15

The Fourth Privilege of Virtue: The Consolations with which the Holy Spirit visits the Just

We might regard charity, or the love of God, as the fourth privilege of virtue, particularly as the Apostle accounts it the first-fruit of the Holy Ghost; but our intention being at present to treat more of the rewards of virtue than of virtue itself, we shall devote this chapter to the consolations of the Holy Ghost, and refer to another part the consideration of charity, the most noble of virtues.

This fourth privilege of virtue is the effect of that divine light of which we spoke in the preceding chapter.

This is the teaching of David when he says, "Light is risen to the just, and joy to the right of heart." (*Ps.* 96:11). The Holy Scriptures furnish abundant proof of this truth. If the path of virtue, O deluded sinner, be as sad and difficult as you represent it, what does the Psalmist mean when he exclaims, "O how great is the multitude of thy sweetness, O Lord, which thou hast hidden for them that fear thee!" (*Ps.* 30:20). And again: "My soul shall rejoice in the Lord, and shall be delighted in his salvation. All my bones [that is, all the powers of my soul] shall say: Lord, who is like to thee?" (*Ps.* 34:9-10).

Do not these texts clearly tell us of the joy with which the souls of the just overflow, which penetrates even to the flesh, and which so inebriates man's whole being that he breaks forth into transports of holy joy? What earthly pleasure can be compared to this? What peace, what love, what delight can equal that of which Thou, O my God, art the inexhaustible source? "The voice of rejoicing and of salvation," continues the prophet, "is in the tabernacles of the just." (*Ps.* 117:15). Yes, only just souls know true joy, true peace, true consolation.

"Let the just feast and rejoice before God, and be delighted with gladness." (*Ps.* 67:4). "They shall be inebriated with the plenty of thy house, and thou shalt make them drink of the torrent of thy pleasure." (*Ps.* 35:9). Could the prophet more powerfully express the strength and sweetness of these consolations? They shall be inebriated, he tells us; for as a man overcome by the fumes of wine is insensible to all outward objects, so the just, who are filled with the wine of heavenly consolations, are dead to the things of this world.

"Blessed is the people," he further says, "that knoweth jubilation." (*Ps.* 88:16). Many would perhaps have said, "Blessed are they who abound in wealth, who are protected by strong walls, and who possess valiant soldiers to defend them!" But David, who had all these, esteemed only that people happy who knew by experience what it was to rejoice in God with that joy of spirit which, according to St. Gregory, cannot find expression in words or actions. Happy are they who are sufficiently advanced in love for God to know this jubilation! It is a knowledge which Plato, with all his wisdom, and Demosthenes, with all his eloquence, could never attain. Since, then, God is the author of this joy, how great must be its strength and sweetness! For if His arm be so terrible when stretched forth to chastise, it is equally tender when extended to caress.

We are told that St. Ephrem was frequently so overcome with the strength of this divine sweetness that he was forced to cry out, "Withdraw from me a little, O Lord, for my body faints under the weight of Thy delights!" (St. John Climachus). Oh! Unspeakable Goodness! Oh! Sovereign Sweetness, communicating Thyself so prodigally to Thy creatures that the human heart cannot contain the effusions of Thy infinite love! In this inebriation of heavenly sweetness the troubles and trials of the world are forgotten, and the soul is strengthened and elevated to joys beyond the power of her natural faculties.

Just as water under the action of fire loses its property of heaviness, and rises in imitation, as it were, of the element by which it is moved, so the soul inflamed with the fire of divine love soars to Heaven, the source of this flame, and burns with desire for the object of her love. "Tell my beloved," she cries, "that I languish with love." (*Cant.* 5:8). These joys, which are the portion of the just in this world, need not excite our wonder, if we consider all that God endured in His Passion. All His sufferings and ignominies were for the sinner as well as for the just. Hence, if He endured so much for the sinner, what will He not do for the happiness of faithful souls?

The devotion and fidelity of the just still further enable us to form some conception of the ardor with which God promotes their happiness. Look into their hearts, and you will find there not a thought or desire which is not for Him whose glory is the end of all their actions; that they spare no sacrifice to serve Him who is continually giving them proofs of His love. If, therefore, frail and inconstant man be capable of such devotedness, what will God not do for him? Isaias, and after him St. Paul, tells us that "eye hath not seen, nor ear heard, neither hath it entered into the heart of man, what things God hath prepared for them that love Him." (*Is.* 64:4 and *1 Cor.* 2:9).

We could cite many other passages from Scripture in proof of this truth, particularly from the Canticle of Canticles, where these divine consolations are represented, sometimes under the figure of generous wine which rejoices the heart of man, or as milk sweeter than honey, containing all strength, and filling the soul with life and joy. But what we have said will suffice to prove to you the joys which are reserved for the good, and how far these heavenly consolations exceed the pleasures of this world. For what comparison can there be between light and darkness, between Christ and Belial? How can the happiness afforded by a creature be compared to that which is given by the Creator? That it is particularly in prayer that just souls enjoy these divine consolations is a truth we now wish to prove.

God Himself tells us, "The children of the stranger that adhere to the Lord, to worship him, and to love his name, to be his servants; every one that keepeth the sabbath from profaning it, and that holdeth fast my covenant, I will bring them into my holy mount, and will make them joyful in my house of prayer." (*Is.* 56:6-7).

Hence St. Lawrence Justinian tells us that the hearts of the just are inflamed in prayer with love for their Creator; that they are frequently raised above themselves and transported in spirit to the abode of the angels, where, in the presence of their God, they unite their praise to that of the celestial choirs. They weep and rejoice, for the sighs of their exile mingle with the anticipations of their blessed country. They feast, but are never filled. They drink, but are never satisfied. They unceasingly long to be transformed into Thee, O Lord, whom they contemplate with faith, whom they adore with humility, whom they seek with desire, whom they possess and enjoy through love.

The powers of their mind are inadequate to comprehend this happiness, which penetrates their whole being, yet they tremble to lose it. Even as Jacob wrestled with the angel, so do their hearts struggle to retain this divine sweetness amid the turmoil and trouble of this world, crying out with the Apostle, "Lord, it is good for us to be here." (*Matt.* 17:4).

When inflamed with this divine fire, the soul longs to be freed from her prison of clay. She waters her bread with her tears, that the hour of her deliverance may not be delayed. She mourns that she has learned so late the enjoyment of these treasures which God has prepared for all men. She longs to proclaim them in public places, crying to the deluded victims of this world, "O unhappy people, senseless men! Whither are you hastening? What is the object of your search? Why will you not seek happiness at its source? 'Taste and see that the Lord is sweet; blessed is the man that hopeth in him.'" (*Ps.* 33:9).

O Lord, "What have I in heaven, and besides thee what do I desire upon earth? For thee my flesh and my heart hath fainted away; thou art the God of my heart, and the God that is my portion for ever." (*Ps.* 72:25-26).

You will probably tell me that these consolations are reserved for those who are already advanced in virtue. No doubt these intimate joys of the soul are known only to more perfect souls, yet the Divine Master grants even beginners ineffable rewards. The happiness of the prodigal, the rejoicing and feasting which resound in his father's house, are an image of the spiritual joy which the soul experiences when she is released from the slavery of the evil one and made an honored child of Christ.

It is very evident that man, bound by the chains of the flesh and the allurements of the world, could not trample pleasure underfoot and resolutely enter the path of virtue, did not God accord him favors which sweeten all his sacrifices. Therefore, when a soul is resolved to turn to God, He smooths the way for her, and removes many obstacles that might cause her to lose courage and fall back.

This is what God did for the children of Israel when He led them out of the land of Egypt: "When Pharao had sent out the people, the Lord led them not by way of the land of the Philistines, which is near, thinking lest perhaps they would repent, if they should see wars arise against them, and would return into Egypt." (*Ex.* 13:17).

This same Providence, which guided the Israelites, continues daily to manifest like care for the faithful, bringing them out of the slavery of the world and leading them to the conquest of Heaven, the true promised land.

We find still another figure of this truth in the Old Testament, where God commanded the first and the last days of the week to be observed with particular solemnity, thus teaching us that He rejoices with His children in the beginning as well as in the consummation of their perfection. Those who are entering the path of virtue are treated by God with the tenderness and consideration which are shown to children. The affection of a mother for her younger sons is not greater than that which she bears those of riper years, yet she tenderly carries the little ones in her arms, and leaves the older ones to walk by themselves. The latter are sometimes obliged to earn their food before it is given them, while the little ones not only receive it unsolicited, but are tenderly fed. This is a faint image of the loving care with which God surrounds those who are beginning to serve Him.

It is no argument against this truth that you do not experience these divine consolations when you think of God. Food is tasteless to a disordered palate, and for a soul vitiated by sin and sensual affections this heavenly manna has no relish. Cleanse your soul with the tears of repentance, and then "taste and see that the Lord is sweet." (*Ps.* 33:9).

What are all the pleasures of this world compared to these ineffable consolations? Why will you not begin to be happy from this moment? "O man!" says Richard of St. Victor, quoting the words of the Gospel, "since Paradise may be thine, why dost thou not sell all thy possessions to purchase this pearl of great price?"

Dear Christian, delay not an affair so important. Every

moment is worth more to you than all the riches of the universe. Even though you attain this heavenly treasure, you will never cease to lament the time you have lost, and to cry out with St. Augustine, "Too late have I known Thee, too late have I loved Thee, O Beauty ever ancient and ever new!" This illustrious penitent, though he unceasingly lamented the lateness of his conversion, gave himself to God with all his heart, and therefore, won an immortal crown. Imitate him, and thus avoid the unhappy lot of lamenting not only the delay of your conversion, but even the loss of your crown.

CHAPTER 16

The Fifth Privilege of Virtue: The Peace of a Good Conscience

God, who gives His creatures all that is necessary for their perfection, has planted the seed of virtue in the soul of man, and has endowed him with a natural inclination for good and an instinctive hatred of evil. This inclination may be weakened and perverted by a habit of vice, but it can never be totally destroyed.

We find a figure of this truth in Job, where we see that, in the calamities which befell the holy man, one servant always escaped to announce the misfortune which had overtaken his master. So the faithful servant, conscience, always remains with the sinner in the midst of his disorders to show him what he has lost and the state to which his sins have reduced him.

This is still another striking proof of that providence we have been considering, and of the value God attaches to virtue. He has placed in the center of our souls a guardian that never sleeps, a monitor that is never silent, a master that never ceases to guide and sustain us. Epictetus, the Stoic philosopher, was deeply impressed with this truth when he said that "as fathers are wont to entrust their children to a tutor who will prudently guard them from vice and lead them to virtue, so God, after creating man, confides him to the care of that interior guide which stimulates him to virtue and warns him against vice."

But conscience, which is such a kind master to the just, becomes a scourge to the wicked. It tortures them with the remembrance of their crimes and embitters all their pleasures. Among these torments of conscience, one of the greatest is the hideousness and deformity of sin, which is so abominable in itself that a heathen philosopher once said, "Though I knew that the gods would pardon me if I sinned, and that men would never know it, yet I would not take upon me a thing so abominable in itself."

Another rod with which conscience scourges the wicked is the sight of the evil caused by sin, which, like the blood of Abel, seems to cry to Heaven for vengeance. Thus we are told that King Antiochus, during his sickness, was so assailed by the thoughts of his past crimes that the grief they occasioned brought on his death. "I remember," he cried, "the evils that I did in Jerusalem, whence also I took away all the spoils of gold and of silver that were in it, and I sent to destroy the inhabitants of Juda without cause. I know, therefore, that for this cause these evils have found me; and behold I perish with great grief in a strange land." (*Mac.* 6:12-13).

The shame and dishonor of sin form another torment for the wicked. It is natural for man to desire esteem, but who can honor the sinner? It is natural for him to wish to be loved, but who is there who does not hate iniquity? To these miseries let us add the fear of death, which never fails to haunt the wicked, unless they are utterly abandoned. What comfort can they have in reflecting on the uncertainty of life, the thought of the terrible account they must render, and the anticipation of eternal torments? Consider the sentiments which such reflections must awaken in the sinner's breast, and you will form some idea of the torments of his conscience.

Of these torments one of the friends of Job spoke when he said, "The wicked man is proud all his days, and the number of the years of his tyranny is uncertain. The sound of dread is always in his ears"—the dread sound of an accusing conscience. "And when there is peace, he always suspecteth treason," for he cannot escape the alarms and the warning cries of conscience. "He believeth not that he may return from darkness to light." He believes it impossible to extricate himself from the terrible darkness which envelops him; he almost despairs of ever again enjoying the peace of a good conscience. "Looking round about for the sword on every side," he is in constant dread of avenging justice. "When he moveth himself to seek bread he knoweth that the day of darkness is at hand." Even at table, the place of mirth and rejoicing, the fear of judgment is upon him. "Tribulation shall terrify him, and distress shall surround him, as a king that is prepared for the battle. For he hath stretched out his hand against God, and hath strengthened himself against the Almighty." (*Job* 15:22-26).

Thus does Holy Scripture portray the torments of which the heart of the sinner is both the theater and the victim. A philosopher has wisely said that by an eternal law of God it is ordained that fear should be the inseparable companion of evil; and this is confirmed by Solomon, who tells us, "The wicked man fleeth when no man pursueth, but the just, bold as a lion, shall be without dread." (*Prov.* 28:1). This thought is also expressed by St. Augustine, who says, "Thou hast ordained, O Lord, that every soul in which disorder reigns should be a torment to herself; and truly it is so." (*Conf.* 1,12).

Nature teaches us the same. Does not every creature suffer for infringing the law of its being? Consider the pain which follows the displacement of a bone in the body. What violence a creature endures when out of its element! How quickly does sickness follow when the different parts of the body are not in harmony! Since, then, it belongs to a rational creature to lead a regular life, how can he escape suffering, how can he fail to become his own torment, when he disregards the laws of reason and the order of Divine Providence? "Who hath resisted God and hath had peace?" (*Job* 9:4). Hence we see that creatures who submit to the order of God enjoy a peace and security which abandon them the moment they resist this divine law. Man, in his innocence, was absolute master of himself; but after his disobedience he lost his peaceful empire and began to experience remorse and an interior warfare against himself.

"Is there any greater torment in this world," asks St. Ambrose, "than remorse of conscience? Is it not a misery more to be feared than sickness, than exile, than loss of life or liberty?" (*De Officiis*, L. 3,4).

"There is nothing," says St. Isidore, "from which man cannot fly, save from himself. Let him go where he will, he cannot escape the pursuit of an accusing conscience." The same Father adds elsewhere, "There is no torment which exceeds that of a guilty conscience. If, then, you desire to live in peace, live in the practice of virtue."

This truth is so manifest that even pagan philosophers acknowledged it. "What doth it avail thee," says Seneca, "to fly from the conversation of men? For as a good conscience may call all the world to witness its truth, so a bad conscience will be tormented by a thousand fears, a thousand anxieties, even in a desert. If thy action be good all the world may witness it; if it be evil what will it avail thee to hide it from others, since thou canst not hide it from thyself? Alas for thee if thou makest no account of such a witness, for its testimony is worth that of a thousand others." (*Epist.* 97).

"Great," says Cicero, "is the power of conscience; nothing can more effectually condemn or acquit a man. It raises the innocent above all fear and keeps the guilty in perpetual alarm." This is one of the eternal torments of the wicked, for it begins even in this life and will continue forever in the life to come. It is the undying worm mentioned by Isaias. (Cf. *Is.* 66:24).

Having thus seen the sad effects of an evil conscience, we will be enabled to realize more fully the blessed peace which the just enjoy.

Virtue shelters them from the remorse and sufferings which have been described as the lot of the wicked. The consolations and sweet fruits of the Holy Ghost fill them with joy and transform the soul into a terrestrial paradise, where He is pleased to take up His abode. "The joy of a good conscience," says St. Augustine, "makes the soul a true paradise." (*De Gen. ad Lit.,* L. 12, c. 34). And elsewhere he says, "Be assured, ye who seek that true peace promised to a future life, that you may here enjoy it by anticipation, if you will but love and keep the commandments of Him who promises this reward; for you will soon find by experience that the fruits of justice are sweeter than those of iniquity. You will learn that the joys of virtue, even in the midst of trials and misfortunes, far exceed all the delights of pleasure and prosperity accompanied by the remorse of a bad conscience." (*Lib. de Cat.* 2,9).

Sin, as we have said, finds in its baseness and enormity its own punishment; so virtue finds in its beauty and worth its own reward. David teaches us this truth: "The judgments of the Lord"—that is, His holy commandments—"are true, justified in themselves. More to be desired than gold and precious stones, and sweeter than honey and the honeycomb." (*Ps.* 18:10-11). This was his own experience, for he says, "I have been delighted in the way of thy testimonies, as in all riches." (*Ps.* 118:14). The chief cause of this joy is the dignity and beauty of virtue, which as Plato declares, is incomparably fair and lovely. Finally, so great are the advantages of a good conscience that, according to St. Ambrose, they constitute in this life the happiness of the just.

The ancient philosophers, as we have seen, though deprived of the light of faith, knew the torments of a guilty conscience. Nor were they ignorant of the joy of a good conscience, as we learn from Cicero, who, in his *Tusculan Questions,* says, "A life spent in noble and honorable deeds brings such consolations with it that just men are either insensible to the trials of life or feel them very little." The same author adds elsewhere that virtue has no more brilliant, no more honorable theater than that in which the applause of conscience is heard. Socrates, being asked who could live free from passion, answered, "He who lives virtuously." And Bias, another celebrated philosopher, gave almost the same reply to a similiar question. "Who," he was asked, "can live without fear?" "He who has the testimony of a good conscience," he replied. Seneca, in one of his epistles, wrote, "A wise man is always cheerful, and his cheerfulness comes from a good conscience."

If pagan philosophers, knowing nothing of future rewards, so justly esteemed the peace of a good conscience, how dearly should a Christian prize it! This testimony of a good conscience does not, however, exclude that salutary fear with which we must work out our salvation; but such a fear, so far from discouraging us, inspires us with marvelous courage in the fulfillment of our duties. We feel, in the depth of our hearts, that our confidence is better founded when moderated by this holy fear, without which it would be only a false security and a vain presumption.

It was of this privilege that the Apostle spoke when he said, "Our glory is this, the testimony of our conscience, that in simplicity of heart and sincerity of God, and not in carnal wisdom, but in the grace of God, we have conversed in this world." (*2 Cor.* 1:12).

We have endeavored to explain this privilege of virtue, but, despite all that could be said, there is nothing save experience that can give us a keen realization of it.

CHAPTER 17

*The Sixth Privilege of Virtue: The
Confidence of the Just*

The joy of a good conscience is always accompanied by that blessed hope of which the Apostle speaks when he tells us to rejoice in hope and to be patient in tribulation. (Cf. *Rom.* 12:12). This is the rich inheritance of the children of God, their general refuge in tribulation, and their most efficacious remedy against all the miseries of life.

Before entering upon this subject we must bear in mind that as there are two kinds of faith, one barren and dead, the other living and strengthened by charity, fruitful in good works; so there are two kinds of hope—one barren, which gives the soul no light in darkness, no strength in weakness, no consolation in tribulation; the other "lively" (Cf. *1 Pet.* 1:3), which consoles us in sorrow, strengthens us in labor, and sustains us in all the dangers and trials of this world.

This living hope works in the soul many marvelous effects, which increase according as the charity which accompanies it becomes more ardent. The first of these effects is the strength which supports man under the labors of life by holding before his eyes the eternal reward reserved for him; for, in the opinion of the saints, the stronger this hope of reward the greater is man's courage in overcoming obstacles in the path of virtue.

"Hope," says St. Gregory, "fixes our hearts so steadfastly upon the joys of Heaven that we are insensible to the miseries of this life." "The hope of future glory," Origen tells us, "sustains the just under the trials of life, as the hope of victory supports the soldier during battle." "If the furious tempests of the sea," says St. Chrysostom, "cannot daunt the sailor; if hard frosts and withering blight cannot discourage the farmer; if neither wounds nor death itself affright the soldier; if neither falls nor blows dishearten the wrestler, because of the fleeting recompense they hope from their labors, how much greater should be the courage of a Christian, who is toiling for an eternal reward! Therefore, consider not the roughness of the path of virtue, but rather the end to which it leads; look not upon the pleasures which strew the path of vice, but rather upon the precipice to which it is hurrying you."

Who is so foolish as willingly to pursue a path, though strewn with flowers, if it lead to destruction? Who, conversely, would not choose a rugged and difficult path if it lead to life and happiness?

Holy Scripture is full of commendations of this blessed hope. "The eyes of the Lord," the prophet Hanani tells King Asa, "behold all the earth, and give strength to them that with a perfect heart trust in him." (*2 Par.* 16:9). "The Lord is good to them that hope in him, and to the soul that seeketh him." (*Lam.* 3:25). "The Lord is good, and giveth strength in the day of trouble, and knoweth them that hope in him." (*Nahum* 1:7).

"If you return and be quiet, you shall be saved; in silence and in hope shall your strength be." (*Is.* 30:15) By silence the prophet here signifies that interior calm and sweet peace experienced by the soul amid all her troubles, and which is the result of that hope in God's mercy which expels all fear. "Ye that fear the Lord, hope in him, and mercy shall come to you for your delight. My children, behold the generations of men, and know ye that no one hath hoped in the Lord and hath been confounded." (*Ecclus.* 2:9,11).

"Mercy shall encompass him that hopeth in the Lord." (*Ps.* 31:10). Mark the strength of this word *encompass,* by which the prophet teaches us that a virtuous man is shielded by God's protection, as a king surrounded by his guards. Read the Psalms, and you will see how beautifully David speaks of the power and merit of divine hope.

In one of his sermons, St. Bernard dwells at some length on this virtue, and concludes by saying, "Faith teaches us that God has inestimable rewards reserved for His faithful servants. Hope answers, 'It is for me that they are prepared'; and charity, inspired by hope, cries out, 'I will hasten to possess them.'"

Behold, then, the happy fruits of hope! It is a port of refuge from the storms of life; it is a buckler against the attacks of the world; it is a storehouse to supply us in the time of famine; it is the shade and tent of which Isaias spoke, to protect us from the heat of summer and the frosts of winter; in fine, it is a remedy for all our evils, for there is no doubt that all we confidently and justly hope from God will be granted to us, if for our welfare. Hence St. Cyprian says that God's mercy is a healing fountain, and hope a vessel into which its waters flow. Therefore, the larger the vessel the more abundantly will we receive of these waters. God told the children of Israel that every place upon which they set their feet should be theirs. So every salutary blessing upon which man fixes his hope will be granted to him. Hope, then, for all blessings, and you will obtain them.

Thus we see that this virtue is an imitation of the divine power; for, says St. Bernard, nothing so manifests the power of God as the omnipotence with which He invests those who hope in Him. Witness Josue, at whose command the sun stood still; or Ezechiel, who bade King Ezechias choose whether he would have the sun advance or go backward in its course, as a sign from God.

In studying the inestimable treasures of hope, you have some idea of one of the blessings of which the wicked are deprived. Whatever hope remains to them is dead; destroyed by sin, it can produce none of the glorious fruits we have been considering. Distrust and fear as inevitably accompany a bad conscience as the shadow does the body. Hence the happiness of the sinner is the measure of his hope. He sets his heart upon the vanities and follies of the world; he rejoices in them; he glories in them; and in them he hopes in the time of affliction.

It is of such hope that God speaks when He says, "The hope of the wicked is as dust, which is blown away with the winds, and as a thin froth which is dispersed by the storm; and a smoke which is scattered abroad by the wind." (*Wis*. 5:15). Can you imagine a weaker or a vainer confidence than this? But it is not only vain, it is deceptive and injurious. "Woe to them that go down to Egypt for help, trusting in horses, and putting their confidence in chariots, because they are many; and in horsemen, because they are very strong; and have not trusted in the Holy One of Israel, and have not sought after the Lord. Egypt is man, and not God; and their horses flesh, and not spirit; and the Lord shall put down his hand, and the helper shall fall, and he that is helped shall fall, and they shall all be confounded together." (*Is*. 31:1,3).

Behold, dear Christian, the difference between the hope of the just and the hope of the wicked. One is of the flesh, the other of the spirit; one is centered in man, the other in God. And even as God exceeds man, so does the hope of the just exceed that of the sinner. Therefore, the prophet exhorts us, "Put not your trust in princes; in the children of men, in whom there is no salvation. Blessed is he who

hath the God of Jacob for his helper, whose hope is in the
Lord his God; who made heaven and earth, the sea, and
all things that are in them." (*Ps.* 114:3,5-6).

"Some trust in chariots, and some in horses; but we will
call upon the name of the Lord our God. They are bound,
and have fallen; but we are risen, and are set upright."
(*Ps.* 19:8-9). Thus we see that our hopes are realized according to that upon which they rest—in ruin and destruction, or in honor and victory.

Therefore, he whose hope is fixed upon the things of
this world is rightly compared to the man in the Gospel
who built his house upon the sand and beheld it beaten
down by the rain and winds; while he whose hope is fixed
upon the things of Heaven is like the man whose house
was built upon a rock, and which stood unshaken amidst
the storms. (Cf. *Matt.* 7:25).

"Cursed be he," cries out the prophet, "that trusteth in
man, and maketh flesh his arm, and whose heart departeth
from the Lord. For he shall be like tamaric [a barren
shrub] in the desert, and he shall not see when good shall
come; but he shall dwell in dryness in the desert, in a salt
land and not inhabited. But blessed be the man that
trusteth in the Lord, and the Lord shall be his confidence;
and he shall be as a tree that is planted by the waters, that
spreadeth out its roots towards moisture; and it shall not
fear when the heat cometh. And the leaf thereof shall be
green, and in the time of drought it shall not be solicitous,
neither shall it cease at any time to bring forth fruit." (*Jer.*
17:5-9).

Can there be any misery compared to life without hope?
To live without hope is to live without God. If this support be taken from man, what remains for him? There is
no nation, however barbarous, that has not some
knowledge of a god whom they worship and in whom they
hope. When Moses was absent for a short time from the

children of Israel, they imagined themselves without God; and in their ignorance they besought Aaron to give them a god, for they feared to continue without one. Thus we see that human nature, though ignorant of the true God, instinctively acknowledges the necessity of a Supreme Being, and, recognizing its own weakness, turns to God for assistance and support.

As the ivy clings to a tree, and as woman naturally depends on man, so human nature in its weakness and poverty seeks the protection and assistance of God. How deplorable, then, is the condition of those who deprive themselves of His support! Whither can they turn for comfort in trials, for relief in sickness? Of whom will they seek protection in dangers, counsel in difficulties? If the body cannot live without the soul, how can the soul live without God? If hope, as we have said, be the anchor of life, how can we trust ourselves without it on the stormy sea of the world? If hope be our buckler, how can we go without it into the midst of our foes?

What we have said must sufficiently show us that an infinite distance separates the hope of the just from that of the wicked. The hope of the just man is in God, and that of the wicked is in the staff of Egypt, which breaks and wounds the hand which sought its support. For when man leans upon such a reed, God wishes to make him sensible of his error by the sorrow and shame of his fall. We have an example of this in God's treatment of Moab: "Because thou hast trusted in thy bulwarks, and in thy treasures, thou also shalt be taken: and Chamos [the god of the Moabites] shall go into captivity, his priests, and his princes together." (*Jer.* 48:7). Consider what a support that is which brings ruin upon those who invoke it.

Behold, then, dear Christian, how great is this privilege of hope, which, though it appears one with the special providence of which we have been treating, differs from it, nevertheless, as the effect differs from the cause. For though the hope of the just proceeds from several causes, such as the goodness of God, the truth of His promises, the merits of Christ, yet its principal foundation is this paternal providence. It is this which excites our hope; for who could fail in confidence, knowing the fatherly care that God has for us all?

CHAPTER 18

The Seventh Privilege of Virtue: The True Liberty of the Just

From the privileges we have been considering, but particularly from the graces of the Holy Spirit and His divine consolations, there arises a seventh, though no less marvelous, privilege, which is true liberty of the soul. The Son of God brought this gift to men; hence He is called the Redeemer, or Deliverer, for He freed mankind from the slavery of sin, and restored them to the true liberty of the children of God. This is one of the greatest of God's favors, one of the most signal benefits of the Gospel, and one of the principal effects of the Holy Ghost. "Where the Spirit of the Lord is, there is liberty." (*2 Cor.* 3:17). This liberty is one of the most magnificent rewards which God has promised to His servants in this life: "If you continue in my word, you shall be my disciples indeed. And you shall know the truth, and the truth shall make you free."

To this the Jews answered, "We are the seed of Abraham, and we have never been slaves to any man; how sayest thou: You shall be free?" Jesus answered them, "Amen, amen I say unto you, that whosoever committeth sin is the servant of sin. Now the servant abideth not in the house for ever; but the son abideth for ever. If, therefore, the son shall make you free, you shall be free indeed." (*Jn.* 8:31-37).

Our Saviour teaches us by these words that there are two kinds of liberty. The first is the liberty of those who are doubtless free in body, but whose souls are enslaved by sin, as Alexander the Great, who, though master of the world, was a slave to his own vices. The second is that true liberty which is the portion of those whose souls are free from the bondage of sin, though their bodies may be held in chains. Witness the great Apostle, whose mind, despite his fetters, soared to Heaven, and whose preaching and doctrine freed the world. To such a condition we unhesitantly give the glorious name of liberty. For the noblest part of man is the soul; in a measure it constitutes man. The body is merely matter vivified by the soul. Hence, only he whose soul is at liberty is truly free, and he whose soul is in bondage, however free his body may be, possesses only the semblance of liberty.

Now, the sinner is in bondage under sin, the most cruel of tyrants. The torments of Hell are but the effects of sin; consider, then, how horrible sin itself must be. It is to this cruel tyrant that the wicked are enslaved, for Our Saviour tells us, "Whosoever committeth sin is the servant of sin." (*Jn.* 8:34). Nor is the sinner a slave to sin only, but to all that incites him to sin—that is, to the world, the devil, and the flesh with all its disorderly appetites. These three powers are the sources of all sin, and, therefore, are called the three enemies of the soul, because they imprison her and surrender her to a most pitiless master.

The first two powers make use of the flesh, as Satan made use of Eve, to tempt and incite us to every kind of iniquity. Therefore, the Apostle calls flesh "sin," giving the name of the effect to the cause, for there is no evil to which man is not incited by the flesh. (*Rom.* 7:25). For this reason theologians term it *fomes peccati*—that is, the germ and fuel of sin; for, like wool and oil, it serves to feed the fire of sin. It is more commonly called sensuality, or concupiscence, which, to speak more plainly, is our sensual appetite. Hence, St. Basil tells us that our desires are the principal arms with which the devil makes war upon us; for, carried away by the immoderate desires of the flesh, we seek to gratify them by any means in our power, regardless of God's law. From this disorder all sins arise.

This appetite of the flesh is one of the greatest tyrants to whom, in the language of the Apostle, the sinner has made himself a slave. By this we do not mean that the sinner loses his free will, for free will is never lost, however great the multitude of his crimes. But sin so weakens the will, and so strengthens the appetites of the flesh, that the stronger naturally prevails over the weaker. What is there more painful than the consequences of such a victory?

Man possesses a soul made to the image of God, a mind capable of rising above creatures to the contemplation of God; yet he despises all these privileges and places himself in subjection to the base appetites of a flesh corrupted by sin and incited and directed by the devil. What can man expect from such a guidance, or rather from such a bondage, but innumerable falls and incomparable misfortunes?

Our souls may be considered as consisting of two parts, which theologians call the superior and the inferior parts. The first is the seat of the will and of reason, the natural light with which God endowed us at creation. This noble and beautiful gift of reason makes man the image of God and capable of enjoying God, and raises him to a companionship with the angels. The inferior part of the soul is the seat of the sensual appetites, which have been given to us to aid us in procuring the necessities of life and in preserving the human race. But these appetites are blind—they must follow the guidance of reason. They are unfitted to command, and, therefore, like good stewards, they should act only in obedience to their master. Alas! How often do we see this order reversed! How often do we behold the servant become the master!

How many men are so enslaved by their appetites that

they will outrage every law of justice and reason to gratify the sensual desires of their hearts! They carry their folly still further, and make the noble faculty of reason wait upon their base appetites and furnish them with means to attain their unlawful desires. For when man devotes the powers of his mind to the invention of new fashions in dress, new pleasures in eating; when he strives to excel his fellow men in wealth and voluptuous luxuries, does he not turn his soul from the noble and spiritual duties suited to her nature, and make her the slave of the flesh? When he devotes his genius to the composition of odes and sonnets to the object of a sinful love, does he not debase his reason beneath this vile passion? Seneca, though a pagan, blushed at such degradation, saying, "I was born for nobler things than to be a slave to the flesh." (*Epist.* 65). Notwithstanding the folly and enormity of this disorder, it is so common among us that we give it little attention. As St. Bernard says, "We are insensible to the odor of our crimes because they are so numerous." In the country of the Moors no one feels affronted if called black, because it is the color of all the inhabitants. So where the vice of drunkenness prevails no one thinks it disgraceful to drink to excess, notwithstanding the degrading nature of this sin.

Yes, the bondage of the flesh is so general that few realize its enormity. How complete, therefore, is this servitude, and how great must be the punishment reserved for one who delivers so noble a creature as reason into the hands of so cruel a tyrant! It is from this slavery that the Wise Man prays to be delivered when he asks that the inordinate desires of the flesh be taken from him, and that he be not given over to a shameless and foolish mind. (Cf. *Ecclus.* 23:6).

If you would know the power of this tyranny you have only to consider the evils it has wrought since the beginning of the world. I will not set before you the inventions of the poets on this subject, or the example of their famous hero, Hercules, who, after destroying or subduing all the monsters of the world, was himself so enslaved by the love of an impure woman that he abandoned his club for a distaff, and all future feats of valor, to sit and spin among the maidens of his haughty mistress. It is a wise invention of the poets to show the arbitrary power this passion exercises over its victims. Nor will I quote from Holy Scripture the example of Solomon, the wisest of men, enslaved by sensual affections, and so far forgetting the true God as to build temples to the idols of his sinful companions. But I will give you an illustration which, alas, is not an uncommon occurrence.

Consider, for instance, all that a married woman risks by abandoning herself to an unlawful love. We choose this passion from among the rest to show you the strength of the others. She cannot but know that should her husband discover her crime he may kill her in his anger, and thus in one moment she will lose her reputation, her children, her life, her soul, and all that she can desire in this life or the next. She knows, moreover, that her disgrace will fall upon her children, her parents, her brothers, her sisters, and all her race; yet so great is the strength of this passion, or rather the power of this tyrant, that she tramples all these considerations underfoot to obey its dictates. Was there ever a master more cruel in his exactions? Can you imagine a more miserable, a more absolute servitude?

Yet such is the bondage in which the wicked live. They are seated "in darkness and the shadow of death," says the prophet, "hungry and bound with chains." (*Ps.* 106:10). What is the darkness, if not the deplorable blindness of the wicked, who neither know themselves nor their Maker, nor the end for which they were created? They see not the vanity of the things upon which they have set their hearts, and they are insensible to the bondage in which they live.

What are the chains which bind them so cruelly, if not the ties of their disorderly affections? And is not this hunger which consumes them the insatiable desire for things which they can never obtain?

Not unfrequently the gratification of man's inordinate desires, so far from satisfying him, only creates other more violent passions, as we learn from the example of Amnon, the wicked son of David, who could neither eat nor rest because of his love for Thamar; but he no sooner obtained possession of her than he hated her even more intensely than he had loved her. (Cf. *2 Kg.* 13:1-16).

Such is the condition of all who are enslaved by this vice. They cease to be masters of themselves; it allows them no rest; they can neither think nor speak of anything else; it fills their dreams at night; and nothing, not even the fear of God, the interests of their souls, the loss of their honor, or life itself, can turn them from their course or break the guilty chains which bind them. Consider also the jealousy and suspicions with which they are tormented, and the dangers of body and soul which they willingly risk for these base pleasures. Was there ever a master who exercised such cruelty towards a slave as this tyrant inflicts upon the heart of his victims? Hence we read that "wine and women make wise men fall off." (*Ecclus.* 19:2). Most fitly are these two passions classed together, for the vice of impurity renders a man as little master of himself, and unfits him for the duties of life, as completely as if robbed of the use of his senses by wine.

The great Latin poet admirably paints the power of this passion in the example of Dido, Queen of Carthage. She no sooner falls in love with AEneas than she abandons the care of public affairs; the walls and fortifications of the city are left unfinished; public works are suspended; the youth are no longer exercised in the noble profession of arms; the harbors are left defenceless, and the city unprotected. Enslaved by this tyrannical passion, Dido is unfitted for the duties of her position; all the powers of her great genius are concentrated upon the object of her love. Oh! Fatal passion! Oh! Pestilential vice, destroying families and overthrowing kingdoms! It is the poison of souls, the death of genius, the folly of old age, the madness of youth, and the bane of mankind.

But this is not the only vice which reduces man to slavery. Study one who is a victim to pride or ambition, and see how eagerly he grasps at honors, how he makes them the end of all his actions. His house, his servants, his table, his dress, his gait, his bearing, his principles are all fashioned to excite the applause of the world; his words and actions are but baits to win admiration. If we wonder at the folly of the Emperor Domitian, armed with a bodkin and spending his leisure in the pursuit of flies, how much more astonishing and pitiable it is to see a man devote not only his leisure but a lifetime to the pursuit of wordly vanities which cannot but end in smoke! Behold how he enslaves himself! He cannot do his own will; he cannot dress to please himself; he cannot go where he chooses; nay, many times he dares not enter a church or converse with virtuous souls, lest his master, the world, should ridicule him.

To satisfy his ambition he imposes upon himself innumerable privations; he lives above his income; he squanders his means; he robs his children of their inheritance, and leaves them only the burden of his debts and the evil example of his follies. What punishment is more fitting for such madness than that which we are told a certain king inflicted upon an ambitious man, whom he condemned to be executed by having smoke poured into his nostrils till he expired, saying to the unhappy victim that as he had lived for smoke, so it was fit that he should die by smoke?

What shall we say of the avaricious man whose money is his master and his god? Is it not in this idol that he finds his comfort and his glory? Is it not the end of all his labors, the object of his hopes? For it does he hesitate to neglect body and soul, to deny himself the necessities of life? Is he restrained even by the fear of God? Can such a man be said to be master of his treasures? On the contrary, is he not their slave as completely as if he were created for his money, and not his money for him?

Can there be a more terrible slavery? We call a man a captive who is placed in prison and bound with chains, but his bondage does not equal that of a man whose soul is the slave of an inordinate affection. Such a man vainly thinks himself free, but no power of his soul enjoys true liberty; his free will, weakened by sin, is the only possession which remains to him. It matters little what fetters bind man, if the nobler part of his soul be captive. Nor does the fact that he has voluntarily assumed these chains make his bondage less real or less ignominious. The sweetness of a poison by no means diminishes its fatal effects.

A man who is the slave of a passion is unceasingly tormented by desires which he cannot satisfy and will not curb. So strong is the bondage of the unhappy victim that when he endeavors to regain his liberty he meets with such resistance that frequently he despairs of succeeding and returns to his chains.

If these miserable captives were held by one chain only, there would be more hope of their deliverance. But how numerous are the fetters which bind them! Man is subject to many necessities, each of which excites some desire; therefore, the greater the number of our inordinate desires, the more numerous our chains. This bondage is stronger in some than in others: there are men of such tenacious disposition that it is only with difficulty they reject what has once taken possession of their imaginations. Others are of a melancholy temperament and cling with gloomy obstinacy to their desires. Many are so narrow-minded that the most insignificant object cannot escape their covetousness. This accords with the saying of Seneca, that to small souls trifles assume vast proportions. Others, again, are naturally vehement in all their desires; this is generally the character of women, who, as a philosopher observes, must either love or hate, for it is difficult for them to observe a just medium.

If the misery of serving one arbitrary master be so great, what must be the suffering of the unhappy man who is enslaved by as many masters as there are ungoverned affections in his heart? If the dignity of man depend upon his reason and free will, what can there be more fatal to this dignity than passion, which obscures the reason and enslaves the will? Without these powers he descends to the level of the brute.

From this miserable slavery the Son of God has delivered us. By the superabundant grace of God we have been redeemed; by the sacrifice of the cross we have been purchased. Hence the Apostle tells us that "our old man [our sensual appetite] is crucified with Christ." (*Rom.* 6:6). By the merits of His crucifixion, we have been strengthened to subdue and crucify our enemies, inflicting upon them the suffering which they caused us to endure, and reducing to slavery the tyrants whom we formerly served. Thus do we verify the words of Isaias: "They shall make them captives that had taken them, and shall subdue their oppressors." (*Is.* 14:2). Before the reign of grace, the flesh ruled the spirit and made it the slave of the most depraved desires. But strengthened by grace, the spirit rules the flesh and makes it the docile instrument of the noblest deeds.

We find a forcible illustration of this defeat of the power of darkness and the triumph of truth in the example of King Adonibezec, whom the children of Israel put to death after cutting off his fingers and toes. In the midst of his suffering the unhappy king exclaimed, "Seventy kings having their fingers and their toes cut off, gathered up the leavings of the meat under my table; as I have done, so God hath requitted me." (*Jud.* 1:7). This cruel tyrant is a figure of the prince of this world, who has disabled the children of God by robbing them of the use of their noblest faculties, thus rendering them powerless to do any good. They being reduced to so helpless a condition, he throws to them, from the store of his vile pleasures, what are fitly called crumbs, for the gratifications which sin brings are never able to satisfy the appetites of the wicked. See, then, that even of the brutal pleasures for which they bargained with Satan, their cruel master will not give them sufficient.

Christ came and by His Passion overcame this enemy and compelled him to endure the same sufferings which he had inflicted on others. He cut off his members—that is, He deprived him of his power and bound him hand and foot. Adonibezec, the Holy Scriptures tell us, suffered death in Jerusalem. In the same city Our Saviour died to destroy the tyrant sin. It was after this great Sacrifice that men learned to conquer the world, the flesh, and the devil. Strengthened by the grace which Christ has purchased for us, neither the pleasures of the world nor the power of Satan can force them to commit a mortal sin.

You will ask, perhaps, what is the source of this liberty and the glorious victory which it enables us to gain. After God, its source is grace, which, by means of the virtues it nourishes in us, subdues our passions and compels them to submit to the empire of reason. Certain men are said to charm serpents to such a degree that, without injuring them or lessening their venom, the snakes are rendered perfectly harmless. In like manner, grace so charms our passions—the venomous reptiles of the flesh—that, though they continue to exist in our nature, they can no longer harm us or infect us with their poison.

St. Paul expresses this truth with great clearness. After speaking at some length of the tyranny of our sensual appetites, he concludes with the memorable words, "Unhappy man that I am, who shall deliver me from the body of this death?" And he answers, "The grace of God by Jesus Christ our Lord." (*Rom.* 7:24,25). The body of death here mentioned by St. Paul is not the natural death of the body which all must undergo, but "the body of sin" (*Rom.* 6:6)—our sensual appetites, the fruitful source of all our miseries. These are the tyrants from which the grace of God delivers us.

A second source of this liberty is the joy of a good conscience and the spiritual consolations experienced by the just. These so satisfy man's thirst for happiness that he can easily resist the grosser pleasures of the flesh. Having found the fountain of all happiness, he desires no other pleasures. As Our Saviour Himself declared: Whoever will drink of the water that He will give him shall thirst no more. (Cf. *Jn.* 4:13).

St. Gregory thus develops this text: He who has experienced the sweetness of the spiritual life rejects the objects of his sensual love. He generously disposes of his treasures. His heart is inflamed with a desire for heavenly things. He sees but deformity in the beauty which formerly allured him. His heart is filled with the water of life, and, therefore, he has no thirst for the fleeting pleasures of the world. He finds the Lord of all things, and thus, in a measure, he becomes the master of all things, for in this one Good every other good is contained.

Besides these two divine favors, there is another means by which the liberty of the just is regained. This is the vigilant care with which the virtuous man unceasingly labors to bring the flesh under the dominion of reason.

The passions are thereby gradually moderated, and lose that violence with which they formerly attacked the soul. Habit does much to cause this happy change, but when aided and confirmed by grace its effects are truly wonderful. Accustomed to the influence of reason, our passions seem to change their nature. They are no longer the fierce assailants of our virtue, but rather its submissive servants.

Hence it is that they who serve God very often find more pleasure, even sensible pleasure, in recollection, silence, pious reading, meditation, prayer, and other devout exercises, than in any wordly amusement. In this happy state the work of subduing the flesh is rendered very easy. Weakened as it is, the attacks it makes on us serve only as occasions of new conquests and new merits. Nevertheless, the ease with which we win these victories should not disarm our prudence or render us less vigilant in guarding the senses as long as we are on earth, however perfectly the flesh may be mortified.

These are the principal sources of that marvelous liberty enjoyed by the just. This liberty inspires us with a new knowledge of God and confirms us in the practice of virtue. This we learn from the prophet: "They shall know that I am the Lord when I shall have broken the bonds of their yoke, and shall have delivered them out of the hand of those that rule over them." (*Ezech.* 34:27). St. Augustine, who experienced the power of this yoke, says, "I was bound by no other fetters than my own iron will, which was in the possession of the enemy. With this he held me fast. From it sprang evil desires, and in satisfying these evil desires I contracted a vicious habit. This habit was not resisted, and, increasing in strength as time passed, finally became a necessity, which reduced me to the most cruel servitude." (*Conf.* 8,5).

When a man who has long been oppressed by the bondage under which St. Augustine groaned turns to God, and sees his chains fall from him, his passions quelled, and the yoke which oppressed him lying at his feet, he cannot but recognize in his deliverance the power of God's grace. Filled with gratitude, he will cry out with the prophet, "Thou hast broken my bonds, O Lord! I will sacrifice to thee a sacrifice of praise, and I will call upon the name of the Lord." (*Ps.* 115:7).

CHAPTER 19

*The Eighth Privilege of Virtue: The Peace
enjoyed by the Just*

The liberty of the children of God is the cause of another
privilege of virtue, no less precious than itself—the interior
peace and tranquillity which the just enjoy. To understand
this more clearly, we must remember that there are three
kinds of peace: peace with God, peace with our neighbor,
and peace with ourselves. Peace with God consists in the
favor and friendship of God, and is one of the results of
justification.

The Apostle, speaking of this peace, says, "Being
justified, therefore, by faith, let us have peace with God
through our Lord Jesus Christ." (*Rom.* 5:1). Peace with our
neighbor consists in a friendly union with our fellow men,
which banishes from us all ill-will towards them. David enjoyed this peace when he said, "With them that hated peace
I was peaceable; when I spoke to them they fought against
me without cause." (*Ps.* 119:7). To this peace St. Paul exhorted the Romans, "As much as is in you, have peace with
all men." (*Rom.* 12:18). Peace with ourselves is the tranquillity arising from a good conscience, and the harmony
existing between the spirit and the flesh when the latter has
been reduced to submission to the laws of reason.

We will first consider the agitation and anxiety of the sinner, in order more keenly to appreciate the blessing of holy
peace. The wicked hearken to the flesh, and, therefore, they

are never free from the disturbance caused by the unceasing and insatiable demands of their passions. Deprived of God's grace which can alone check their unruly appetites, they are a prey to innumerable desires. Some hunger for honors, titles, and dignities, others long for riches, honorable alliances, amusements, or sensual pleasures.

But none of them will ever be fully satisfied, for passion is as insatiable as the daughters of the horse-leech, which continually cry out for more and more. (Cf. *Prov.* 30:15). This leech is the gnawing desire of our hearts, and its daughters are necessity and concupiscence. The first is a real thirst, the second a fictitious thirst; but both are equally disturbing. Therefore, it is evident that without virtue man cannot know peace, either in poverty or riches; for in the former, necessity allows him no ease, and in the latter, sensuality is continually demanding more. What rest, what peace, can one enjoy in the midst of ceaseless cries which he cannot satisfy? Could a mother know peace surrounded by children asking for bread which she could not give them?

This, then, is one of the greatest torments of the wicked. "They hunger and thirst," says the prophet, "and their souls faint within them." (*Ps.* 106:5). Having placed their happiness in earthly things, they hunger and thirst for them as the object of all their hope. The fulfillment of desire, says Solomon, is the tree of life. (Cf. *Prov.* 8:12). Consequently, there is nothing more torturing to the wicked than their unsatisfied desires. And the more their desires are thwarted, the stronger and more intense they become. Their lives, then, are passed in wretched anxiety, constant war raging within them.

The prodigal is a forcible illustration of the unhappy lot of the wicked. Like him, they separate themselves from God and plunge into every vice. They abuse and squander all that God has given them. They go into a far country where famine rages; and what is this country but the world, so far removed from God, where men hunger with desires which can never be satisfied, where, like ravenous wolves, they are constantly seeking more? And how do such men understand the duties of life? They recognize no higher duty than that of feeding swine. To satisfy the animal within them, to feed their swinish appetites, is their only aim.

If you would be convinced of this, study the life of a worldling. From morning until night, and from night until morning, what is the object of his pursuit? Is it not the gratification of some pleasure of sense, either of sight, of hearing, of taste, or of touch? Does he not act as if he were a follower of Epicurus and not a disciple of Christ? Does he seem to be conscious that he possesses any faculty but those which he has in common with the beasts? For what does he live but to enjoy the grossest pleasures of the flesh? What is the end of all his revels, his feasts, his balls, his gallantry, his luxurious couches, his enervating music, his degrading spectacles, but to afford new delights to the flesh?

Give all this what name you will—fashion, refinement, elegance—in the language of God and the Gospel it is feeding swine. For as swine love to wallow in the mire, so these depraved hearts delight to wallow in the mire of sensual pleasures.

But what is most deplorable in this condition is that a son of such noble origin, born to partake of the Bread of Angels at God's own table, would feed upon husks which cannot even satisfy his hunger. In truth, the world cannot gratify its votaries. They are so numerous that, like swine grunting and fighting for acorns at the foot of an oak, they quarrel and wrest from one another the pleasures and gratifications for which they hunger.

This is the miserable condition which David described when he said, "They wandered in a wilderness, in a place without water. They were hungry and thirsty; their soul fainted in them." (*Ps.* 106:4-5). A terrible characteristic of this hunger is that it is increased by the gratifications which are meant to appease it. The poisoned cup of this world kindles in the hearts of the wicked a fire to which pleasures only add renewed heat. Is it strange that they are consumed by a burning thirst? Unhappy man! Whence is it that you thirst so cruelly, if it be not that you "have forsaken the fountain of living waters, and sought broken cisterns which can hold no water"? (*Jer.* 2:13). You have mistaken the source of happiness. You wander in a wilderness, and, therefore, you faint with hunger and thirst.

When Holofernes besieged Bethulia he cut off the aqueducts, leaving to the besieged but a few little streams which served only to moisten their lips. The besieged city is an image of your condition. You have cut yourselves off from the source of living waters, and you find in creatures the little springs which may moisten your lips, but, far from allaying your thirst, will only increase it.

The blindness and vehemence of our desires often make us long for what we cannot possibly obtain; and when, after violent efforts, the object of our pursuit eludes our grasp, anger is added to our disappointment, and both combine to throw us into a state of confusion. This gives rise to that internal warfare mentioned by St. James when he asks, "Whence are wars and contentions among you? Are they not from your concupiscences, which war in your members? You covet, and have not." (*James* 4:1-2). Another lamentable feature of this condition is that very often when men have attained the summit of their wishes they are seized with a desire for some other worldly advantage, and if their caprice is not gratified, all they possess is powerless to comfort them. Their unsatisfied desire is a continual thorn. It poisons all their pleasure.

"There is also another evil," says Solomon, "which I have seen under the sun, and which is frequent among men. A man to whom God hath given riches, and substance, and

honor, and his soul wanteth nothing of all that he desireth;
yet God doth not give him power to eat thereof, but a
stranger shall eat it up. This is vanity and a great misery."
(*Eccles.* 6:1-2). Does not the Wise Man here clearly point
out the wretched condition of one in the midst of abundance, and yet unhappy because of his unsatisfied desires?

If such be the condition of those who possess the goods of
the world, how miserable must be the lot of those who are in
need of everything! For the human heart in every state is
alike subject to unruly appetites, is alike the theater of a
most bitter warfare which rages among its opposing passions. When these importunate desires are unsatisfied at every point, the misery of their victim must be beyond de-
scription.

The condition of the wicked which we have been considering will enable us by contrast to set a true value on the
peace of the just. Knowing how to moderate their appetites
and passions, they do not seek their happiness in the
pleasures of this life, but in God alone. The end of their
labors is not to acquire the perishable goods of this world,
but the enduring treasures of eternity. They wage unceasing
war upon their sensual appetites, and thus keep them entirely subdued. They are resigned to God's will in all the
events of their lives, and, therefore, experience no rebellion
of their will or appetites to disturb their interior peace.

This is one of the principal rewards which God has
promised to virtue. "Much peace have they that love thy
law, and to them there is no stumbling-block." (*Ps.*
118:165).

"Oh! That thou hadst hearkened to my commandments;
thy peace had been as a river, and thy justice as the waves
of the sea." (*Is.* 48:18). Peace is here represented by the
prophet under the figure of a river, because it extinguishes
the fire of concupiscence, moderates the ardor of our
desires, fertilizes the soil of our heart, and refreshes our

soul. Solomon no less clearly asserts this same truth: "When the ways of man shall please the Lord, he will convert even his enemies to peace." (*Prov.* 16:7). He will convert his enemies, the sensual appetites and passions, to peace, and by the power of grace and habit He will subject them to the spirit.

Virtue meets with much opposition in its first efforts against the passions, but as it begins to be perfected, this opposition ceases and its course becomes calm and peaceful. The truth of this is most keenly realized by the just in their practices of piety. They cannot but contrast their present peace with the restless fears and jealousies to which they were a prey when they served the world.

Now that they have given themselves to God and placed all their confidence in Him, none of these alarms can reach them. Their calm resignation to His will has wrought such a change in them that they can hardly believe themselves the same beings. In truth, grace has transformed them by creating in them new hearts. Can we, then, be surprised that such souls enjoy a peace which, the Apostle says, surpasses all understanding?

He who enjoys this favor cannot but turn to the Author of so many marvels and cry out with the prophet, "Come and behold ye the works of the Lord, what wonders he hath done upon earth, making wars to cease even to the ends of the earth. He shall destroy the bow, and break the weapons; and the shields he shall burn in the fire." (*Ps.* 45:9-10). What, then, is more beautiful, more worthy of our ambition, than this peace of soul, this calm of conscience, which is the work of grace and the privilege of virtue?

As one of the twelve fruits of the Holy Ghost, peace is the effect of virtue and its inseparable companion. It is one of those blessings which give us on earth many of the joys of Heaven. For the Apostle tells us, "The kingdom of God is not meat and drink; but justice, and peace, and joy in the

Holy Ghost." (*Rom.* 14:17). According to the Hebrew version, justice here means the perfection of virtue, which, together with its beautiful fruits, peace and joy, gives the just a foretaste of eternal happiness. If you would have still further proof that this peace flows from virtue, hear the words of the prophet: "The work of justice shall be peace, and the service of justice quietness and security for ever." (*Is.* 32:17).

A second cause of this peace is the liberty which the just enjoy. This liberty is gained by the triumph of the nobler part of the soul over the inferior appetites, which, after they have been subjugated, are easily prevented from causing any disturbance. The great spiritual consolations which we considered in a preceding chapter form another source of this peace. They soothe the affections and appetites of the flesh by making them content to share in the joys of the spirit, which they afterwards begin to relish as the sovereign sweetness of God becomes better known. Seeking, therefore, no other delights, they are never disappointed, and consequently never feel the attacks of anger. The happy result of all this is the reign of peace in the soul.

Finally, this great privilege proceeds from the just man's confidence in God, which is his comfort in all trials and his anchor in all storms. He knows that God is his Father, his Defender, his Shield. Hence, he can say with the prophet, "In peace in the selfsame I will sleep and I will rest; for thou, O Lord, singularly hast settled me in hope." (*Ps.* 4:9-10).

CHAPTER 20

*The Ninth Privilege of Virtue: The Manner
in which God hears the Prayers of the Just*

To comprehend what we are about to say upon this subject, you must remember that there have been two universal
deluges, one material, the other moral. The former took
place in the time of Noe and destroyed everything in the
world but the ark and what it contained. The moral deluge,
much greater and more fatal than the material, arose from
the sin of our first parents. Unlike the flood in the days of
Noe, it affected not only Adam and Eve, its guilty cause,
but every human being. It affected the soul even more than
the body. It robbed us of all the spiritual riches and supernatural treasures which were bestowed upon us in the person of our first parent.

From this first deluge came all the miseries and necessities under which we groan. So great and so numerous are
these that a celebrated doctor, who was also an illustrious
pontiff, has devoted to them an entire work. (Innocent III,
De Vilitate Conditionis Humanae). Eminent philosophers,
considering on the one hand man's superiority to all other
creatures, and on the other the miseries and vices to which
he is subject, have greatly wondered at such contradictions
in so noble a creature. Unenlightened by revelation, they
knew not the cause of this discord. They saw that of all
animals man had most infirmities of body; that he alone was
tormented by ambition, by avarice, by a desire to prolong

his life, by a strange anxiety concerning his burial, and, as it appeared to them, by a still stranger anxiety concerning his condition after death. In fine, they saw that he was subject to innumerable accidents and miseries of body and soul, and condemned to earn his bread by the sweat of his brow.

His wretchedness was briefly but forcibly described by Job when he said that "the life of man upon earth is a warfare; and his days are like the days of a hireling." (*Job* 7:1). Many of the ancient philosophers were so impressed with this truth that they doubted whether nature should not be called a stepmother rather than a mother, so great are the miseries to which she subjects us. Others argued that it would be better never to be born, or to die immediately after birth. And some have said that few would accept life could they have any experience of it before it was offered them.

Reduced to this miserable condition, and deprived of our possessions by the first deluge, what resource, what remedy, has been left us by the Master who has punished us so severely? There is but one remedy for us, and that is to have recourse to Him, crying out with the holy king Josaphat, "We know not what to do; we can only turn our eyes to thee." (*2 Par.* 20:12). Ezechias, powerful monarch though he was, knew that this was his only refuge, and therefore declared that he would cry to God like a swallow and would moan before Him as a dove. (Cf. *Is.* 38:14).

And David, though a still greater monarch, placed all his confidence in this heavenly succor. Inspired with the same sentiment, he exclaimed, "I cried to the Lord with my voice; to God with my voice, and he gave ear to me. In the day of my trouble I sought God, with my hands lifted up to him in the night, and I was not deceived." (*Ps.* 76:2-3). Thus when all other avenues of hope were closed against him, when all other resources failed him, he had recourse to prayer, the sovereign remedy for every evil.

You will ask, perhaps, whether this is truly the sovereign remedy for every evil. As this depends solely upon the will of God, they alone can answer it who have been instructed in the secrets of His will—the Apostles and prophets. "There is no other nation so great, that hath gods so nigh them, as our God is present to all our petitions." (*Deut.* 4:7).

These are the words of God Himself, though expressed by His servant. They assure us with absolute certainty that our prayers are not addressed in vain, that God is invisibly present with us to receive every sigh of our soul, to compassionate our miseries, and to grant us what we ask, if it be for our welfare. What is there more consoling in prayer than this guarantee of God's assistance? But still more reassuring are the promises of God Himself in the New Testament where He tells us, "Ask, and you shall receive; seek, and you shall find; knock, and it shall be opened to you." (*Matt.* 7:7). What stronger, what fuller pledge could we find to allay our doubts?

Is it not evident that this is one of the greatest privileges enjoyed by the just, to whom these consoling words are in a special manner addressed? "The eyes of the Lord are upon the just, and his ears unto their prayers." (*Ps.* 33:16). "Then shalt thou call, and the Lord shall hear; thou shalt cry, and he shall say: Here I am." (*Is.* 58:9). By the same prophet God promises more—to grant the prayers of the just even before they are addressed to Him. And yet none of these promises equal those of Our Saviour in the New Testament. "If you abide in me," He says, "and my words abide in you, you shall ask whatever you will, and it shall be done unto you." (*Jn.* 15:7).

"Amen, amen I say to you: if you ask the Father any thing in my name, he will give it you." (*Jn.* 16:23).

Oh! Promise truly worthy of Him who utters it! What other power could offer such a pledge? Who but God could fulfill it? Does not this favor make man, in a measure, the lord of all things? Is he not thereby entrusted with the keys of Heaven? "Whatsoever you shall ask"—provided it lead to your salvation—"shall be given to you." There is no limitation, no special blessing—all the treasures of grace are offered to us.

Ah! If men knew how to appreciate things at their true value, with what confidence would these words inspire them! If men glory in possessing the favor of an earthly monarch who places his royal power at their disposal, how much more reason have we to rejoice in the favor and protection of the King of kings!

If you would learn how such promises are fulfilled, study the lives of the saints and see what marvels they effected by prayer. What did not Moses accomplish by prayer in Egypt and throughout the journey of the Israelites in the desert? How wonderful were the works of Elias and his disciple Eliseus! Behold the miracles which the Apostles wrought! Prayer was the source of their power. It is, moreover, the weapon with which the saints have fought and overcome the world. By prayer they ruled the elements, and converted even the fierce flames into refreshing dew. By prayer they disarmed the wrath of God and opened the fountains of His mercy. By prayer, in fine, they obtained all their desires.

It is related that our holy Father, St. Dominic, once told a friend that he never failed to obtain a favor which he asked from God. Whereupon his friend desired him to pray that a celebrated doctor named Reginald might become a member of his order. The saint spent the night in prayer for this disciple, and early in the morning, as he was beginning the first hymn of the morning office, Reginald suddenly came into the choir, and, prostrating himself at the feet of the saint, begged for the habit of his order. Behold the recompense with which God rewards the obedience of the just. They are docile to the voice of His commandments, and He is equally attentive to the voice of their supplications. Hence Solomon tells us that "an obedient man shall speak of victory." (*Prov.* 21:28).

How differently are the prayers of the wicked answered! "When you stretch forth your hands," the Almighty tells them, "I will turn away my eyes from you; and when you multiply prayer I will not hear." (*Is.* 1:15). "In the time of their affliction," says the prophet, "they will say to the Lord, Arise, and deliver us." But God will ask, "Where are the gods whom thou hast made thee? Let them arise and deliver thee." (*Jer.* 2:27-28).

"What is the hope of the hypocrite, if through covetousness he takes by violence? Will God hear his cry when distress shall come upon him?" (*Job* 27:8).

"Dearly beloved," says St. John, "if our heart do not reprehend us, we have confidence towards God; and whatsoever we shall ask, we shall receive of him, because we keep his commandments, and do those things which are pleasing in his sight." (*1 Jn.* 3:21-22).

"If I have looked at iniquity in my heart," the royal prophet tells us, "the Lord will not hear me"; but I have not committed iniquity, and "therefore God hath heard me, and attended to the voice of my supplication." (*Ps.* 65:18-19).

It would be easy to find in Holy Scripture many similar passages, but these will suffice to manifest the difference between the prayers of the just and those of the wicked, and, by consequence, the incomparable privileges which the former enjoy. The just are heard and treated as the children of God; the wicked are rejected as His enemies. This should not astonish us, for a prayer unsupported by good works, devoid of fervor, charity, or humility, cannot be pleasing to God.

Nevertheless, the sinner who reads these lines must not give way to discouragement. It is only the obstinately wicked who are rejected. It is only those who wish to continue in their disorders who are thus cut off. Though your sins are as numerous as the sands on the shore, though your life has been wasted in crime, never forget that God is your Father, that He awaits you with open arms and open heart, that He is continually calling upon you to return and be reconciled to Him. Have the desire to change your life; be resolved to walk in the path of virtue, and turn to God in humble prayer, with unshaken confidence that you will be heard. "Ask, and you shall receive; seek, and you shall find; knock, and it shall be opened to you."

CHAPTER 21

*The Tenth Privilege of Virtue: The
Consolation and Assistance with which
God sustains the Just in their Afflictions*

As we have already remarked, there is no sea more
treacherous or more inconstant than this life. No man's
happiness is secure from the danger of innumerable accidents and misfortunes. It is, therefore, important to observe how differently the just and the wicked act under
tribulation. The just, knowing that God is their Father
and the Physician of their souls, submissively and
generously accept as the cure for their infirmities the bitter chalice of suffering. They look on tribulation as a file
in the hands of their Maker to remove the rust of sin
from their souls, and to restore them to their original
purity and brightness. They have learned in the school of
the Divine Master that affliction renders a man more
humble, increases the fervor of his prayers, and purifies
his conscience.

Now, no physician more carefully proportions his
remedies to the strength of his patient than this Heavenly
Physician tempers trials according to the necessities of
souls. Should their burdens be increased, He redoubles
the measure of their consolations. Seeing from this the
riches they acquire by sufferings, the just no longer fly
from them, but eagerly desire them, and meet them with
patience and even with joy. They regard not the labor,

but the crown; not the bitter medicine, but the health to be restored to them; not the pain of their wounds, but the goodness of Him who has said that He loves those whom He chastises. (Cf. *Heb.* 12:6).

Grace, which is never wanting to the just in the hour of tribulation, is the first source of the fortitude which they display. Though He seems to have withdrawn from them, God is never nearer to His children than at such a time. Search the Scriptures and you will see that there is no truth more frequently repeated than this. "Call upon me in the day of trouble," says the Lord; "I will deliver thee, and thou shalt glorify me." (*Ps.* 49:15). "When I called upon the Lord," David sings, "the God of my justice heard me; when I was in distress, thou hast enlarged me." (*Ps.* 4:2).

Hence the calmness and fortitude of the just under suffering. They are strong in the protection of a powerful Friend who constantly watches over them. Witness the three young men who were cast into the burning furnace. God sent His angel to accompany them, and "He drove the flame of the fire out of the furnace, and made the midst of the furnace like the blowing of a wind bringing dew, and the fire touched them not, nor troubled them, nor did them any harm . . . Then Nabuchodonosor was astonished, and rose up in haste, and said to his nobles: Did we not cast three men bound into the midst of the fire? They answered the king and said: True, O king. He answered and said: Behold I see four men loose, and walking in the midst of the fire, and there is no hurt in them, and the form of the fourth is like the Son of God." (*Dan.* 3:49-50 and 91-92). Does this not teach us that God's protection never fails the just in the hour of trial?

A no less striking example is that of Joseph, with whom God's protection "descended into the pit, and left him not till he was brought to the scepter of the kingdom, and power against those that had oppressed him, and showed them to be liars that had accused him, and gave him everlasting glory." (*Wis.* 10:13-14). Such examples prove more powerfully than words the truth of God's promise, "I am with him in tribulation; I will deliver him and I will glorify him." (*Ps.* 90:15). Oh! Happy affliction which merits for us the companionship of God! Let our prayers, then, be with St. Bernard: "Give me, O Lord, tribulations through life, that I may never be separated from Thee!" (*Serm.* 17 in *Ps.* 90).

To the direct action of grace we must add that of the virtues, each of which, in its own way, strengthens the afflicted soul. When the heart is oppressed, the blood rushes to it to facilitate its movement, to strengthen its action. So, when the soul is oppressed by suffering, the virtues hasten to assist and strengthen it.

First comes faith, with her absolute assurance of the eternal happiness of Heaven and the eternal misery of Hell. She tells us, in the words of the Apostle, that "the sufferings of this time are not worthy to be compared with the glory to come that shall be revealed in us." (*Rom.* 8:18). Next comes hope, softening our troubles and lightening our burdens with her glorious promises of future rewards. Then charity, the most powerful help of the soul, so inflames our will that we even desire to suffer for love of Him who has endured so much for love of us.

Gratitude reminds us that as we have received good things from God, we should also be willing to receive evil. (Cf. *Job* 2:10). Resignation helps us recognize and cheerfully accept God's will or permission in all things. Humility bows the heart before the wind of adversity, like a young tree swept by the storm. Patience gives us strength above nature to enable us to bear the heaviest burden. Obedience tells us that there is no holocaust more pleasing to God than that which we make of our

will by our perfect submission to Him. Penance urges
that it is but just that one who has so often resisted God's
will should have his own will denied in many things.
Fidelity pleads that we should rejoice to be able to prove
our devotion to Him who unceasingly showers His
benefits upon us.

Finally, the memory of Christ's Passion and the lives of
the saints show us how cowardly it would be to complain
of our trials. Yet among all the virtues, hope consoles us
most effectually. "Rejoice in hope," says the Apostle; "be
patient in tribulation" (*Rom.* 12:12), thus teaching us
that our patience is the result of our hope. Again, he
calls hope an anchor (*Heb.* 6:19), because it holds firm
and steady the frail barque of our life in the midst of the
most tempestuous storms.

Strengthened by these considerations and by God's unfailing grace, the just endure tribulation not only with invincible fortitude, but even with cheerfulness and gratitude. They know that the duty of a good Christian does
not consist solely in praying, fasting, or hearing Mass,
but in proving their faith under tribulation, as did
Abraham, the father of the faithful, and Job, the most
patient of men. Consider also the example of Tobias,
who, after suffering many trials, was permitted by God to
lose his sight. The Holy Ghost bears witness to his invincible patience and virtue. "Having always feared God
from his infancy, and kept his commandments, he
repined not against God because the evil of blindness had
befallen him, but continued immovable in the fear of
God, giving thanks to God all the days of his life." (*Tob.*
2:13-14). We could cite numerous examples of men and
women who—even in our time—have cheerfully and
lovingly borne cruel infirmities and painful labors, finding honey in gall, calm in tempest, refreshment and peace
in the midst of the flames of Babylon.

But we feel that we have said sufficient to prove that God consoles the just in their sufferings, and therefore we shall next consider the unfortunate condition of the wicked when laboring under affliction. Devoid of hope, of charity, of courage, of every sustaining virtue, tribulation attacks them unarmed and defenceless. Their dead faith sheds no ray of light upon the darkness of their afflictions. Hope holds out no future reward to sustain their failing courage. Strangers to charity, they know not the loving care of their Heavenly Father. How lamentable a sight to behold them swallowed in the gulf of tribulation! Utterly defenceless, how can they breast the angry waves? How can they escape being dashed to pieces against the rocks of pride, despair, rage, and blasphemy?

Have we not seen unhappy souls lose their health, their reason, their very life in the excess of their misery? While the just, like pure gold, come out of the crucible of suffering refined and purified, the wicked, like some viler metal, are melted and dissolved. While the wicked shed bitter tears, the just sing songs of gladness. "The voice of rejoicing and of salvation is in the tabernacles of the just" (*Ps.* 117:15), while the habitations of sinners resound with cries of sorrow and despair.

Observe, moreover, the extravagant grief of the wicked when those they love are taken from them by death. They storm against Heaven; they deny God's justice; they blaspheme His mercy; they accuse His providence; they rage against men; and not unfrequently they end their miserable lives by their own hands. Their curses and blasphemies bring upon them terrible calamities, for the Divine Justice cannot but punish those who rebel against the providence of God.

Unhappy souls! The afflictions which are sent for the cure of their disorders only increase their misery. May we not say that the pains of Hell begin for them even in this life? Consider, too, the loss which they suffer by their murmurings and impatience. No man can escape the trials of life, but all can lighten their burden and merit eternal reward by bearing their sorrows in patience. Not only is this precious fruit lost by the wicked, but to the load of misery which they are compelled to carry they add the still more intolerable burden of their impatience and rebellion. They are like a traveler who, after a long and weary journey through the night, finds himself in the morning further than ever from the place he wished to reach.

What a subject is this for our contemplation! "The same fire," says St. Chrysostom, "which purifies gold, consumes wood; so in the fire of tribulation the just acquire new beauty and perfection, while the wicked, like dry wood, are reduced to ashes." (*Hom.* 14 in *Matt.* 1). St. Cyprian expresses the same thought by another illustration: "As the wind in harvest time scatters the chaff but cleanses the wheat, so the winds of adversity scatter the wicked but purify the just." (*De Unitate Eccl.*).

The passage of the children of Israel through the Red Sea is still another figure of the same truth. Like protecting walls the waters rose on each side of the people, and gave them a safe passage to the dry land; but as soon as the Egyptian army with its king and chariots had entered the watery breach, the same waves closed upon them and buried them in the sea. In like manner the waters of tribulation are a preservation to the just, while to the wicked they are a tempestuous gulf which sweeps them into the abyss of rage, of blasphemy, and of despair.

Behold the admirable advantage which virtue possesses over vice. It was for this reason that philosophers so highly extolled philosophy, persuaded that its study rendered man more constant and more resolute in adversity. But this was one of their numerous errors. True constancy, like true virtue, cannot be drawn from the teaching of worldly philosophy. It must be learned in the school of the Divine Master, who from His cross consoles us by His example, and from His throne in Heaven sends us His Spirit to strengthen and encourage us by the hope of an immortal crown.

CHAPTER 22

The Eleventh Privilege of Virtue: God's
Care for the Temporal Needs of the Just

The privileges of virtue which we considered in the preceding chapters are the spiritual blessings accorded to the just in this life, independently of the eternal reward of Heaven. As, however, there may be some who, like the Jews of old, cling to the things of the flesh rather than to those of the spirit, we shall devote this chapter to the temporal blessings which the virtuous enjoy.

The Wise Man says of wisdom, which is the perfection of virtue, that "length of days is in her right hand, and in her left hand riches and glory." (*Prov.* 3:16). Perfect virtue, then, possesses this double reward with which she wins men to her allegiance, holding out to them with one hand the temporal blessings of this life, and with the other the eternal blessings of the life to come. Oh, no; God does not leave His followers in want! He who so carefully provides for the ant, the worm, the smallest of His creatures, cannot disregard the necessities of His faithful servants.

I do not ask you to receive this upon my word, but I do ask you to read the Gospel according to St. Matthew, in which you will find many assurances and promises on this subject. "Behold the birds of the air," says Our Saviour, "for they neither sow, nor do they reap, nor gather into barns; and your heavenly Father feedeth them. Are not you of much more value than they? . . . Be not solicitous, therefore, saying: What shall we eat, or what shall we drink, or wherewith shall we be clothed? For after all these things do the heathen seek. For your Father knoweth that you have need of all these things. Seek ye, therefore, first the kingdom of God, and his justice, and all these things shall be added unto you." (*Matt.* 6:26, 31-33).

"Fear the Lord, all ye his saints," the psalmist sings, "for they that fear him know no want. The rich have wanted, and have suffered hunger; but they that seek the Lord shall not be deprived of any good." (*Ps.* 33:10-11). "I have been young, and now am old, and I have not seen the just forsaken nor his seed seeking bread." (*Ps.* 36:25).

If you would satisfy yourself still further concerning the temporal blessings conferred on the just, read the divine promises recorded in Deuteronomy: "If thou wilt hear the voice of the Lord thy God, to do and keep all his commandments which I command thee this day, the Lord thy God will make thee higher than all the nations that are on the earth. And all these blessings shall come upon thee and overtake thee, if thou hear his precepts. Blessed shalt thou be in the city, and blessed in the field. Blessed shall be the fruit of thy womb, and the fruit of thy ground, and the fruit of thy cattle, the droves of thy herds, and the folds of thy sheep. Blessed shall be thy barns and blessed thy stores. Blessed shalt thou be coming in and going out. The Lord shall cause thy enemies that rise up against thee to fall down before thy face; one way shall they come out against thee, and seven ways shall they flee before thee. The Lord will send forth a blessing upon thy storehouses, and upon all the works of thy hands, and will bless thee in the land that thou shalt receive.

"The Lord will raise thee up to be a holy people to himself, as he swore to thee, if thou keep the commandments of the Lord thy God and walk in his ways. And all the people of the earth shall see that the name of the Lord is invoked upon thee, and they shall fear thee. The Lord will make thee abound with all goods, with the fruit of thy womb, and the fruit of thy cattle, with the fruit of thy land which the Lord swore to thy fathers that he would give thee. The Lord will open his excellent treasure, the heaven, that it may give rain in due season; and he will bless all the works of thy hands." (*Deut.* 28:1-12).

What riches can be compared to such blessings as these? And they have been promised not only to the Jews, but to all Christians who are faithful to God's law. Moreover, they are bestowed with two extraordinary advantages unknown to the wicked. The first of these is the wisdom with which God awards them. Like a skillful physician, He gives His servants temporal blessings according to their necessities, and not in such measure as to inflate them with pride or endanger their salvation. The wicked despise this moderation and madly heap up all the riches they can acquire, forgetting that excess in this respect is as dangerous to the soul as excess of nourishment is injurious to the body. Though a man's life lies in his blood, too copious a supply only tends to choke him.

The second of these advantages is that temporal blessings afford the just, with far less disturbance or display, that rest and contentment which all men seek in worldly goods. Even with a little, the just enjoy as much repose as if they possessed the universe. Hence St. Paul speaks of himself as having nothing, yet possessing all things. (Cf. *2 Cor.* 6:10). Thus the just journey through life, poor but knowing no want, possessing abundance in the midst of poverty. The wicked, on the contrary, hunger in the midst of abundance, and though, like Tantalus, they are surrounded by water, they can never satisfy their thirst. (Tantalus, according to the fable of the ancients, was a king of Corinth, condemned by the gods, for divulging their secrets, to be placed in Hell in the midst of water which reached his chin, but which he could not even taste; to have fruit suspended over his head which he could not eat; and to be always in fear of a large stone falling on his hand.).

For like reasons Moses earnestly exhorted the people to the observance of God's law. "Lay up these words in thy heart," he says; "teach them to thy children; meditate upon them sitting in thy house, walking on thy journey, sleeping and rising. Bind them as a sign upon thy hand; keep them before thy eyes; write them over the entrance to thy house, on the doors of thy house. Do that which is pleasing and good in the sight of the Lord, that it may be well with thee all the days of thy life in the land which God shall give thee." (*Deut.* 6:6-10).

Having been admitted to the counsels of the Most High, Moses knew the inestimable treasure contained in the observance of the law. His prophetic mind saw that all temporal and spiritual blessings, both present and future, were comprised in this. It is a compact which God makes with the just, and which, we may feel assured, will never be broken on His part. Nay, rather, if we prove ourselves faithful servants we will find that God will be even more generous than His promises.

"Godliness," says St. Paul, "is profitable to all things, having promise of the life that now is, and of that which is to come." (*1 Tim.* 4:8). Behold how clearly the Apostle promises to piety, which is the observance of God's commandments, not only the blessings of eternity but those of this life also.

If you desire to know the poverty, miseries, and afflictions which are reserved for the wicked, read the twenty-eighth chapter of the Book of Deuteronomy. Therein Moses, in the name of God, utters most terrible threats and maledictions against the impious. "If thou wilt not hear the voice of the Lord thy God, to keep and to do all his commandments and ceremonies which I command thee this day, all these curses shall come upon thee and overtake thee. Cursed shalt thou be in the city, cursed in the field. Cursed shall be thy barn, and cursed thy stores. Cursed shall be the fruit of thy womb, and the fruit of thy ground, the herds of thy oxen, and the flocks of thy sheep. Cursed shalt thou be coming in and going out. The Lord shall send upon thee famine and hunger, and a rebuke upon all the works which thou shalt do, until he consume and destroy thee quickly for thy most wicked inventions, by which thou hast forsaken me. May the Lord set the pestilence upon thee until he consume thee out of the land which thou shalt go in to possess.

"May the Lord afflict thee with miserable want, with the fever and with cold, with burning and with heat, and with corrupted air and with blasting, and pursue thee till thou perish. Be the heaven that is over thee of brass, and the ground thou treadest on of iron. The Lord give thee dust for rain upon thy land, and let ashes come down from heaven upon thee till thou be consumed. The Lord make thee fall down before thy enemies; one way mayst thou go out against them, and flee seven ways, and be scattered throughout all the kingdoms of the earth. And be thy carcass meat for all the fowls of the air and the beasts of the earth, and be there none to drive them away. The Lord strike thee with madness and blindness, and fury of mind. And mayst thou grope at midday as the blind is wont to grope in the dark, and not make straight thy ways. And mayst thou at all times suffer wrong, and be oppressed with violence, and mayest thou have no one to deliver thee. May thy sons and thy daughters be given to another people, thy eyes looking on, and languishing at the sight of them all the day, and may there be no strength in thy hand.

"May a people which thou knowest not eat the fruits of thy land, and all thy labors, and mayst thou always suffer oppression, and be crushed at all times. May the Lord strike thee with a very sore ulcer in the knees and in the legs, and be thou incurable from the sole of thy foot to the top of thy head . . . And all these curses shall come upon thee, and shall pursue and overtake thee, till thou perish; because thou heardst not the voice of the Lord thy God, and didst not keep his commandments. Because thou didst not serve the Lord thy God with joy and gladness of heart for the abundance of all things, thou shalt serve thy enemy whom the Lord will send upon thee, in hunger, in thirst, and nakedness, and in want of all things; and he shall put an iron yoke upon thy neck till he consume thee. The Lord will bring upon thee a nation from afar, and from the uttermost ends of the earth, a most insolent nation, that will show no regard to the ancient, nor have pity on the infant, and will devour the fruit of thy cattle, and the fruits of thy land, until thou be destroyed, and will leave thee no wheat, nor wine, nor oil, nor herds of oxen, nor flocks of sheep, till he consume thee in all thy cities, and thy strong and high walls be brought down, wherein thou trustedst in all thy land. Thou shalt be besieged within thy gates, and thou shalt eat the fruit of thy womb, and the flesh of thy sons and thy daughters, in the distress and extremity wherewith thy enemies shall oppress thee."

Let us not forget that these maledictions are recorded in Holy Scripture, with many others, equally terrible, which we have not cited. Learn from them the rigor with which Divine Justice pursues the wicked, and the hatred God must bear to sin, which He punishes with such severity in this life and with still greater torments in the next.

Think not these were idle menaces. No; they were words of prophecy, and were terribly verified in the Jewish nation. For we read that during the reign of Achab, King of Israel, his people were besieged by the army of the King of Syria, and reduced to such straits that they fed upon pigeons' dung, which sold at a high price, and that a mother devoured her own child. (Cf. *4 Kg.* 6). And these scenes the historian Josephus tells us, were repeated during the siege of Jerusalem. The captivity of this people and the complete destruction of their kingdom and power are well-known to all.

Think not that these calamities were reserved for the Jewish people only. All the nations that have known God's law and despised it have been the objects of His just and terrible anger. "Did not I bring up Israel out of the land of Egypt, and the Philistines out of Cappadocia, and the Syrians out of Cyrene? Behold the eyes of the Lord God are upon the sinful kingdom, and I will destroy it from the face of the earth." (*Amos* 9:7-8). From this we can understand that wars and revolutions, the downfall of some kingdoms and the rise of others, are due to the sins of men.

Read the annals of the early ages of the Church, and you will find that God has dealt in like manner with the wicked, especially with those who were once enlightened by His law, and who afterwards rejected it. See how He has punished infidelity in Christian nations. Vast portions of Europe, Asia, and Africa, formerly filled with Christian churches are now in the hands of infidels and barbarians. Behold the ravages wrought in Christian nations by the Goths, the Huns, and the Vandals! In the time of St. Augustine they laid waste all the countries of Africa, sparing none of the inhabitants, not even women and children. At the same time Dalmatia and the neighboring towns were so devastated by the barbarians that St. Jerome, who was a native of that kingdom, said that a traveler passing through the country would find only earth and sky, so universal was the desolation.

Is it not evident, therefore, that virtue not only helps us attain the joys of eternity, but that it also secures for us the blessings of this life?

Let, then, the consideration of this privilege, with the others which we have mentioned, excite you to renewed ardor in the practice of virtue, which is able to save you from so many miseries and procure you so many blessings.

CHAPTER 23

The Twelfth Privilege of Virtue: The Happy Death of the Just

The end, it is said, crowns the work, and, therefore, it is in death that the just man's life is most fittingly crowned, while the departure of the sinner is a no less fitting close to his wretched career. "Precious in the sight of the Lord is the death of his saints" (*Ps.* 115:15), says the Psalmist, but "the death of the wicked is very evil." (*Ps.* 33:22). Commenting upon the latter part of this text, St. Bernard says, "The death of the wicked is bad because it takes them from this world; it is still worse because it separates the soul from the body; and it is worst because it precipitates them into the fire of Hell, and delivers them a prey to the undying worm of remorse."

To these evils which haunt the sinner at the hour of death add the bitter regrets which gnaw his heart, the anguish which fills his soul, and the torments which rack his body. He is seized with terror at the thought of the past; of the account he must render; of the sentence which is to be pronounced against him; of the horrors of the tomb; of separation from wife, children, and friends; of bidding farewell to the things he has loved with an inordinate and a guilty love—wealth, luxuries, and even the gifts of nature, the light of day and the pure air of heaven. The stronger his love for earthly things has been, the more bitter will be his anguish in separating from them. As St. Augustine says, we cannot part without grief from that which we have possessed with love. It was in the same spirit that a certain philosopher said that he who has fewest pleasures in life has least reason to fear death.

But the greatest suffering of the wicked at the hour of death comes from the stings of remorse, and the thought of the terrible future upon which they are about to enter. The approach of death seems to open man's eyes and make him see all things as he never saw them before. "As life ebbs away," says St. Eusebius, "man is free from all distracting care for the necessities of life. He ceases to desire honors, emoluments, or dignities, for he sees that they are beyond his grasp. Eternal interests and thoughts of God's justice demand all his attention. The past with its pleasures is gone; the present with its opportunities is rapidly gliding away; all that remains to him is the future, with the dismal prospect of his many sins waiting to accuse him before the judgment-seat of the just God."

"Consider," the saint again says, "the terror which will seize the negligent soul when she is entering eternity; the anguish with which she will be filled when, foremost among her accusers, her conscience will appear with its innumerable retinue of sins. Its testimony cannot be denied; its accusations will leave her mute and helpless; there will be no need to seek further witnesses, for the knowledge of this life-long companion will confound her."

Still more terrible is the picture of the death of the sinner given by St. Peter Damian. "Let us try to represent to ourselves," he says, "the terror which fills the soul of the sinner at the hour of death and the bitter reproaches with which conscience assails him. The commandments he has despised and the sins he has committed appear before him to haunt him by their presence. He sighs for the time which he has squandered, and which was given to him to do penance; he beholds with despair the account he must render before the dread tribunal of God. He longs to arrest the moments, but they speed relentlessly on, bearing him nearer and nearer to his doom.

"If he looks back, his life seems but a moment, and before him is the limitless horizon of eternity. He weeps bitterly at the thought of the unspeakable happiness which he has sacrificed for the fleeting pleasures of the flesh. Confusion and shame overwhelm him when he sees he has forfeited a glorious place among the angelic choirs, through love for his body, which is about to become the food of worms. When he turns his eyes from the abode of these beings of light to the dark valley of this world, he sees how base and unworthy are the things for which he has rejected immortal glory and happiness. Oh! Could he but regain a small portion of the time he has lost, what austerities, what mortifications he would practice! What is there that could overcome his courage? What vows would he not offer, and how fervent would be his prayers! But while he is revolving these sad thoughts, the messengers of death appear in the rigid limbs, the dark and hollow eyes, the heaving breast, the foaming lips, the livid face. And as these exterior heralds approach, every thought, word, and action of his guilty life appears before him.

"Vainly does he strive to turn his eyes from them; they will not be banished. On one side—and this is true of every man's death—Satan and his legions are present, tempting the dying man, in the hope of seizing his soul even at the last minute. On the other side are the angels of Heaven, helping, consoling, and strengthening him. And yet it is his own life that will decide the contest between the spirits of darkness and the angels of light. In the case of the good, who have heaped up a treasure of meritorious works, the victory is with the angels of light. But the impious man, whose unexpiated crimes are crying for vengeance, rejects the help that is offered to him, yields to despair, and as his unhappy soul passes from his pampered body, the demons are ready to seize it and bear it away."

What stronger proof does man require of the wretched condition of the sinner, and what more does he need to make him avoid a career which ends so deplorably? If, at this critical hour, riches could help him as they do at many other periods of life, the evil would be less. But he will receive no succor from his riches, his honors, his dignities, his distinguished friends. The only patronage which will then avail him will be that of virtue and innocence. "Riches," says the Wise Man, "shall not profit in the day of revenge, but justice shall deliver from death." (*Prov.* 11:4).

As the wicked, therefore, receive at the hour of death the punishment of their crimes, so do the just then receive the reward of their virtues. "With him that feareth the Lord," says the Holy Ghost, "it shall go well in the latter end; and in the day of his death he shall be blessed." (*Ecclus.* 1:13). St. John declares this truth still more forcibly when he tells us that he heard a voice from Heaven commanding him, "Write: Blessed are the dead who die in the Lord. From henceforth, saith the Spirit, they rest from their labors, for their works follow them." (*Apoc.* 14:13). With such a promise from God Himself, how can the just man fear? Can he dread that hour in which he is to receive the reward of his life's labors?

Since, as we read in Job, he has put away iniquity, brightness like that of the noonday shall arise to him at evening, and when he shall think himself consumed he shall rise as the day-star. (Cf. *Job* 11:14,17). Explaining these words, St. Gregory says that the light which illumines the close of the just man's life is the splendor of that immortal glory which is already so near. When others, therefore, are weighed down by sadness and despair, he is full of confidence and joy. For this reason Solomon has said that the wicked shall be rejected because of their wickedness, but the just man hath hope in the hour of his death. (Cf. *Prov.* 14:32).

What more striking example of this confident hope can we find than that of the glorious St. Martin? Seeing the devil beside his bed at the hour of death, he cried out, "What art thou doing here, cruel beast? Thou wilt find no mortal sin in my soul by which thou mayest bind me. I go, therefore, to enjoy eternal peace in Abraham's bosom." Equally touching and beautiful was the confidence of our holy Father, St. Dominic. Seeing the religious of his order weeping around his bed, he said to them, "Weep not, my children, for I can do you more good where I am going than I could ever hope to do on earth." How could the fear of death overcome one who so confidently hoped to obtain Heaven, not only for himself, but also for his disciples?

Far, then, from fearing death, the just hail it as the hour of their deliverance and the beginning of their reward. In his commentary on the Epistle of St. John, St. Augustine writes, "It cannot be said that he who desires to be dissolved and to be with Christ endures death with patience, but rather that he endures life with patience and embraces death with joy." It is not, therefore, with cries and lamentations that the just man sees his end approaching, but—like the swan, which is said to sing as death draws near—he departs this life with words of praise and thanksgiving on his lips.

He does not fear death, because he has always feared God, and he who fears God need fear nothing else. He does not fear death, because his life has been a preparation for death, and he who is always armed and ready need not fear the enemy. He does not fear death, because he has sought during life to secure in virtue and good works powerful advocates for that terrible hour. He does not fear death, because he has endeavored, by devoted service, to incline his Judge in his favor. Finally, he does not fear death, because to the just, death is only a sweet sleep, the end of toil, and the beginning of a blessed immortality.

Nor can the accompanying accidents and pains of death alarm him, for he knows that they are but the throes and pangs in which he must be brought forth to eternal life. He is not dismayed by the memory of his sins or the rigor of God's justice, since he has Christ for his Friend and Advocate. He does not tremble at the presence of Satan and his followers, for his Redeemer, who has conquered Hell and death, stands at his side. For him the tomb has no terrors, for he knows that he must sow a natural body in order that it may rise a spiritual body, that this corruptible must put on incorruption. (Cf. *1 Cor.* 15:42,44).

Since, as we have already remarked, the end crowns the work, and, as Seneca tells us, the last day condemns or justifies the whole life, how can we, beholding the peaceful and blessed death of the just and the miserable departure of the wicked, seek for any other motive to make us embrace a life of virtue?

Of what avail will be the riches and prosperity which you may enjoy during your short stay in this life, if your eternity will be spent in the endless torments of Hell? Or how can you shrink from the temporary sufferings that will win for you an eternity of happiness? Of what advantage are learning and skill, if the sinner uses them only to acquire those things which flatter his pride, feed his sensuality, confirm him in sin, make him unfit to practice virtue, and thus render death as bitter and unwelcome as his life was pleasant and luxurious? We consider him a wise and skillful physician who prudently seeks by every fit means to restore the health of his patient, since this is the end of his science. So is he truly wise who regulates his life with a view to his last end, who constantly employs all the means in his power to fit himself for a happy death.

Behold, then, dear Christian, the twelve fruits of virtue in this life. They are like the twelve fruits of the tree of life seen by St. John in his prophetic vision. (Cf. *Apoc.* 22:2). This tree represents Jesus Christ, and is also a symbol of virtue with its abundant fruits of holiness and life. And what fruits can be compared to those which we have been considering? What is there more consoling than the fatherly care with which God surrounds the just? What blessings equal those of divine grace, of heavenly wisdom, of the consolations of the Holy Spirit, of the testimony of a good conscience, of invincible hope, of unfailing efficacy in prayer, and of that peaceful and happy death with which the just man's life is crowned? But one of these fruits, rightly known and appreciated, should suffice to make us embrace virtue.

Think not that you will ever regret any labor or any sacrifice made in pursuit of so great a good. The wicked do not strive to attain it, for they know not its value. To them the kingdom of Heaven is like a hidden treasure. (Cf. *Matt.* 13:44). And yet it is only through the divine light and the practice of virtue that they will learn its beauty and worth. Seek, therefore, this light, and you will find the pearl of great price.

Do not leave the source of eternal life to drink at the turbid streams of the world. Follow the counsel of the prophet, and taste and see that the Lord is sweet. Trusting in Our Saviour's words, resolutely enter the path of virtue, and your illusions will vanish. The serpent into which the rod of Moses was converted was frightful at a distance, but at the touch of his hand it became again a harmless rod. To the wicked, virtue wears a forbidding look; to sacrifice their worldly pleasures for her would be to buy her at too dear a rate. But when they draw near they see how lovely she is, and when they have once tasted the sweetness she possesses they cheerfully surrender all they have to win her friendship and love. How gladly did the man in the Gospel hasten to sell all he had to purchase the field which contained a treasure! (Cf. *Matt.* 13:44).

Why, then, do Christians make so little effort to obtain this inestimable good? If a companion assured you that a treasure lay hidden in your house, you would not fail to search for it, even though you doubted its existence. Yet though you know, on the infallible word of God, that you can find a priceless treasure within your own breast, you do nothing to discover it. Oh! That you would realize its value! Would that you knew how little it costs to obtain it, and how "nigh is the Lord unto all them that call upon him, that call upon him in truth" (*Ps.* 144:18)!

Be mindful of the prodigal, of so many others who have returned from sin and error, to find, instead of an angry Judge, a loving Father awaiting them. Do penance, therefore, for your sins, and God will no longer remember your iniquities (Cf. *Ezech.* 18:21-22). Return to your loving Father; rise with the dawn and knock at the gates of His mercy; humbly persevere in your entreaties, and He will not fail to reveal to you the treasure of His love. Having once experienced the sweetness which it contains, you will say with the spouse in the Canticle, "If a man should give all the substance of his house for love, he shall despise it as nothing." (*Cant.* 8:7).

CHAPTER 24

The Folly of those who Defer their Conversion

The considerations offered in the preceding chapters should be more than sufficient to excite men to the love and practice of virtue. However, sinners never seem to be in want of excuses to defend their loose lives. "A sinful man," says the Scripture, "will flee reproof, and will find an excuse according to his will." (*Ecclus.* 32:21).

"He that hath a mind to depart from a friend seeketh occasions." (*Prov.* 18:1). Thus the wicked, who flee reproach, who wish to withdraw from God, are never without an excuse. Some defer this important affair of salvation to an indefinite future; others till the hour of death. Many allege that it is too difficult and arduous an undertaking. Many presume upon God's mercy, persuading themselves that they can be saved by faith and hope without charity. Others, in fine, who are enslaved by the pleasures of the world, are unwilling to sacrifice them for the happiness which God promises. These are the snares most frequently employed by Satan to allure men to sin, and to keep them in its bondage until death surprises them.

At present we intend to answer those who defer their conversion, alleging that they can turn to God more efficaciously at another time. With this excuse was St. Augustine kept back from a virtuous life. "Later, Lord," he cried—"later I will abandon the world and sin."

It will not be difficult to prove that this is a ruse of the father of lies, whose office since the beginning of the world has been to deceive man. We know with certainty that there is nothing which a Christian should desire more earnestly than salvation. It is equally certain that to obtain it the sinner must change his life, since there is no other possible means of salvation. Therefore, all that remains for us is to decide when this amendment should begin. You say, at a future day. I answer, at this present moment. You urge that later it will be easier. I insist that it will be easier now. Let us see which of us is right.

Before we speak of the facility of conversion, tell me who has assured you that you will live to the time you have appointed for your amendment. Do you not know how many have been deceived by this hope? St. Gregory tells us that "God promises to receive the repentant sinner when he returns to Him, but nowhere does He promise to give him tomorrow." St. Caesarius thus expresses the same thought: "Some say, 'In my old age I will have recourse to penance'; but how can you promise yourself an old age, when your frail life cannot count with security upon one day?"

I cannot but think that the number of souls lost in this way is infinite. It was the cause of the ruin of the rich man in the Gospel, whose terrible history is related by St. Luke: "The land of a certain rich man brought forth plenty of fruits; and he thought within himself, saying: What shall I do, because I have no room where to bestow my fruits? And he said: This will I do: I will pull down my barns, and will build greater, and into them will I gather all things that are grown to me, and my goods; and I will say to my soul: Soul, thou hast much goods laid up for many years; take thy rest, eat, drink, make good cheer. But God said to him: Thou fool, this night do they require thy soul of thee; and whose shall those things be which thou hast provided?" (*Lk.* 12:16-21). What greater folly than thus to dispose of the future, as if time were our own!

God, says St. John (Cf. *Apoc.* 1:18), holds the keys of life and death. Yet a miserable worm of the earth dares usurp this power. Such insolence merits the punishment which the sinner usually receives. Rejecting the opportunity God gives him for amendment, he is denied the time he has presumptuously chosen for penance, and thus miserably perishes in his sins. Since the number who are thus chastised is very great, let us profit by their misfortunes and heed the counsel of the Wise Man: "Delay not to be converted to the Lord, and defer it not from day to day. For his wrath shall come on a sudden, and in the time of vengeance he will destroy thee." (*Ecclus.* 5:8-9).

But, even granting that you will live as long as you imagine, will it be easier to begin your conversion now or some years hence? To make this point clear we shall give a brief summary of the causes which render a sincere conversion difficult. The first of these causes is the tyranny of bad habits. So strong are these that many would die rather than relinquish them. Hence St. Jerome declares that a long habit of sin robs virtue of all its sweetness. For habit becomes second nature, and to overcome it we must conquer nature itself, which is the greatest victory a man can achieve.

"When a vice is confirmed by habit," says St. Bernard, "it cannot be extirpated except by a very special and even miraculous grace." Therefore, there is nothing which a Christian should dread more than a habit of vice, because, like other things in this world, vice claims prescription, and once that is established it is almost impossible to root it out. A second cause of this difficulty is the absolute power which the devil has over a soul in sin. He is then the strongly-armed man mentioned in the Gospel, who does not easily relinquish what he has acquired.

Another cause of this difficulty is the separation which sin makes between God and the soul. Though represented in Scripture (Cf. *Is.* 60) as a sentinel guarding the walls of Jerusalem, God withdraws further and further from a sinful soul, in proportion as her vices increase. We can learn the deplorable condition into which this separation plunges the soul from God Himself, who exclaims by His prophet, "Woe to them, for they have departed from me. Woe to them when I shall depart from them." (*Osee* 7:13 and 9:12). This abandonment by God is the second woe of which St. John speaks in the Apocalypse.

The last cause of this difficulty is the corruption of sin, which weakens and impairs the faculties of the soul, not in themselves, but in their operations and effects. Sin darkens the understanding, excites the sensual appetites, and, though leaving it free, so weakens the will that it is unable to govern us. Being the instruments of the soul, what but trouble and disorder can be expected from these faculties in their weak and helpless state? How, then, can you think that your conversion will be easier in the future, since every day increases the obstacles you now dread, and weakens the forces with which you must combat them? If you cannot ford the present stream, how will you pass through it when it will have swollen to an angry torrent? Perhaps you are now a prey to a dozen vices, which you tremble to attack. With what courage, but especially with what success, will you attack them when they will have increased a hundredfold in numbers and power? If you are now baffled by a year or two of sinful habits, how can you resist their strength at the end of ten years? Do you not see that this is a snare of the archenemy, who deceived our first parents, and who is continually seeking to deceive us also?

Can you, then, doubt that you only increase the

difficulties of your conversion by deferring it? Do you think that the more numerous your crimes, the easier it will be to obtain a pardon? Do you think that it will be easier to effect a cure when the disease will have become chronic? "A long sickness is troublesome to the physician, but a short one"—that is, one which is taken in the beginning—"is easily cut off." (*Ecclus.* 10:11-12).

Hear how an angel disabused a holy solitary of an illusion like yours: Taking him by the hand, he led him into a field and showed him a man gathering fagots. Finding the bundle he had collected too heavy, the woodcutter began to add to it; and perceiving that he was still less able to lift it, he continued to add to the quantity, imagining that he would thus carry it more easily. The holy man wondering at what he saw, the angel said to him: Such is the folly of men, who, unable to remove the present burden of their sins, continue to add to it sin after sin, foolishly supposing that they will more easily lift a heavier burden in the future.

But among all these obstacles, the greatest is the tyranny of evil habits. Would that I could make you understand the power with which they bind us! As each blow of the hammer drives a nail further and further into the wood, until it can hardly be withdrawn, so every sinful action is a fresh blow which sinks vices deeper and deeper into our souls until it is almost impossible to uproot them. Thus it is not rare to see the sinner in his old age a prey to vices which have dishonored his youth, in which he is no longer capable of finding pleasure, and which his years and the weakness of nature would repel, were he not bound to them by long-continued habit. Are we not told in Scripture that "the bones of the sinner shall be filled with the vices of his youth, and that they shall sleep with him in the dust"? (*Job* 20:11). Thus we see that even death does not terminate the habit of vice; its terrible effects pass into eternity. It becomes a second nature, and is so imprinted in the sinner's flesh that it consumes him like a fatal poison for which there is scarcely any remedy.

This Our Saviour teaches us in the resurrection of Lazarus. He had raised other dead persons by a single word, but to restore Lazarus, who had been four days in the tomb, He had recourse to tears and prayers, to show us the miracle God effects when he raises to the life of grace a soul buried in a habit of sin. For, according to St. Augustine, the first of these four days represents the pleasure of sin; the second, the consent; the third, the act; and the fourth, the habit of sin. Therefore, the sinner who has reached this fourth day can only be restored to life by the tears and prayers of Our Saviour.

But let us suppose that you will not be disappointed, that you will live to do penance. Think of the inestimable treasures you are now losing and how bitterly you will regret them when too late. While your fellow Christians are enriching themselves for Heaven, you are idling away your time in the childish follies of the world.

Besides this, think of the evil you are accumulating. We should not, says St. Augustine, commit one venial sin even to gain the whole world. How, then, can you so carelessly heap up mortal sins, when the salvation of a thousand worlds would not justify one? How dare you offend with impunity Him at whose feet you must kneel for mercy, in whose hands lies your eternal destiny? Can you afford to defy Him of whom you have such urgent need?

"Tell me," says St. Bernard, "you who live in sin, do you think God will pardon you or not? If you think He will reject you, is it not foolish to continue to sin when you have no hope of pardon? And if you rely upon His goodness to pardon you, notwithstanding your innumerable offences, what can be more base than the ingratitude with which you presume upon His mercy, which, instead of exciting you to love Him, only leads you to offend Him?" How can you answer this argument of the saint?

Consider also the tears with which you will expiate your present sins. If God visits you one day, if He causes you to hear His voice (and alas for you if He does not!), be assured that the remorse for your sins will be so bitter that you will wish you had suffered a thousand deaths rather than have offended so good a Master. David indulged but a short time in sinful pleasures, yet behold how bitter was his sorrow, how long he wept for his sins. "I have labored in my goanings," he cried; "every night I will wash my bed, I will water my couch with my tears." (*Ps.* 6:7). Why, then, will you sow what you can only reap in tears? Consider, moreover, the obstacles to virtue which continual sin establishes in us. Moses compelled the children of Israel, in punishment of their idolatry, to drink the ashes of the golden calf which they had adored. (Cf. *Ex.* 32:20). God often inflicts a like punishment upon sinners, permitting their very bones to become so impregnated with the effects of sin that the idol which they formerly worshipped becomes for them a punishment and a constant source of torment.

Let me call your attention to the foolish choice you make in selecting old age as a time for repentance, and permitting your youth to go fruitlessly by. What would you think of a man who, having several beasts of burden, put all the weight upon the weakest, letting the others go unloaded? Greater is the folly of those Christians who assign all the burden of penance to old age, which can hardly support itself, and who spend in idleness the vigorous years of youth. Seneca has admirably said that he who waits until old age to practice virtue clearly shows that he desires to give to virtue only the time of which he can make no other use. (*De Brev. Vitae,* cap. 15).

And do not lose sight of the satisfaction God requires for sin, which is so great that, in the opinion of St. John

Climachus, man can with difficulty satisfy each day for the faults he commits each day. Why, then, will you continue to accumulate the debt of sin and defer its payment to old age, which can so poorly satisfy for its own transgressions? St. Gregory considers this the basest treason, and says that he who defers the duty of penance to old age falls far short of the allegiance he owes to God, and has much reason to fear that he will be a victim of God's justice rather than the object of that mercy upon which he has so rashly presumed.

But apart from all these considerations, if you have any sense of justice or honesty, will not the benefits you have received and the rewards you are promised induce you to be less sparing in the service of so liberal a Master? How wise is the counsel we read in Ecclesiasticus: "Let nothing hinder thee from praying always, and be not afraid to be justified even to death; for the reward of God continueth for ever." (*Ecclus.* 18:22). Since the reward is to continue as long as God remains in Heaven, why should not your service continue as long as you remain upon earth? If the duration of the recompense is limitless, why will you limit the time of your service?

You hope, no doubt, to be saved; therefore, you must believe yourself of the number of those whom God has predestined. Will you, then, wait until the end of your life to serve Him who has loved you and chosen you heir to His kingdom from all eternity? Will you be so ungenerous with Him whose generosity to you has been boundless? The span of human life is so limited, how can you dare rob this generous Benefactor of the greatest part, leaving Him only the smallest and most worthless portion? "Dregs alone," says Seneca, "remain at the bottom of a vessel." "Cursed is the deceitful man," says God, "that hath in his flock a male, and making a vow offereth in sacrifice that which is feeble to the Lord; for I am a great King, saith the Lord of hosts, and my name is dreadful among the Gentiles." (*Mal.* 1:14).

In other words, none but great services are worthy of His greatness. Imperfect offerings are an affront to His majesty. Will you, then, give the best and most beautiful part of your life to the service of the devil, and reserve for God only that portion which the world refuses? He has said that there shall not be in thy house a greater measure and a less; that thou shalt have a just and true weight. (Cf. *Deut.* 25:14-15). Yet, in contradiction to this law, you have two unequal measures—a great one for the devil, whom you treat as your friend, and a small one for God, whom you treat as your enemy.

If all these benefits fail to touch you, do not be insensible to the favor your Heavenly Father has conferred upon you in giving His Divine Son to redeem you. Were you possessed of an infinite number of lives, you would owe them all in payment—and they would be but a small return—for that Life, more precious than that of angels and men, which was offered for you. How, then, can you refuse the service of your miserable life to Him who sacrificed Himself for you?

I shall conclude this chapter with a passage from Ecclesiastes in which man is exhorted to give himself to the service of his Creator in his youth, and not to defer it till old age, the infirmities of which are described under curious and admirable figures: "Remember thy Creator in the days of thy youth, before the time of affliction comes, and the years draw nigh of which thou shalt say: They please me not. Before the sun, and the light, and the moon, and the stars be darkened ... when the keepers of the house [that is, the hands] shall tremble, and the strong men [the legs, which support the frame] shall stagger, and the teeth shall be few and idle; when they that looked through the eyes [the faculties of the soul] shall be darkened; when they shall shut the doors in the street [that is, the senses by which we communicate with the outer world] ... when man shall rise with the bird [for old age requires little sleep]; when all the daughters of music shall grow deaf [for the organs of the voice grow weak and narrow]; when man shall fear high things and be afraid in the way [for old age shuns a steep and rugged way, and trembles as it walks]; when the almond tree shall flourish [that is, when the head shall be crowned with white hair] . . . when man shall enter the house of his eternity [which is the tomb]; when his friends shall lament and mourn for him . . . and when dust shall return to the earth whence it came, and the spirit shall return to God who gave it." (*Eccles.* 12:1-7).

Therefore, defer not your repentance until old age, when virtue will seem a necessity rather than a choice, and when it may be said that your vices have left you, rather than that you have left them. Remember, however, that old age is generally what youth has been: For as the sacred writer observes, "how shalt thou find in thy old age the things thou hast not gathered in thy youth?" (*Ecclus.* 25:5). Let me urge you, then, in the words of the same inspired author, to "give thanks whilst thou art living and in health, to praise God and glory in His mercies." (*Ecclus.* 17:27).

Among those who waited at the pool of Bethsaida (Cf. *Jn.* 5:4), he only was cured who first plunged into the water after it had been moved by the angel. The salvation of our soul, in like manner, depends upon the promptness and submission with which we obey the inspiration with which God moves us. Delay not, therefore, dear Christian, but make all the haste you can; and if, as the prophet says, "you shall hear his voice today" (*Ps.* 94:8), defer not your answer till tomorrow, but set about a work the difficulty of which will be so much lessened by a timely beginning.

CHAPTER 25

Of those who Defer their Conversion until the Hour of Death

The arguments we have just stated should certainly be sufficient to convince men of the folly of deathbed repentances; for if it be so dangerous to defer penance from day to day, what must be the consequence of deferring it until the hour of death? But as this is a very general error, causing the ruin of many souls, we shall devote a special chapter to it. The reflections which we are about to make may alarm and discourage weak souls, but the consequences of presumption are still more fatal, for a greater number is lost through false confidence than through excessive fear. Therefore, we, who are one of the sentinels mentioned by Ezechiel, must warn you of these dangers, that you may not rush blindly to your ruin, and that your blood may not be upon us. As the safest light for us is that of Holy Scripture, interpreted by the Fathers and Doctors of the Church, we shall first study their opinions on this subject, and afterwards we shall learn what God Himself teaches us by His inspired writers.

Before entering upon the subject we must bear in mind an undeniable principle, concerning which St. Augustine and all the holy Doctors are agreed—namely, that as true repentance is the work of God, so He can inspire it when and where he wills. Hence if the heart of the sinner, even at the hour of death, be filled with true contrition for his sins, it will avail him for salvation. But, to show you how rare such examples of repentance are, I shall give you the testimony of the saints and Doctors of the Church. I do not ask you to believe me, but believe them, the chosen instruments of the Holy Ghost.

And first hear St. Augustine. In a work entitled, *True and False Penance* he says, "Let no one hope to do penance when he can no longer sin. God wishes us to perform this work cheerfully and not through compulsion. Therefore, he who, instead of leaving his sins, waits until they leave him, acts from necessity rather than from choice. For this reason they who would not return to God when they could, but are willing to seek Him when they are no longer able to sin, will not so easily obtain what they desire." Speaking of the character of true conversion, he says, "He is truly converted who turns to God with his whole heart, who not only fears punishment but earnestly desires to merit God's graces and favors. Should anyone turn to God in this way, even at the end of his life, we would have no reason to despair of his salvation. But as examples of this perfect conversion are very rare, we cannot but tremble for one who defers his repentance until the hour of death.

"Moreover, if he obtain the pardon of his sins, their temporal punishment is not remitted; he must expiate them in the fire of Purgatory, the pain of which is greater than any suffering known on earth. Never did the martyrs in their most terrible torments, never did malefactors, though subjected to all the cruelties which human malice could invent, endure sufferings equal to those of Purgatory. Let him, then, if he would avoid these dreadful punishments after death, begin from this time to amend his life."

St. Ambrose, in his book on penance, which some attribute to St. Augustine, treats of this subject at great length. Here is one of the many excellent things he tells us: "If a man ask for the sacrament of penance on his deathbed, we do not refuse him what he asks, but we are far from assuring you that if he dies after it he is on the way to Heaven. It is more than we dare affirm or promise, for we would not deceive you. But if you would be relieved of this uncertainty, if you would dissipate this doubt, do penance for your sins while you are in health, and then I can positively assure you that you will be in a good way, for you will have repented for your crimes when you might have been increasing them. If, on the contrary, you defer your repentance until you are no longer able to sin, it will not be that you have abandoned your sins, but rather that they have abandoned you."

St. Isidore forcibly expresses the same truth: "If you would have a hope of being pardoned your sins at the hour of death, do penance for them while you are able. But if you spend your life in wickedness, and still hope for forgiveness at your death, you are running a most serious risk. Though you are not sure that you will be damned, your salvation is by no means more certain."

The authorities which we have just quoted are very alarming; yet the words of St. Jerome, uttered as he lay in sackcloth upon the ground awaiting his last hour, are still more terrifying. I dare not give his words in all their rigor, lest I should discourage weak souls; but I refer him who desires to read them to an epistle on the death of St. Jerome written by his disciple, Eusebius, to a bishop named Damasus. I will quote only this passage: "He who daily perseveres in sin will probably say: 'When I am going to die I shall do penance.' Oh! Melancholy consolation! Penance at the hour of death is a very doubtful remedy for him who has always done evil, and has thought of penance only as a dream, to be realized in the uncertain future. Wearied by suffering; distracted with grief at parting from family, friends, and worldly possessions which he can no longer enjoy; a prey to bitter anguish—how will he raise his heart to

God or conceive a true sorrow for his sins? He has never done so in life, and he would not do it now had he any hope of recovery. What kind of penance must that be which a man performs when life itself is leaving him? I have known rich wordlings who have recovered from bodily sickness only to render the health of their souls still more deplorable. Here is what I think, what I know, for I have learned it by a long experience: If he who has been a slave to sin during life die a happy death, it is only by an extraordinary miracle of grace."

St. Gregory expresses himself not less strongly upon this subject. Writing upon these words of Job, "What is the hope of the hypocrite, if through covetousness he take by violence? Will God hear his cry when distress shall come upon him?" (*Job* 27:8-9) he says, "If a man be deaf to God's voice in prosperity, God will refuse to hear him in adversity, for it is written: 'He that turneth away his ears from hearing the law, his prayer shall be an abomination.'" (*Prov.* 28:9). And Hugh of St. Victor, comprehending in one sentence the teaching of the Fathers, says, "It is very difficult for that penance to be true which comes at the hour of death, for we have much reason to suspect it because it is forced."

You now know the sentiments of these great Doctors of the Church on deathbed repentance. See, then, what folly it would be in you to contemplate without fear a passage of which the most skillful pilots speak with terror. A lifetime is not too long to learn how to die well. At the hour of death our time is sufficiently occupied in dying. We have then no leisure to learn the lesson of dying well.

The teaching of the Fathers which we have just given is also the teaching of the doctors of the schools. Among the many authorities whom we could quote we shall select Scotus, one of the most eminent, who, after treating this subject at great length, concludes that conversion at the hour of death is so difficult that it is rarely true repentance. He supports his conclusion by these four reasons:

First, because the physical pains and weakness which precede death prevent a man from elevating his heart to God or fulfilling the duties of true repentance. To understand this you must know that uncontrolled passions lead man's free will where they please. Now, philosophers teach that the passions which excite sorrow are much stronger than those which cause joy. Hence it follows that no passions, no sentiments, exceed in intensity the passions and sentiments awakened by the approach of death; for, as Aristotle tells us, death is the most terrible of all terrible things. To sufferings of body it unites anguish of soul awakened by parting from loved ones and from all that bind our affections to this world. When, therefore, the passions are so strong and turbulent, whither can man's will and thoughts turn but to those things to which these violent emotions draw them? We see how difficult it is even for a man exercised in virtue to turn his thoughts to God or spiritual things when his body is racked with pain. How much more difficult will it be for the sinner to turn his thoughts from his body, which he has always preferred to his soul!

I myself knew a man who enjoyed a reputation for virtue, but who, when told that his last hour was at hand, was so terrified that he could think of nothing but applying remedies to ward off the terrible moment. A priest who was present exhorted him to turn his thoughts to his soul's interests; but he impatiently repelled his counsels, and in these disedifying dispositions soon after expired. Judge by this example the trouble which the presence of death excites in those who have an inordinate love for this life, if one who loves it in moderation clings to it so tenaciously, regardless of the interests of the life to come.

The second reason given by Scotus is that repentance

should be voluntary, not forced. Hence St. Augustine tells us that a man must not only fear, but also love his Judge. We cannot think that one who has refused to repent during life, and only has recourse to this remedy at the hour of death, seeks it freely and voluntarily.

Such was the repentance of Semei for his outrage against David when he fled from his son Absalom. When King David returned in triumph, Semei went forth to meet him with tears and supplications; but though David then spared his life, on his deathbed he enjoined his son Solomon to deal with the traitor according to his deserts. (Cf. *2 Kg.* 16 and 17 and *3 Kg.* 2). Similar is the repentance of Christians who, after outraging God with impunity during life, piteously claim His mercy at the hour of death. We may judge of the sincerity of such repentance by the conduct of many who have been restored to health, for they are no sooner released from the imminent fear of death than they relapse into the same disorders. The salutary sentiments excited by fear, and not by virtue, vanish when the danger is past.

The third reason is that a habit of sin confirmed by long indulgence accompanies man as inseparably as the shadow does the body, even to the tomb. It becomes, as we have said, a second nature which it is almost impossible to conquer. How often do we see old men on the verge of the grave as hardened to good, and as eager for honors and wealth, which they know they cannot take with them, as if they were at the beginning of their career!

This is a punishment, says St. Gregory, which God frequently inflicts upon sin, permitting it to accompany its author even to the tomb; for the sinner, who has forgotten God during life, too often forgets his own eternal interest at this terrible hour. We have frequent and striking proof of this, for how often do we hear of persons who refuse to be separated from the objects of their sinful love even at their last hour, and, by a just judgment of God, expire wholly forgetful of what is due to their Maker and their own souls!

The fourth reason given by Scotus is taken from the value of actions done at such a time; for it is manifest to all who have any knowledge of God that He is much less pleased with services offered at this hour than with the same services offered under different circumstances. "What merit is there," says the virgin and martyr St. Lucy, "in giving up what you are forced to leave," in pardoning an injury which it would be a dishonor to avenge, or in breaking sinful bonds which you can no longer maintain?

From these reasons this doctor concludes that repentance at the hour of death is a dangerous and difficult matter. He goes even further, and affirms that the act by which a Christian deliberately resolves to defer his conversion till the hour of death is in itself a mortal sin, because of the injury he thereby inflicts on his soul, and because of the peril to which he exposes his salvation.

As the final decision of this question depends on the word of God, I pray you to hear what He teaches us through Holy Scripture. The Eternal Wisdom, after inviting men to practice virtue, utters by the mouth of Solomon the following malediction against those who are deaf to His voice: "Because I called, and you refused: I stretched out my hand, and there was none that regarded. You have despised all my counsels, and have neglected my reprehensions. I also will laugh in your destruction, and will mock when that shall come to you which you feared. When sudden calamity shall fall on you, and destruction, as a tempest, shall be at hand; when tribulation and distress shall come upon you, then shall they call upon me, and I will not hear. They shall rise in the morning, and shall not find me, because they have hated instruction, and received not the fear of the Lord, nor consented to my counsel, but despised all my reproof." (*Prov.* 1:24-31).

We have the authority of St. Gregory for saying that these words of the Holy Ghost apply to our present subject. Are they not sufficient to open your eyes and determine you to save yourself from God's vengeance by a timely preparation for this terrible hour?

In the New Testament we find no less striking authority. Our Saviour, when speaking to His Apostles of the day of His coming, never fails to warn them to be always ready. "Blessed is that servant," He says, "whom when his lord shall come he shall find watching. Amen I say to you, he shall place him over all his goods. But if the evil servant shall say in his heart: My lord is long coming, and shall begin to strike his fellow servants, and shall eat and drink with drunkards, the lord of that servant shall come in a day that he hopeth not, and at an hour that he knoweth not, and shall separate him, and appoint his portion with the hypocrites. There shall be weeping and gnashing of teeth." (*Matt.* 24:46-51). In this parable Our Saviour, who reads the secret designs of the wicked, tells them what they are to expect and what will be the result of their vain confidence. You are this bad servant, since you cherish the same designs in your heart, and seize the present time to eat and drink and gratify every passion. Why do you not fear the wrath of Him who is all-powerful to execute what He threatens? It is to you that His menaces are addressed. Awake, unhappy soul, and hasten to profit by the time that remains to you!

We are devoting much time to this subject, which ought to be clear to all, but we must do so, since there are so many unhappy Christians who endeavor to satisfy their consciences with this false excuse. Hear, then, another lesson of Our Saviour: "Then shall the Kingdom of heaven," He says, "be like to ten virgins who, taking their lamps, went out to meet the bridegroom and the bride." What time does Our Saviour indicate by "then"? The hour of general judgment and of each particular judgment, St. Augustine replies, for the sentence uttered in secret immediately after death will be ratified before all men on the last day. Five of these virgins were wise and five were foolish, Our Saviour continues. The foolish virgins took no oil with them for their lamps, and when at midnight—a time of profoundest slumber, when men give least thought to their interests—a cry was heard, "The bridegroom cometh," all the virgins arose, and they who had trimmed their lamps and furnished them with oil went in to the marriage, and the door was shut. When the foolish virgins, who had gone to seek oil for their lamps, came, saying: "Lord, Lord, open to us," He answered them saying, "Amen I say to you, I know you not." Our Saviour concludes the parable with these words: "Watch, therefore, because you know not the day nor the hour." Could we ask a plainer warning than this? Could we desire a clearer condemnation of the folly of those who rely on deathbed repentances?

You will perhaps urge in opposition to all this that the good thief was saved at the last hour. St. Augustine answers this objection by saying that the good thief received in one hour the grace of conversion and baptism, which being immediately followed by death, his soul went directly to Paradise. Moreover, the conversion of the good thief was one of the many miracles which marked Our Saviour's coming, one of the chief testimonies to His glory. The rocks were rent; the earth trembled; the sun refused to give its light; the graves were opened and the dead came forth to bear witness to the divinity of Him who was crucified. For a like purpose the grace of repentance was bestowed on the good thief, whose confession of Christ was no less wonderful than his conversion, for he acknowledged Christ when the Apostles fled from Him and denied Him; he glorified Christ when the world blasphemed and insulted Him. This miracle being one of the extraordinary marvels marking the coming of Christ, it is folly to expect that it will be repeated in our behalf. No; St. Paul tells us that the end of the wicked corresponds to their works. This is a truth which is constantly repeated in Holy Scripture. It is sung by the psalmist, foretold by the prophets, announced by the Evangelists, and preached by the Apostles.

Others argue that attrition joined to the sacraments suffices to obtain the pardon of sin, and claim that at the hour of death they will have at least attrition. But they should remember that the attrition which, joined to the sacraments, obtains the pardon of sin, is a special degree of sorrow, and God only can know whether they possess it.

The holy Doctors were not ignorant of the efficacy of attrition joined to the sacraments; yet see how little confidence they had in deathbed repentances. "We give the sacrament of Penance to such a sinner who asks for it," says St. Ambrose, "but we give him no assurance of salvation."

If you cite the example of the Ninivites, whose conversion was the effect of fear, I would remind you not only of the rigorous penance they performed, but of the amendment which was wrought in their lives. Let there be the same amendment in your life, and you will not fail to find equal mercy. But when I see that you no sooner recover your health than you relapse into your former disorders, what am I to think of your repentance?

What we have said in this and the preceding chapters is not intended to close the door of hope or salvation against anyone. Our only intention is to rout the sinner from the stronghold in which he entrenches himself that he may continue to sin. Tell me, dear Christian, for the love of God, how you dare expose yourself to such peril when the Fathers of the Church, the saints, Holy Scripture, and reason itself unite in warning you of the dangers attending a repentance deferred until the hour of death? In what do you place your confidence? In the prayers and Masses you will have offered for you? In the money you will leave for good works?

Alas! The foolish virgins filled their lamps at the last hour, but they called in vain upon the Bridegroom. Do you think your tears will avail you at that time? Tears, no doubt, are powerful, and blessed is he who weeps in sincerity; but your tears, like those of Esau, who sold his birthright to satisfy his gluttony, will flow, not for your sins, but for what you have lost; and like his, as the Apostle tells us, they will flow in vain. (Cf. *Heb.* 12:17). Will your promises and good resolutions help you? Good resolutions are excellent when sincere, but remember what edifying and valiant resolutions Antiochus formed when the hand of God had been laid upon him. Yet Holy Scripture tells us, "This wicked man prayed to the Lord, of whom he was not to obtain mercy." (*2 Mac.* 9:13). And why? Because his good purposes and resolutions sprang not from love, but from servile fear, which, though commendable, is not sufficient of itself to justify the sinner. The fear of Hell can arise from the love man naturally bears himself, but love of self gives us no right to Heaven. As no one clothed in sackcloth could enter the palace of Assuerus (Cf. *Esther* 4:2), so no one can enter Heaven clothed in the dress of a slave—that is, with the garment of servile fear. We must be clothed with the wedding garment of love, if we would be admitted to the palace of the King of kings.

I conjure you, then, dear Christian, to think of this hour which must inevitably come to you. And it may not be far distant. But a few years, and you will experience the truth of my predictions. You will find yourself distracted with pain, filled with anguish and terror at the approach of death and at the thought of the eternal sentence which is about to be pronounced upon you. Vainly will you then essay to change it, to soften its rigor. But that which will be impossible then is not only possible but easily accomplished now, for it is in your own power to make your sentence what you will wish it at the hour of death. Lose no time, therefore; hasten to propitiate your Judge. Follow the counsel of the prophet, and "seek the Lord while he may be found; call upon him while he is near." (*Is.* 55:6). He is now near to hear us, though we cannot see Him. On the day of judgment we shall see Him, but He will not hear us, unless we now live so as to merit this blessing from Him.

CHAPTER 26

Of those who Continue in Sin, trusting in the Mercy of God

Besides those who defer their conversion till the hour of death, there are others who persevere in sin, trusting in the mercy of God and the merits of His Passion. We must now disabuse them of this illusion.

You say that God's mercy is great, since He died on the cross for the salvation of sinners. It is indeed great, and a striking proof of its greatness is the fact that He bears with the blasphemy and malice of those who so presume upon the merits of His death as to make His cross, which was intended to destroy the kingdom of evil, a reason for multiplying sin. Had you a thousand lives you would owe them all to Him, yet you rob Him of that one life which you have and for which He died. This crime was more bitter to Our Saviour than death itself. For it He reproaches us by the mouth of His prophet, though He does not complain of His sufferings: "The wicked have wrought upon my back; they have extended their iniquity." (*Ps.* 128:3).

Who taught you to reason that because God was good you could sin with impunity? Such is not the teaching of the Holy Spirit. On the contrary, those who listen to His voice reason thus: God is good; therefore, I must serve Him, obey Him, and love Him above all things. God is good; therefore, I will turn to Him with all my heart; I will hope for pardon, notwithstanding the number and enormity of my sins. God is good; therefore, I must be good if I would imitate Him. God is good; therefore, it would be base ingratitude in me to offend Him by sin.

Thus, the greater you represent God's goodness the more heinous are your crimes against Him. Nor will these offenses remain unpunished, for God's justice, which protects His mercy, cannot permit your sinful abuse of it to remain unavenged.

This is not a new pretext; the world has long made use of it. In ancient times it distinguished the false from the true prophets. While the latter announced to the people, in God's name, the justice with which He would punish their iniquities, the former, speaking in their own name, promised them mercy which was but a false peace and security.

You say God's mercy is great; but if you presume upon it you show that you have never studied the greatness of His justice. Had you done so you would cry out to the Lord with the psalmist: "Who knoweth the power of thy anger, and for thy fear who can number thy wrath?" (*Ps.* 89:11-12).

But to dissipate your illusion, let me ask you to contemplate this justice in the only way in which we may have any knowledge of it—that is, in its effects here below.

Besides the result we are seeking, we shall reap another excellent advantage by exciting in our hearts the fear of God, which, in the opinion of the saints, is the treasure and defence of the soul. Without the fear of God the soul is like a ship without ballast; the winds of human or divine favor may sweep it to destruction. Notwithstanding that she may be richly laden with virtue, she is in continual danger of being wrecked on the rocks of temptation, if she be not stayed by this ballast of the fear of God. Therefore, not only those who have just entered God's service, but those who have long been of His household, should continue in this salutary fear; the former by reason of their past transgressions, the latter on account of their weakness, which exposes them to danger at every moment.

This holy fear is the effect of grace, and is preserved in the soul by frequent meditation. To aid you in this reflection we shall here propose a few of the practical proofs of the greatness of God's justice.

The first work of God's justice was the reprobation of the angels. "All the ways of God are mercy and justice" (Cf. *Ps.* 24:10), says David; but until the fall of the angels, divine justice had not been manifested. It had been shut up in the bosom of God like a sword in the scabbard, like that sword of which Ezechiel speaks with alarm, foretelling the ruin it will cause. (Cf. *Ezech.* 21). This first sin drew the sword of justice from its scabbard, and terrible was the destruction it wrought. Contemplate its effects; raise your eyes and behold one of the most brilliant beings of God's house, a resplendent image of the divine beauty, flung with lightning-like rapidity from a glorious throne in Heaven to the uttermost depths of Hell, for one thought of pride. (Cf. *Lk.* 10:18). The prince of heavenly spirits becomes the chief of devils. His beauty and glory are changed into deformity and ignominy. God's favorite subject is changed into His bitterest enemy, and will continue such for all eternity. With what awe this must have filled the angels, who knew the greatness of his fall! With what astonishment they repeat the words of Isaias: "How art thou fallen from heaven, O Lucifer, who didst rise in the morning"? (*Is.* 14:12).

Consider also the fall of man, which would have been no less terrible than that of the angels, if it had not been repaired. Behold in it the cause of all the miseries we suffer on earth: original and actual sin, suffering of body and mind, death, and the ruin of numberless souls who have been lost forever. Terrible are the calamities it brought upon us; and even greater would be our misfortunes had not Christ, by His death, bound the power of sin and redeemed us from its slavery. How rigorous, therefore, was the justice of God in thus punishing man's rebellion; but how great was His goodness in restoring him to His friendship!

In addition to the penalties imposed on the human race for the sin of Adam, new and repeated punishments have at different times been inflicted upon mankind for the crimes they have committed. In the time of Noe, the whole world was destroyed by the deluge. (Cf. *Gen.* 7). Fire and brimstone from Heaven consumed the wicked inhabitants of Sodom and Gomorrha. (Cf. *Gen.* 19). The earth opened and swallowed alive into Hell Core, Dathan, and Abiron for resisting the authority of Moses. (Cf. *Num.* 16). Nadab and Abiu, sons of Aaron, were destroyed by a sudden flame from the sanctuary because they offered strange fire in the sacrifice. (Cf. *Lev.* 10). Neither their priestly character, nor the sanctity of their father, nor the intimacy with God of their uncle, Moses, could obtain for them any remission for their fault.

Recall the example of Ananias and Sapphira, struck dead by God for telling a lie. (Cf. *Acts* 5). But the strongest proof of the rigor of God's justice was the satisfaction required for sin, which was nothing less than the death of His only-begotten Son. Think of this Price of man's Redemption, and you will begin to realize what sin is and how the justice of God regards it. Think, too, of the eternity of Hell, and judge of the rigor of that justice which inflicts such punishment. This justice terrifies you, but it is no less certain than the mercy in which you trust. Yes, through endless ages, God will look upon the indescribable torments of the damned, but they will excite in Him no compassion; they will not move Him to limit their sufferings or give them any hope of relief. Oh! Mysterious depths of divine justice! Who can reflect upon them and not tremble?

Another subject to which I would call your serious attention is the state of the world. Reflect on this, and you will begin to realize the rigors of God's justice.

As an increase in virtue is the effect and reward of virtue, so likewise an increase in sin is the effect and punishment of sin. Indeed, it is one of the greatest chastisements that can be inflicted on us, when we are permitted, through blindness and passion, to rush headlong down the broad road of vice, adding sin to sin every day and hour of our lives. This is but just; for when man once mortally sins he loses all right to any help from God. It is owing solely to the divine mercy when he is converted. Look, therefore, over the world, and behold the greatness of its iniquity. Think of the millions who are living in infidelity and heresy. Think how many calling themselves Christians are daily betraying their name by their scandalous lives.

Why is this sad condition permitted? Ah! It is owing to man's crimes. God is disobeyed, insulted, and mocked by the majority of men, and His long-suffering justice, being wearied by their wickedness, permits them to go on in their mad career. St. Augustine is an illustrious example of this. "I was plunged," he says, "in iniquity, and Thy anger was aroused against me, but I knew it not. I was deaf to the noise which the chains of my sins made. But this ignorance, this deafness, were the punishments of my pride."

Reflect on this. Men act freely when they sin, for no man is forced to do wrong. But when they have fallen they cannot rise without the divine assistance. Now, God owes this to no man. It is His gratuitous gift when He restores the sinner to His favor. Hence He but exercises His justice when He permits him to remain in his misery, and even to fall lower.

When, therefore, we behold so much iniquity, have we not reason to feel that God's justice permits men to become so blinded and hardened? I say *permits,* for man is the cause of his own miseries; God urges him only to what is good. If, then, you perceive in yourself any mark of such divine anger, be not without fear. Remember that you need no help but your own passions and the devil's temptations to carry you along the broad road to destruction. Stop while you have time. Implore the divine mercy to aid you in retracing your steps till you discover that narrow way which leads to everlasting life. Having found it, walk manfully in it, ever mindful of the justice of God, and of the terrible truth that while thousands throng the road to death, there are few who find the way of life.

Tremble for your salvation, and, while always maintaining an unshaken hope, have no less fear of Hell. You have no reason to expect that God should treat you differently from other men. Bear in mind the law of His justice, as it has been explained, and so live that you may never expose yourself to its terrible effects here and hereafter.

Be not the victim of a vain confidence which you may flatter yourself is hope, while it is naught but presumption. Rather, in the words of the Eternal Wisdom, "Be not without fear about sin forgiven, and add not sin upon sin. And say not: The mercy of the Lord is great; he will have mercy on the multitude of my sins. For mercy and wrath quickly come from him, and his wrath looketh upon sinners." (*Ecclus.* 5:5-7). If, then, we must tremble even for sin which has been remitted, how is it that you do not fear to add daily to your crimes? And mark well these words: "His wrath looketh upon sinners"; for as the eyes of His mercy are upon the good, so are the eyes of His anger upon the wicked. And this agrees with what David says in one of the psalms: "The eyes of the Lord are upon the just, and His ears unto their prayers. But the countenance of the Lord is against them that do evil, to cut off the remembrance of them from the earth." (*Ps.* 33:16-17).

"The hand of God," says the inspired author of the book of Esdras, "is upon all them that seek him in goodness; and his power and strength and wrath upon all them that forsake him." (*1 Esd.* 8:22). Be reconciled, therefore, with God;

amend your life; and then you can confidently hope for the mercy promised to His faithful servants. "Hope in the Lord and do that which is good," we are told by the psalmist; "offer the sacrifice of justice, and trust in the Lord." (*Ps.* 36:3 and 4:6). This is hope; any other confidence is presumption. The ark of the true Church will not save its unworthy members from the deluge of their iniquities, nor can you reap any benefit from the mercy of God if you seek His protection in order to sin with impunity.

"Men go to Hell," says St. Augustine, "through hope, as well as through despair: through a *presumptuous* hope during life, and through despair at the hour of death." (*De Verbo Dei,* Serm. 147). I entreat you, therefore, O sinner, to abandon your false hope, and let God's justice inspire you with a fear proportioned to the confidence which His mercy excites in you. For, as St. Bernard tells us, "God has two feet, one of justice and the other of mercy. We must embrace both, lest justice separated from mercy should cause us to despair, or mercy without justice should excite in us presumption." (*In Cantica,* Serm. 80).

CHAPTER 27

*Of those who allege that the
Path of Virtue is too Difficult*

As virtue is entirely conformable to reason, there is nothing in its own nature which renders it burdensome. The difficulty, therefore, which is here objected arises not from virtue, but from the evil inclinations and appetites implanted in us by sin. Thus the Apostle tells us, "The flesh opposes the spirit, and the spirit opposes the flesh; for these are contrary one to another. For I am delighted with the law of God, according to the inward man; but I see another law in my members, fighting against the law of my mind, and captivating me in the law of sin, that is in my members." (*Gal.* 5:17 and *Rom.* 7:22-23). By these words we are taught that the law of God is acceptable to the superior part of the soul, the seat of the will and understanding, but that we are opposed, in obeying it, by the corruption of our appetites and passions, which reside in the inferior part of the soul.

When man rebelled against God, the passions rebelled against reason—and from this arose all the difficulties which we encounter in the practice of virtue. Thus we see that many who appreciate virtue refuse to practice it, just as sick men earnestly desire health, but refuse the unpalatable remedies which alone would restore it. As this repugnance is the principal barrier to virtue, which, when known, is always valued and loved, if we succeed in proving that there

217

is little foundation for such repugnance we shall have accomplished a good work.

The principal cause of this illusion is that we only regard the obstacles to virtue, and do not consider the grace which God gives us to overcome these obstacles. The servant of Eliseus was frightened at the numbers who were coming armed against his master, until God, at the prayer of the prophet, opened his eyes and caused him to see that Eliseus was surrounded by a still greater number of defenders. A like fear leads men to reject virtue, when they know not the succors which God reserves for it.

But if the way of virtue is so difficult, how could David express himself as he does? "I have been delighted in the way of thy testimonies, as in all riches. Thy commandments are more to be desired than gold and many precious stones, and sweeter than honey and the honeycomb." (*Ps.* 118:14 and 18:11). Not only does he award to virtue the excellence which all ascribe to it, but praises it for that pleasure and sweetness which the world denies it. Whoever, therefore, speaks of virtue as a heavy yoke shows that he has not yet penetrated this mystery.

Tell me, you who claim to be a Christian, why did Christ come into the world? Why did He shed His Blood? Why did He institute the sacraments? Why did He send down the Holy Ghost? What is the meaning of the Gospel, of grace, of the name of Jesus, whom you adore? If you know not, hear the angel, who says, "Thou shalt call his name Jesus, for he shall save his people from their sins." (*Matt.* 1:21).

Now, what is saving from sin, if not obtaining the pardon of past faults and the grace to avoid others in the future? What was the end of Our Saviour's coming, if not to help you in the work of your salvation? Did He not die on the cross to destroy sin? Did He not rise from the dead to enable you to rise to a life of grace? Why did He shed His Blood, if not to heal the wounds of your soul? Why did He institute the sacraments, if not to strengthen you against sin? Did not His coming render the way to Heaven smooth and straight, according to that of Isaias, who said, in prophesying of Him, "The crooked shall become straight, and the rough ways plain"? (*Is*. 40:4). Why did He send the Holy Spirit, if not to change you from flesh into spirit? Why did He send Him under the form of fire but to enlighten you, to inflame you, and to transform you into Himself, that thus your soul might be fitted for His own divine kingdom?

What, in fine, is the object of grace, with the infused virtues which flow from it, but to sweeten the yoke of Christ, to facilitate the practice of virtue, to make you joyful in tribulations, hopeful in danger, and victorious in temptation? This comprises the teaching of the Gospel. Adam, an earthly and sinful man, made us earthly and sinful. Jesus Christ, a heavenly and just Man, makes us spiritual and just. This is the sum of the doctrine proclaimed by the evangelists, preached by the Apostles, and promised by the prophets.

But, to study the subject more in detail, what is the cause of the difficulty you find in practicing virtue? You say it is the evil inclinations of your heart, as well as the perpetual conflict between the spirit and the flesh, which has been conceived in sin. But why should you be dismayed, when you have the infallible promise of God that He will take away these corrupt sources of sin, and, giving you a new heart, will establish you in strength and courage to conquer all your enemies? "I will give them," He says, "a new heart, and I will put a new spirit in their bowels; and I will take away the stony heart out of their flesh, and I will give them a heart of flesh, that they may walk in my commandments, and keep my judgments and do them, and that they may be my people, and I may be their God." (*Ezech*. 11:19-20). What, then, can arrest you in the path of virtue? Do you fear that the promise will not be fulfilled, or that with the assistance of God's grace you will not be able to keep His law? Your doubts are blasphemous; for, in the first instance, you question the truth of God's words, and, in the second, you respect Him as unable to fulfill what He promises, since you think Him capable of offering you succor insufficient for your needs.

No, doubt not, but be assured that in addition to all this He will give you the necessary strength to overcome the passions which torment you. This is one of the principal benefits purchased for us by the Blood of Our Saviour, one of the most precious fruits of the tree of life. "Our old man is crucified with Jesus Christ, that the body of sin may be destroyed, and that we may serve sin no longer." (*Rom.* 6:6). By the "old man" and the "the body of sin" the Apostle designates our sensual appetite with its evil inclinations. He tells us that it was crucified with Jesus Christ, because the sacrifice of the cross obtained for us grace and strength to overcome it. This is the victory which God promises us by Isaias, who says, "Fear not, for I am with thee; turn not aside, for I am thy God; I have strengthened thee, and have helped thee, and the right hand of my just one—Jesus Christ—hath upheld thee. Behold all that fight against thee shall be confounded and ashamed; they shall be as nothing, and the men shall perish that strive against thee. Thou shalt seek them, and shalt not find the men that resist thee. They shall be as nothing, and the men that war against thee shall be as a thing consumed. For I am the Lord thy God, who take thee by the hand and say to thee: Fear not, for I have helped thee." (*Is.* 41:10-13). With such assistance who will yield to discouragement? Who will be daunted by fear of his evil inclinations, over which grace obtains such a glorious victory?

You will urge, perhaps, that the just are not without their secret failings, which, as Job says (Cf. *Job* 16:9), bear witness against them. To this I reply, in the words of Isaias, that "they shall be as if they never had been." (*Is.* 41:12). If they remain, it is only to exercise our virtue, not to overcome us; to stimulate us, not to master us; to serve as an occasion of merit, not of sin; for our triumph, not for our downfall; in a word, to try us, to humble us, to make us acknowledge our own weakness and render to God the glory and thanksgiving which are due Him. They are a source of real profit to us. For as wild animals, when domesticated, can be made most serviceable to man, so our passions, when moderated and controlled, aid us in the practice of virtue.

"If God be for us, who is against us?" (*Rom.* 8:31). "The Lord is my light and my salvation; whom shall I fear? The Lord is the protector of my life; of whom shall I be afraid? If armies in camp should stand together against me, my heart shall not fear. If a battle should rise up against me, in this will I be confident." (*Ps.* 26:1-4). Surely, my dear Christian, if such promises do not encourage you to serve God, your cowardice is very great. If you have no confidence in them your faith is very weak. God assures you that He will give you a new spirit, that He will change your heart of stone into a heart of flesh, that He will mortify your passions to such a degree that you will not know yourself. You will seek in vain for the evil inclinations which warred against you; they will be as a thing consumed, for He will weaken all their forces. What more can you desire? Have, then, a lively faith and firm hope, and cast yourself into the arms of God.

But, perhaps, you will still object that your sins are so numerous that God must refuse you His grace. Away with such a thought! It is one of the greatest insults you could offer to God. By it you virtually say either that God cannot or will not assist His creatures when they implore His aid. Do not yield to such a blasphemy. Rather let your prayer be, with St. Augustine, "Give me grace, Lord, to do what

Thou commandest, and command what Thou pleasest." (*Conf.* L.10,31). This prayer will always be answered, for God is ever ready to cooperate with man in doing good. God is the principal cause, man is the secondary. God aids man, as a painter aids a pupil whose hand he guides, that he may produce a perfect work. Both concur in the labor, but equal honor is not due to both. Thus does God deal with man, without prejudice to his free will. When the work, therefore, is accomplished, he glorifies God, and not himself, saying with the prophet, "Thou, Lord, hast wrought all our works for us." (*Is.* 26:12).

Lean, then, on the power of God, and you will ever fulfill His will. Be mindful of the words He addresses to you through Moses: "This commandment that I command thee this day is not above thee nor far off from thee. Nor is it in heaven, that thou shouldst say: Which of us can go up to heaven to bring it to us, that we may hear and fulfill it in work? Nor is it beyond the sea, that thou mayest excuse thyself, saying: Which of us can cross the sea and bring it unto us, that we may hear and do that which is commanded? But the word is very nigh unto thee, in thy mouth and in thy heart, that thou mayest do it." (*Deut.* 30:11-14).

Let these words assure you that however difficult God's commandments may appear, His grace will render their observance very easy, and if faithful to them, you will soon experience that His yoke is sweet and His burden light.

Moreover, call to mind the assistance which charity affords us in the pursuit of virtue. Charity, or the love of God, renders the law sweet and delightful; for, as St. Augustine says, love knows no fatigue. How willingly men fond of hunting, riding, or fishing bear the labor of these sports! What makes a mother insensible to the fatigue she endures for her child? What keeps a devoted wife day and night at the bedside of her sick husband? What excites even in animals the solicitude, the self-denial, with which they care for their young, and the courage with which they defend them? I answer that it is the great power of love. Strong by this power was St. Paul when he exclaimed, "Who, then, shall separate us from the love of Christ? Shall tribulation, or distress, or famine, or nakedness, or danger, or persecution, or the sword?" (*Rom.* 8:35).

It was love which caused St. Dominic and so many other saints to sigh for martyrdom. It was love which raised the martyrs above their sufferings and gave them refreshments in the midst of the most cruel torments. "True love of God," says St. Peter Chrysologus, "finds nothing hard, nothing bitter, nothing difficult. What weapon, what wounds, what pains, what death, can conquer true love? As an impenetrable armor it defies all attacks, and fears not even death, but triumphs over all things." (*Serm.* 147, "De Incarnat.").

But perfect love is not content with these victories. It longs to combat for the Beloved. Hence the thirst of the just for martyrdom; hence their desire to shed their blood for Him who shed His precious Blood for them. And when this desire is not satisfied, they become their own executioners and martyr their bodies with hunger, thirst, cold, and every kind of mortification. Thus they find their happiness in suffering for Christ.

Doubtless this language is not understood by worldlings. They cannot conceive that one should love what they abhor, or abhor what they love. Yet so it is. Holy Scripture tells us that the Egyptians worshipped certain animals as gods. The Israelites justly called these false gods abominations, and sacrificed them to the honor of the true God. In like manner the virtuous regard as abominations the idols which the world adores—pleasures, riches, and honors— and sacrifice them to the glory of God. Let him, therefore, who would offer a pleasing sacrifice to God observe what the world adores, and let him offer that as a victim to the Lord. It was thus that the Apostles acted when they came forth from the council, rejoicing that they had received the honor of suffering for Christ. Can you, then, believe that the power which rendered the prison, the scourge, the stake, welcome to God's servants, will not be able to lighten the yoke of His commandments for you? Will not that power which supported the just under fasts, vigils, austerities, and sufferings of every kind enable you to bear the burden of the commandments? Alas! How feebly you comprehend the force of charity and divine grace!

But let us suppose that the path of virtue is sown with difficulties and hardships. Will this prove that you ought not to walk in it? Oh, no! Are you not expected to do something for the salvation of your soul? Will you not do at least as much for this grand purpose, for *eternity,* as you do for your body and for time, which for you is rapidly passing away and will soon leave you at the tomb? What is a little suffering in this life, if you are spared everlasting torments? Think of the rich glutton, now burning in Hell. What would he not do to expiate his sins, could he return to this world? There is no reason why you should not now do as much, if you feel that you have ever offended God.

Consider, moreover, what God has done for you and what He has promised you. Reflect on the many sins you have committed. Think of the sufferings endured by the saints, particularly the Saint of saints. If such thoughts will not make you blush for your past life of ease, and incite you to suffer something for the love of God, I know not what will move you to abandon the things in which you formerly delighted and by which you formerly sinned. Thus St. Bernard tells us that the tribulations of this life bear no proportion to the glory we hope for, to the torments we fear, to the sins we have committed, or to the benefits we have received from our Creator. Any of these considerations ought to suffice to make us embrace a life of virtue, however hard and laborious.

Though we acknowledge that in every condition of life there are trials and difficulties, yet the path of the wicked is far more thickly strewn with hardships than is that of the just. One necessarily grows weary on a long journey, but a blind man who stumbles at every step will certainly tire sooner than the traveler who clearly sees and guards against the obstacles in his way. In the journey of life we must expect to feel fatigue and experience hardships until we reach our destination. The sinner, guided by passion, walks blindly, and therefore often falls. The just man, guided by reason, sees and avoids the rocks and precipices, and thus travels with less fatigue and more safety.

"The path of the just," says Solomon, "as a shining light, goeth forward and increaseth even to perfect day; but the way of the wicked is darksome, and they know not where they fall." (*Prov.* 4:18,19). And not only is it dark, but also slippery, as holy David tells us. (Cf. *Ps.* 34:6). Judge, then, what a difference there is between these two paths. Behold how excessive are the difficulties which beset the wicked. Reflect, moreover, that the just find a thousand means of alleviating their trials which the sinner does not experience. They have God's fatherly providence to guide them; the grace of the Holy Spirit to enlighten and encourage them; the sacraments to sanctify them; the divine consolations to refresh them; the example of the pious to animate them; the writings of the saints to instruct them; the testimony of a good conscience to comfort them; the hope of future glory to sustain them, besides the numerous other favors which the virtuous enjoy. Hence they are ever ready to sing to the Lord with the prophet, "How sweet are thy words to my palate, more than honey to my mouth." (*Ps.* 118:103).

Reflect on these truths, and you will soon understand the Scriptures where they seem to speak in contradictory terms of the ease or difficulty of practicing virtue. At one time David says, "For the sake of the words of thy lips I have kept hard ways." (*Ps.* 16:4). At another: "I have been delighted in the way of thy testimonies, as in all riches." (*Ps.* 118:14). Both declarations are true, for the path of virtue is difficult to nature, easy to grace.

Our Saviour Himself tells us this when He says, "My yoke is sweet and my burden light." (*Matt.* 11:30). By the word *yoke* He expresses the difficulty which nature experiences. By calling it sweet, He shows us the power of grace to enable us to carry it. This He accomplishes by sharing our burden, according to the prophet: "I will be to them as one that taketh off the yoke from their jaws." (*Osee* 11:4). Is it, then, astonishing that the yoke is light which God Himself bears? The Apostle experienced this when he said, "In all things we suffer tribulation, but are not distressed; we are straitened, but are not destitute; we suffer persecution, but are not forsaken; we are cast down, but we perish not." (*2 Cor.* 4:8-9). Behold on one side the weight of tribulation and on the other the sweetness which God communicates to it.

Isaias expressed this even more clearly: "They that hope in the Lord shall renew their strength; they shall take wings as eagles; they shall run and not be weary; they shall walk and not faint." (*Is.* 40:31). Learn from this that the yoke is removed by grace, and the strength of the flesh is changed into that of the spirit, or rather the strength of God replaces that of man. Remember also that the prophet says the just will run, though taking no pains; they will walk, and not faint. Be not dismayed, therefore, by the roughness of a road on which you find so many aids to render your journey smooth and pleasant.

If, like the Apostle St. Thomas, you are still incredulous and ask for further proof, I will not deny it. Take, for example, a man who has led a wicked life, but who has finally turned to God by the power of grace. Such a man will be an excellent judge in this matter, for he has not only heard of these two lives, but he has experienced them. Ask him which he found the sweeter. He will tell you of the marvels effected in the depths of his soul by grace.

There is nothing in the world more astonishing, no more interesting spectacle, than that afforded by the action of grace upon the soul of a just man. How it transforms him, sustains him, strengthens him and comforts him! How it subdues and governs him exteriorly and interiorly! How it altars his affections, making him love what he formerly abhorred, and abhor what he formerly loved! How strong it makes him in combat! What peace it gives him! What light it pours into his soul to enable him to learn God's will, to realize the vanity of the world, and to set a true value on the spiritual blessings which he formerly despised! And still more wonderful is the short space of time in which these great changes are made. It is not necessary to spend long years in study, or to wait until old age helps us by experience. Men in the fire of youth are sometimes so changed in the space of a few days that they hardly seem the same beings. Hence St. Cyprian says that the sinner finds himself converted even before he has learned how to bring about such a change, for it is the work of grace, which needs neither study nor time, but which acts in an instant, like a spiritual charm.

St. Cyprian, already mentioned, who was for a time a prey to the illusions of the world, gives, while writing to his friend Donatus, some beautiful and forcible thoughts on this subject:

"When I walked in darkness, when I was tossed about by the tempests of this world, I knew not what my life was, because I was deprived of light and truth. I regarded as impossible all that God's grace promised to do for my conversion and salvation. I would not believe that man could be born again (Cf. *Sn.* 3:5), and by virtue of Baptism receive a new life and spirit, which, while leaving his exterior untouched, would entirely reform him within. I urged that it was impossible to uproot vices implanted in us by our corrupt nature and confirmed by the habits of years. Is temperance possible, I asked, to one long accustomed to a sumptuous table? Will he who has been clothed in purple willingly put on a plain and modest dress? Will he who found all his happiness in honors and dignities willingly forego them and be content to lead a quiet and obscure life? Will he who was accustomed to travel with a grand retinue now be content to travel unattended? Former habits will cling to him and struggle for mastery. Intemperance will solicit him, pride will inflate him, honors will allure him, anger will inflame him, and sensuality will blind and overpower him. These were the reflections in which I frequently indulged. I was bound by numerous habits of vice from which I felt I never could be freed, and which I encouraged and strengthened by this very distrust.

"But my sins were no sooner washed away in the waters of Baptism than a new light shone upon my soul, now purified from all stains. By the reception of the Holy Spirit I was born to a new life. Suddenly, as if by a miracle, doubt gave place to certainty; my darkness was dissipated; what heretofore appeared difficult had now become easy; the insurmountable obstacles I feared had vanished completely. I clearly saw that the life of the flesh with all its failings was of man, and that the new life to which I had come was of God. You know, dear Donatus, from what the Holy Spirit has delivered me, and what He has bestowed upon me. He has delivered me from the slavery of vice and has restored me to the true liberty of virtue. You know all this, and that, so far from boasting, I am only publishing the glory of God. It is not pride but a sentiment of gratitude which prompts me to speak of this wonderful transformation, which is due only to God. For it is evident that the power to abandon sin is no less the effect of the divine grace than the will to commit it is the effect of human frailty." (L. 2, *Ep.* 2).

These words of St. Cyprian perfectly describe the illusion which paralyzes the efforts of many Christians. They measure the difficulties of virtue according to their own strength, and thus deem its acquisition impossible. They do not consider that if they firmly resolve to abandon sin, and cast themselves into the strong arms of God's mercy, His grace will smooth the roughness of their way and remove all the obstacles which formerly alarmed them. The example of St. Cyprian proves this, for the truth of what he relates is incontestable. If you imitate his sincere return to God, the grace which was given him will not be denied you.

Another no less remarkable example is that of St. Augustine, who, in his *Confessions,* tells us that when he began to think seriously of leaving the world a thousand difficulties presented themselves to his mind. On one side appeared the past pleasures of his life, saying, "Will you part from us forever? Shall we no longer be your companions?" On the other, he beheld virtue with a radiant countenance, accompanied by a multitude of persons of every state in life who had led pure lives, and a voice said to him, "Can you not do what so many others have done? Was their strength in themselves? Was it not God who enabled them to do what they did? While you continue to rely upon yourself you must necessarily fall. Cast yourself without fear upon God; He will not abandon you." In the midst of this struggle the saint tells us that he began to weep bitterly, and, throwing himself upon the ground, he cried from the depth of his heart, "How long, Lord, how long wilt Thou be angry? Remember not my past iniquities. How long shall I continue to repeat, 'tomorrow, tomorrow'? Why not now? Why should not this very hour witness the end of my disorders?" (*Confess.,* L. 8, c. 11).

No sooner had Augustine taken this resolution than his heart was changed, so that he ceased to feel the stings of the flesh or any affection for the pleasures of the world. He was entirely freed from all the irregular desires which formerly tormented him, and broke forth into thanksgiving for the liberty which had been restored to him: "O Lord! I am Thy servant; I am Thy servant and the son of Thy handmaid. Thou hast broken my bonds. I will sacrifice to Thee a sacrifice of praise. (Cf. *Ps.* 115).

"Let my heart and my tongue praise Thee. Let all my bones say: Who is like unto Thee, O Lord? Where was my free will all these years, O Jesus, my Redeemer and Helper, that it did not return to Thee? From what an abyss hast Thou suddenly drawn it, causing me to bend my neck to Thy sweet yoke and to take upon me the easy burden of Thy law? How delighted I am with the absence of those pleasures which I formerly sought with so much eagerness! How I rejoice no longer to possess those follies which I formerly trembled to lose! O Thou true and sovereign Good! Thou hast driven all false pleasures from my soul; Thou hast banished them and hast Thyself taken their place, O Joy exceeding all joy! O Beauty exceeding all beauty!" (*Conf.* L.9).

Behold the efficacy of grace! What, then, prevents you from imitating the example of these great saints? If you believe what I have related, and that the grace which wrought such a change in St. Augustine is at the disposal of all who earnestly seek it, what is there to prevent you from breaking your sinful bonds and embracing this Sovereign Good who so solicitously calls you? Why do you prefer, by a hell on earth, to gain another Hell hereafter, rather than by a paradise here to gain Heaven hereafter? Be not discouraged. Put your trust in God, and resolutely enter the path of virtue. Have an unshaken confidence that you will meet Him there with open arms, to receive you as the father received his prodigal son. (Cf. *Lk.* 15).

Were a charlatan to assert that he could teach the art of

changing copper into gold, how many would be eager to test his suggestion! God offers to teach us that art of changing earth into Heaven for our welfare, of converting us from flesh into spirit, from men into angels, and how many there are who refuse to hear Him! Be not of their unhappy number.

Sooner or later you must acknowledge this truth, if not in this life, surely in the next. Think, therefore, of the confusion and anguish which on the day of judgment will overwhelm all those who will then have been condemned for abandoning the path of virtue. Too late they will recognize how excellent is this path, and how far it exceeds that of sin, not only for the happiness it affords in this life, but for the security with which it leads us to eternal joy.

CHAPTER 28

*Of those who refuse to practice Virtue
because they love the World*

If we examine the hearts of those who refuse to practice virtue, we shall frequently find a delusive love for the world to be one of the chief causes of their faint-heartedness. I call it a delusive love because it is founded on that imaginary good which men suppose they will find in the things of this world. Let them examine with closer attention these objects of their affection, and they will soon recognize that they have been pursuing shadows. If we study the happiness of the world, even under its most favorable aspects, we shall find that it is ever accompanied by six drawbacks, which tend very much to lessen its sweetness. No one will question the truth of this, for who can deny that the happiness of this life is brief, that it is exposed to changes, that it leads to danger or blindness, and that it frequently ends in sin and deceit?

As to the first of these, who will say that that is enduring which at best must end with the brief career of man on earth? Ah! We all know the shortness of human life, for how few attain even a hundred years? There have been popes who reigned but a month; bishops who have survived their consecration but little longer; and married persons whose funerals have followed their weddings in still less time. These are not remarkable occurrences of the past only; they are witnessed in every age. Let us suppose, however, that your life will be one of the longest. "What," asks St. Chrysostom, "are one hundred, two hundred, four hundred years spent in the pleasures of this world compared to eternity?" For "if a man live many years, and have rejoiced in them all, he must remember the darksome time, and the many days; which when they shall come, the things passed shall be accused of vanity." (*Eccles.* 11:8).

All happiness, however great, is but vanity when compared to eternity. Sinners themselves acknowledge this: "Being born, forthwith we ceased to be; we are consumed in our wickedness." (*Wis.* 5:13). How short, then, will this life seem to the wicked! It will appear as if they had been hurried immediately from the cradle to the grave. All the pleasures and satisfactions of this world will then seem to them but a dream. Isaias admirably expressed this when he said, "As he that is hungry dreameth and eateth, but when he is awake his soul is empty; and as he that is thirsty dreameth and drinketh, and after he is awake is yet faint with thirst, and his soul is empty, so shall be the multitude that fought against Mount Sion." (*Is.* 29:8). Their prosperity will be so brief that it will seem like a fleeting dream. What more, in fact, remains of the glory of monarchs and of princes? "Where," asks the prophet, "are the princes of the nations, and they that rule over the beasts that are upon the earth? They that take their diversion with the birds of the air; that hoard up silver and gold wherein men trust, and there is no end of their getting; that work in silver and are solicitous, and their works are unsearchable? They are cut off and are gone down to hell, and others are risen up in their place." (*Baruch* 3:16-20).

What has become of the wise men, the scholars, the searchers into the secrets of nature? Where is the famous Alexander? Where is the mighty Assuerus? Where are the Caesars and the other kings of the earth? What does it now avail them that they lived in pomp and glory, that they had legions of soldiers, and servants, and flatterers almost without number? All have vanished like a shadow or a dream. In one moment all that constitutes human happiness fades away as the mist before the morning sun. Behold, then, dear Christian, how brief it is.

Consider also the innumerable changes to which human happiness is exposed in this valley of tears, this land of exile, this tempestuous sea which we call the world. The days of man on earth scarcely suffice to number his sorrows, for almost every hour brings new cares, new anxieties, or new miseries. Who can fitly describe these? Who can count all the infirmities of the body, all the passions of the soul, all the disasters which come upon us not only from our enemies, but even from our friends and from ourselves? One disputes your inheritance; another attempts your life. You are pursued by hatred, calumny, envy, revenge, and by a lying tongue, the most dangerous of all.

Add to these miseries the innumerable accidents which daily befall us. One man loses an eye; another an arm; a third one is thrown from a horse or falls from a window; while still another loses all he possesses through succoring a friend. If you would know more of these miseries, ask worldlings to tell you the sum of their sorrows and their joys. If balanced in the scales of truth, you will find that their disappointments far outweigh their pleasures.

Since, then, human life is so short, and so constantly beset with miseries, what possibility is there of knowing real happiness in this world? The vicissitudes of which we have been speaking are common to the good and the wicked, for both sail on the same sea and are exposed to the same storms. There are other miseries, however, which, as the fruits of iniquity, are the portion of the wicked. "We wearied ourselves in the way of iniquity and destruction," they tell us by the Wise Man, "and have walked through hard ways, but the way of the Lord we have not known."

(*Wis.* 5:7). Thus, while the just pass from a paradise in this life to Heaven in the next, from the peace of virtue to the rest of their eternal reward, the wicked pass from a hell in this life to an eternal Hell in the next, from the torments of an evil conscience to the unspeakable tortures of the undying worm.

Different causes multiply the miseries of the sinner. God, who is a just Judge, sends them suffering, that crime may not remain unavenged; for though the punishment of sin is generally reserved for the next world, it sometimes begins in this. The government of Divine Providence equally embraces nations and individuals. Thus we see that sin, when it has become general, brings upon the world universal scourges, such as famines, wars, floods, pestilences and heresies. God also frequently inflicts on individuals punishments proportioned to their crimes. For this reason He said to Cain, "If thou do well, shalt thou not receive? but if ill, shall not sin"—that is, thy punishment—"forthwith be present at the door?" (*Gen.* 4:7). Moses gave a like warning to the Jewish people: "Thou shalt know that the Lord thy God is a strong and faithful God, keeping his covenant and mercy to them that love him, and to them that keep his commandments, unto a thousand generations; and repaying forthwith them that hate him, so as to destroy them without further delay, immediately rendering to them what they deserve." (*Deut.* 7:9-10).

Observe how strongly the idea of punishment in this life is shown by the expressions *forthwith, without delay, immediately.* They clearly indicate that besides the future punishment of their crimes, the wicked will suffer for them even in this world. Hence the many calamities which they endure. Hence the incessant trials, anxieties, fatigues, and necessities, of which they are keenly sensible, and which, in their blindness, they regard as the inevitable conditions of nature rather than the punishment of their sins. For as they do not recognize natural advantages as benefits from God, and therefore do not thank Him for them, neither do they regard the calamities which overtake them as the marks of His displeasure, and consequently receive no benefit from them.

Other misfortunes, such as imprisonment, banishment, loss of fortune, come upon the wicked through God's representatives upon earth, the ministers of justice. Dearly bought, then, is the pleasure of sin, for which they pay a hundredfold even in this life.

Man's irregular appetites and passions are another and inexhaustible source of afflictions. What, in fact, can you expect from immoderate affections, inordinate sorrow, groundless fears, uncertain hopes, unreasonable solicitude, but violent shocks and continual anxieties which take from man all freedom and peace of heart? Living in the midst of tumult, he scarcely ever prays, he knows not the sweets of repose. From man himself, from his uncontrolled appetites, spring all these miseries. Judge, then, what happiness is possible under such conditions.

Were there only bodily sufferings to harass us, we would not have so much reason to fear. But the world is full of dangers that are far more terrible, because they menace the soul. Of these the prophet spoke when he said, "He shall rain snares upon sinners." (*Ps.* 10:7). How numerous must be these snares which the holy king compares to drops of rain! He expressly tells us that they shall rain upon sinners, for they are so indifferent in watching over their hearts and guarding their senses, so careless in avoiding the occasions of sin or providing themselves with spiritual remedies, that they rush into the very midst of the flames of the world, and therefore cannot but encounter a thousand dangers.

Snares exist for them everywhere—in youth, in old age; in riches, in poverty; in honor, in dishonor; in society, in solitude; in adversity, in prosperity; in the eyes, in the tongue, in all the senses. Were God to enlighten us as He did St. Anthony, we would see the world covered with snares like a network, and we would exclaim with the holy solitary: Who, O Lord, can avoid all these? Behold the cause of the destruction of the many souls who daily perish! St. Bernard said with tears that there was hardly one ship out of ten lost on the sea, but on the ocean of life there is hardly one soul saved out of ten. Who, then, will not tremble in the midst of so many perils? Who will not seek to avoid the treacherous snares of this world? Who will venture to go unarmed into the midst of so many enemies? Who will not fly from this Egypt (Cf. *Ex.* 7), from this Babylon (Cf. *Jer.* 25), from the flames of this Sodom and Gomorrha? (Cf. *Gen.* 19). "Can a man," says Solomon, "hide fire in his bosom, and his garments not burn? Or can he walk upon hot coals, and his feet not be burnt?" (*Prov.* 6:27-28). "He that toucheth pitch shall be defiled with it, and he that hath fellowship with the proud shall put on pride."(*Ecclus.* 13:1).

The blindness and darkness which prevail in the world render these snares still more dangerous. This blindness of worldlings is represented by the Egyptian darkness, which was so thick that it could be felt, and which, during the three days it lasted, prevented everyone from leaving the place in which he was or beholding the face of his neighbor. (Cf. *Ex.* 10:21-23). The darkness which reigns in the world is even more palpable. For could there be greater blindness than to believe what we believe and yet live as we are living?

Is it not a blindness equal to madness to pay so much attention to men and to be so wholly regardless of God? To be so careful in the observance of human laws and so indifferent in the observance of God's laws? To labor so earnestly for the body, which is but dust, and to neglect the soul, which is the image of the Divine Majesty? To amass treasure upon treasure for this life, which may end tomorrow, and to lay up nothing for the life to come, which will endure for all eternity? To live as if we were never to die, wholly forgetful of the irrevocable sentence which immediately follows death? If his life were never to end, the sinner could scarcely act with more unbridled license. Is it not absolute blindness to sacrifice an eternal kingdom for the momentary gratification of a sinful appetite? To be so careful of one's estate and so careless of one's conscience? To desire that all we possess should be good except our own life?

The world is so full of such blindness that men seem bewitched. They have eyes, and see not; they have ears, and hear not. They have eyes as keen as those of the eagle in discerning the things of this world; but they are as blind as beetles to the things of eternity. Like St. Paul, who could see nothing, though his eyes were open, when he was thrown to the ground on his way to Damascus, their eyes are open to this life, but utterly blind to the life to come.

In the midst of such darkness and so many snares, what can worldlings expect but to stumble and fall? This is one of the greatest miseries of life, one that should inspire us with strong aversion for the world. St. Cyprian, desiring to excite in a friend contempt for the world, makes use of this argument only. (L. 2 *Ep.* 2 *ad Donat*). He goes with him in spirit to a high mountain, whence he points out to him lands, seas, courts of justice, palaces and public places, all defiled with the abominations of sin. At the same time he shows his friend, from this spectacle, how justly such a world merits his contempt, and how great should be his gratitude to God for having rescued him from all these evils.

Imitate this saint, and, rising in spirit above the world, gaze on the scene laid before you. You will be overwhelmed by the sight of so much falsehood, treachery, perjury, fraud, calumny, envy, hatred, vanity, and iniquities of every kind,

but particularly by the total forgetfulness of God which prevails in the world. You will see the majority of men living
like beasts, following the blind impulse of brutal passions,
and living as regardless of justice or reason as if they were
pagans, ignorant of the existence of God, and knowing no
other object than to live and die. You will see the innocent
oppressed, the guilty acquitted, the just despised, the
wicked honored and exalted, and interest always more
powerful than virtue. You will see justice bribed, truth dis-
figured, modesty unknown, arts ruined, power abused,
public places corrupted.

You will see knaves, worthy of rigorous punishment,
who, having become rich through fraud and rapine, are
universally feared and honored. You will see creatures like
these, having little more than the appearance of men, filling
high places and holding honorable offices. You will see
money worshipped instead of God, and its corrupting influence causing the violation of all laws, both human and
divine. Finally, you will behold in the greater part of the
world justice existing only in name. Then will you understand with how much reason the prophets said, "The Lord
hath looked down from heaven upon the children of men, to
see if there be any that understand and seek God. They are
all gone aside, they are become unprofitable together; there
is none that doth good, no, not one." (*Ps.* 13:2,3). "There is
no truth, and there is no mercy, and there is no knowledge
of God in the land. Cursing, and lying, and killing, and
theft, and adultery have overflowed, and blood hath
touched blood." (*Osee* 4:1-2).

Moreover, if you would know the world still better, consider him who governs it. As Jesus Christ tells us that the
devil is the prince of this world—that is, of wicked men—
what must be a body with such a head, a commonwealth
with such a ruler? What must it be but a den of thieves, an
army of brigands, a prison of galley slaves, a nest of ser-

pents and basilisks? Why, then, will you not long to leave a place so vile, so filled with treachery and snares; a place from which justice, religion, and loyalty seem banished; where all vices reign; where honesty counts for so little among friends; where the son desires the death of his father, the husband that of his wife, and the wife that of her husband; where the majority of men of every station rob one another under plausible pretexts, and where the fires of impurity, anger, cupidity, ambition, and every other passion continually rage?

Who would not fly from such a world? "Who will give me in the wilderness a lodging place ... and I will leave my people," says the prophet, "because they are all adulterers, an assembly of transgressors." (*Jer.* 9:2). All that we have said on this subject applies to the wicked, for there are good men in all ranks of life, for whose sake God bears with the rest of mankind.

Judge, therefore, by the picture we have given you how much reason you have to hate a world so full of corruption, where evil spirits and crimes are more numerous than the atoms we behold in the rays of the sun. Nourish and increase the desire to fly, at least in spirit, from this world, saying with David, "Who will give me wings like a dove, and I will fly and be at rest?" (*Ps.* 54:7).

These miseries inseparable from wordly happiness should suffice to show you that it contains more gall than honey, more bitterness than sweetness. Nor have I described all the wretchedness that accompanies the pleasures of this life. In addition to its shortness it is impure, for it reduces men to the level of the brute, and raises the animal above the spiritual part of their nature. It is intoxicating, clouding the mind and distorting judgment. It is inconstant, and makes men the same. It is treacherous, for it abandons us when we need it most.

But there is one of its evil characteristics of which I must speak—that is, its delusive appearance. It pretends to be what it is not, and promises what it cannot give. In this way it allures men to their eternal ruin. As there are real and counterfeit jewels and true and false gold, so there are real and counterfeit virtues and true and false happiness. Aristotle says that as falsehood sometimes has more appearance of truth than truth itself, so many things which are evil appear more fair than others which are really good. Such is the happiness of the world, and therefore the ignorant are allured by it, as fish are drawn to their destruction by a glittering bait. It is the nature of worldly things to present themselves under a bright and smiling exterior which promises much joy. But experience soon dissipates our illusions; we feel the sting of the hook almost as soon as we take the bait.

Take, for example, the happiness of a newly married couple. In many cases how brief it is! How soon it is interrupted by troubles and anxieties; by the cares of children; by sickness; by absence; by jealousy; by misfortunes; by grief; and sometimes by death itself, which suddenly changes it for one or the other into a desolate widowhood! How smilingly the bride goes to the altar, seeing only the exterior of what is before her! Were it given to her see the weight of responsibility which she takes upon her that day, tears would replace her smiles. Eagerly as Rebecca desired children, when they were given her, and fought for mastery over each other, she exclaimed, "Why was my desire granted me?" How many have uttered the same cry when they found the realization of their hopes so far below what they promised!

And honors, dignities, preferments—how attractive they appear! But what anxieties, what jealousies, what passions, what hardships their false splendor conceals! What shall we say of unlawful love? How pleasing is the prospect which it presents to the senses! But once the sinner has entered this dark labyrinth he finds himself astray, the victim of a thousand harrowing torments. This forbidden tree is guarded by a furious dragon. With the sword of an injured parent or a jealous husband he frequently deprives the sinner, by one blow, of his reputation, his honor, his fortune, his life, and his soul. Study also the covetous man, or the worldling whose aim is glory to be attained through arms or the favor of the great. How often do their lives form a complete tragedy, beginning with prosperity and ending in ruin! Truly the cup of Babylon is golden without, but filled with abominations. (Cf. *Apoc.* 17:4).

What, then, is human glory but the song of the siren which lures men to destruction, a sweet but poisoned cup, a viper of brilliant colors breathing only venom? It attracts us only to deceive us; it elevates us only to crush us. Consider, moreover, what a return it exacts for all that it gives. Grief at the loss of a child far exceeds the joy of its birth. Loss gives us more pain than profit gives us joy. The affliction of sickness far exceeds the pleasure of health. An insult wounds us more than honor flatters us; for nature dispenses joys and sorrows so unequally that the latter affect us much more powerfully than the former. These reflections manifestly prove the delusiveness of worldly happiness.

You have here, dear Christian, a true picture of the world, however contrary it is to what the world appears to be. Judge, therefore, of its happiness, so brief, so uncertain, so dangerous, and so delusive. What is this world, then, but a land of toil, as a philosopher has wisely said, a school of vanity, an asylum of illusions, a labyrinth of errors, a prison of darkness, a highway of thieves, a stream of infected water, an ocean of perpetual storms? It is a barren soil, a stony field, a thorny wood, a meadow whose flowers conceal serpents, a garden full of blossoms but yielding no fruit, a river of tears, a fountain of cares, a deceptive poison, a perfect fiction, a pleasing frenzy. Its good is false, its evil real, its peace is restless, its security unfounded, its fears groundless, its labor profitless, its tears fruitless, its hope vain, its joy false, its grief real.

Behold what a striking representation of Hell the world affords. Hell is a place of sin and suffering, and in the world these evils also abound. "Day and night iniquity shall surround it upon its walls, and in the midst thereof are labor and injustice." (*Ps.* 54:11). These are the fruits the world produces, *labor* and *injustice;* these are the merchandise in which it traffics. On every side we behold sin and its punishment. Hence St. Bernard said that were it not for the hope of a better life, there would be little difference between this world and Hell. (*Serm.* 4 *de Ascen.*)

It now remains for us to prove that true happiness can only be found in God. Were men convinced of this, they would cease to pursue the pleasures of this world. My intention is to prove this important truth less by the authorities and testimonies of faith than by arguments drawn from reason.

It will readily be granted that no creature can enjoy perfect happiness until it has attained its last end—that is, the highest degree of perfection of which it is capable. Until it has reached this it cannot enjoy rest, and therefore it cannot be perfectly happy, for it feels the want of something necessary to its completeness. Now, what is man's last end, on the attainment of which depends his happiness? That it is God is undeniable; for since He is our first beginning, He must necessarily be our last end. As it is impossible for man to have two first beginnings, so it is impossible for him to have two last ends, for this would suppose the existence of two Gods.

God, then, is man's last end, and consequently his beatitude. For since it is impossible for him to have more than one last end, it follows that in God alone can his happiness be found. As the glove is only made for the hand, and the scabbard only for the sword, so is the human heart created only for God, and in God only will it find rest. In Him alone will it know happiness. Without Him it will be poor and miserable. The reason of this is because as long as the understanding and the will, the noblest faculties of the soul and the principal seats of happiness, are unsatisfied, man cannot be at peace.

Now, it is evident that these faculties can only be completely satisfied in God. For, according to St. Thomas, the understanding can never be so filled that it will not desire to grasp more while there remains more to be learned; and the will can never love and relish so much good that it will not desire to possess more, if more be possible. Consequently these two powers will never know rest until they have attained a universal object containing all good, which, once known and loved, leaves no other truth to be known, no other good to be desired. Hence no created thing, were it the whole universe, can satisfy man's heart. God alone, for whom he was created, can do this. Plutarch tells of a man who, having risen from the rank of a simple soldier to that of emperor, was accustomed to say that he had tried all conditions of life, and in none had he found happiness. How could it be otherwise, since in God alone, man's sole supreme end, can he find supreme rest?

Let us illustrate this by an example. Consider the needle of the compass. God has given it certain properties which cause it invariably to turn to the north. Change its direction and you will see how restless it becomes until it resumes its normal position. Man, in like manner, naturally turns to God as toward the pole of his existence, his first beginning and last end. Let his heart be directed to any other object, and he becomes a prey to trouble and disquiet. The possession and enjoyment of all the world's favors cannot give him rest. But when he returns to God, he immediately finds happiness and repose. Hence he alone will be happy who possesses God, and therefore he is nearest to happiness who is nearest to God. For this reason only the just, who ever draw near to God, and whose joy is unknown to the world, are truly happy.

To understand this more fully, remember that true happiness does not consist in sensible or corporal pleasures, as the disciples of Epicurus and Mahomet assume. In the same class we may place bad Christians whose lips deny the doctrines of these men, but whose lives are entirely in accordance with them. For do not the majority of the rich, who spend their lives in the mad pursuit of pleasure, tacitly acknowledge with Epicureans that pleasure is their last end, and with Mahometans that sensual delight is their paradise? O disciples worthy of such masters! Why do you not abhor the lives of those whose teachings you profess to condemn? If you will have the paradise of Mahomet, you must expect to lose that of Christ.

True happiness is not to be found in the body nor in corporal advantages, but in the spirit and in spiritual goods, as the greatest philosophers have asserted, and as Christianity confirms, though in a far more elevated sense. The possession of these blessings will afford you more peace and happiness than the kings of the earth know amidst their power and splendor. How many of them have testified to this truth by joyfully forsaking their crowns after tasting the sweetness of God's friendship! St. Gregory, who reluctantly left his monastery to ascend the papal throne, never ceased to sigh for his humble cell as ardently as a captive among infidels sighs for liberty and his native land.

As St. Augustine says, it is not merely the possession of goods, but the gratification of his just desires and the attainment of his real wants, that make man happy. These are to be found only in God. Whatever else man possesses, he knows not the blessing of peace. Aman, the favorite of Assuerus, and powerful by his wealth and influence, was yet so disturbed because Mardochai did not salute him that he declared he found no comfort in all he possessed. See how small a thing can poison all the happiness which prosperity gives.

Observe further how much more accessible man is to misery than to happiness in this life; for but one ungratified desire suffices to make him miserable, and so many things are required to make him happy. Is there, then, any prince or potentate sufficiently powerful to have everything according to his will and thus free himself from contradictions? Even could he bend men to his will, what would protect him from the infirmities of nature, bodily pains, and the anxieties and groundless fears to which the mind is often a prey? How can you expect to find immunity from suffering and contradiction, which the greatest monarchs, with all their power, have never attained? Only that which contains in itself all good can give you happiness. Why, then, will you seek it so far from God, who is the supreme Good?

If these reasons be insufficient to convince you, listen to Solomon, than whom no man had a greater share of worldly happiness. What are the words in which he tells us the result of his experience? "Vanity of vanities, vanity of vanities, and all is vanity." (*Eccles.* 1:2). Do not hesitate to accept his testimony, for he speaks from experience. Do not imagine that you can find what he could not discover. Consider how limited anyone's knowledge must be compared to his; for was there ever a wiser, a richer, a more prosperous, a more glorious monarch than this son of David? Who ever enjoyed a greater variety of amusements? All things contributed to his pleasure, yet he gives this result of his almost unlimited prosperity: "Vanity of vanities, and all is vanity."

Can you, then, expect to realize what Solomon found impossible to attain? You live in the same world, and your resources for happiness are certainly not better than his. His pursuit of pleasure was constant, but in it he found no happiness, but rather, as St. Jerome supposes, the occasion of his fall. As men more readily accept the lessons of experience than those of reason, God may have permitted Solomon to drink so deeply at the fountain of pleasures to teach us how worthless they are, and to save others from a similar misfortune.

How long, then, O sons of men, will you be dull of heart? Why will you love vanity and seek after lies? (Cf. *Ps.* 4:3). Wisely does the psalmist term them vanity and lies, for if there were nothing in worldly things but vanity, which signifies nothingness, their evil would be tolerable. But their most dangerous characteristic is the false assurance with which they persuade us to believe that they are what they claim to be. In this, the world manifests its excessive hypocrisy. Hypocrites endeavor to conceal the faults they have committed, and worldlings the miseries under which they groan. Some who are sinners would pass for saints. Others who are miserable would pass for the favorites of fortune. But draw near to them, study the pulsations of their restless hearts, and you will see what a difference there is between appearances and reality.

There are plants which at a distance appear very beautiful, but touch them and they give forth a disagreeable odor. So it is with the rich and powerful of this world. When you behold the dignity of their position, the splendor of their dwellings, and the luxury of their surroundings, you would suppose them the happiest of men; but draw near to them, search the secret recesses of their souls, the hidden corners of their homes, and you will find how false is much of the happiness they seem to enjoy.

O children of men, created to the image of God, redeemed by His Blood, destined to be the companions of angels, why do you love vanity and seek after a lie? Why do you seek in false blessings a peace which they cannot give? Why do you leave the table of angels to feed with beasts?

Will not the calamities with which the world visits you determine you to break the chains of this cruel tyrant?

Reason and experience clearly prove that the happiness we seek is to be found only in God. Is it not madness to seek it elsewhere? "Go where you will," says St. Augustine, "visit all lands, but you will not find happiness until you go to God."

As we have now arrived at the conclusion of our arguments in favor of virtue and in praise of its rewards, let us briefly resume what we have said. As there is no good which is not included in virtue, we must regard it as a universal good, comparable only to God Himself. God contains in His Being all perfections and all good. In a certain manner the same may be said of virtue. All creatures have each some characteristic perfection. Some are beautiful, others honest, others honorable, and others agreeable. Those among them that possess the greatest number of these perfections have most claims to our love. What, then, is more worthy of our love than virtue, in which all these perfections are combined?

If we seek honesty, what is more honest than virtue, the root of all honesty? If we look for honor, what is more honorable than virtue? If beauty attracts us, what is more beautiful than virtue, of which Plato said that were its beauty only seen the whole world would follow it? If we desire profit, what will we find more profitable than virtue, whose hopes are so exalted and whose reward is the Sovereign Good?

"Length of days is in her right hand, and in her left hand riches and glory." (*Prov.* 3:16). If we seek pleasure, what is comparable to the pure pleasures of a good conscience, of peace, of charity, of the liberty of the children of God, of the consolations of the Holy Spirit which always accompany virtue? Do we desire renown? "The memory of the just is with praises; and the name of the wicked shall rot."

(*Prov.* 10:7). If we aspire to wisdom, the greatest of all wisdom is to know God and to understand how to direct our life to its last end. If we would have the esteem and affection of men, nothing will secure it more effectually than virtue; for, to use a comparison of Cicero, as the corporal beauty we admire results from the regularity and symmetry in the members of the body, so from the order and regularity of a good life results a beauty which is pleasing not only to God and the angels, but even to the wicked and to our very enemies.

Virtue is an absolute good; it admits of no alloy of evil. For this reason God sends to the just this short but glorious message: "Say to the just man that it is well." (*Is.* 3:10). In all things, even in pain and toil, he shall find good, and therefore happiness, because "to them that love God all things work together unto good." (*Rom.* 8:28). Though the elements war upon him, and though the heavens fall, he can hold up his head without fear, for the day of his redemption is at hand. He shall be delivered from supreme evil, which is the company of Satan, for God, the Supreme Good, will be his portion. God the Father will adopt him as His son; God the Son will receive him as His brother; and God the Holy Ghost will dwell in him as His temple. Having sought first the kingdom of God and His justice, every blessing has been given to him. From all things he has drawn profit. Every creature has been an aid to him in serving God. Will you, then, be so cruel as to deprive yourself of a help so powerful and so profitable?

As philosophers tell us, good is the object of our will, which is the seat of love. Consequently the better a thing is, the more deserving it is of our love. What, then, has so corrupted your will that it rejects this incomparable good? Why will you not imitate David, who, though he had the care of a kingdom, tells us that he had the law of the Lord in the midst of his heart? (Cf. *Ps.* 39:9). He put all other considerations aside, and gave to virtue the noblest place, the center of his heart. How different is the conduct of worldlings, who give vanity the first place in their hearts, and God's law the lowest!

Do you desire any other motive to persuade you to follow this wise example and embrace so great a good? If you consider obligation, can there be any greater than the obligation which binds us to serve God because of what He is in Himself? We have already shown you that all other obligations compared to this are as if they did not exist. If you can be moved by benefits, what benefits are comparable to those you have received from God? Besides the grand benefits of creation and redemption, have you any good of soul or body that is not from Him? If interest be your aim, what greater could you have than to avoid eternal misery and gain eternal joy? If you aspire to happiness in this life, what happiness equals that of the just? The least of the privileges of virtue which we have described affords more true happiness than the possession of all the treasures of the world. If you reject these evidences in favor of virtue, you do so in willful blindness, for you close your eyes to the light of truth.

CHAPTER 29

*The First Remedy against Sin: A Firm
Resolution not to commit it*

It is not sufficient to persuade men to love virtue; we must
also teach them how to acquire it. The first condition, a
wise man has said, is the absence of vice. We shall therefore
first treat of the most common vices and their remedies, and
afterwards of the virtues and the means of acquiring them.

Before entering upon this subject, bear in mind that there
are two principles in which you must be firmly established
if you would change your life and give yourself to God. The
first is a just appreciation of the importance of the labor you
are about to undertake; you must be convinced that this is
the sole interest, the sole profit, the sole wisdom in the
world. This is what the Holy Ghost Himself teaches us:
"Learn where is wisdom, where is strength, where is understanding, that thou mayst know also where is length of days
and life, where is the light of the eyes, and peace." (*Bar.*
3:14). "Let not the wise man glory in his wisdom, and let
not the strong man glory in his strength, and let not the rich
man glory in his riches; but let him that glorieth glory in
this, that he understandeth and knoweth me." (*Jer.*
9:23-24).

The second principle with which you must be imbued is
that as this is such a glorious and profitable engagement,
you must undertake it with vigor and a firm determination
to conquer. Be persuaded that all the dangers which you

will encounter will be of little moment compared to the sublime end you have in view. It is a law of nature that nothing great is accomplished without labor and trouble. You will no sooner have resolved to give yourself to God than Hell will send out its forces against you. The flesh, corrupted from its birth by the poison of the serpent, will assail you with its insatiable desires and alluring pleasures. Evil habits as strong as nature itself will fiercely resist this change of life and exaggerate the difficulties which you will encounter.

To turn a river from its course is hardly more laborious than to change a life confirmed by inveterate habits. The world, as powerful as it is cruel, will wage a fierce war against you. Armed with its pleasures and bad examples, it will hasten to compass your downfall. At one time it will seek to captivate your heart with its pomps and vanities. At another time it will strive to entangle you in the net of its ways and maxims. Again it will boldly attack you with ridicule, raillery, and persecution. The devil himself, the arch-deceiver, will renew his warfare and turn all his forces against you. Enraged at your desertion from his party, he will leave nothing undone to ruin you.

Be prepared, therefore, to meet with difficulties. Remember the words of the Wise Man: "Son, when thou comest to the service of God, stand in justice and in fear, and prepare thy soul for temptation." (*Ecclus.* 2:1). Do not think you are called to enjoyment alone. You must struggle and combat; for, notwithstanding the abundant succor which is offered to us, we must expect hard labor and difficulties in the beginning of our conversion. That you may not be discouraged, bear in mind that the prize for which you are striving is worth more than all you can ever give to purchase it. Remember that you have powerful defenders ever near you. Against the assaults of corrupt nature you have God's grace. Against the snares of the devil you have the almighty power of God. Against the allurements of evil habits you have the force of good habits confirmed by grace. Against a multitude of evil spirits you have numberless angels of light. Against the bad example and persecutions of the world you have the good example and strengthening exhortations of the saints. Against the sinful pleasures and vain joys of the world you have the pure joys and ineffable consolations of the Holy Ghost.

Is it not evident that all that are for you are stronger than all that are against you? Is not God stronger than the devil? Is not grace superior to nature? Are not the good angels more powerful than the fallen legions of Satan? Are not the pure and ineffable joys of the soul far more delightful than the gross pleasures of sense and the vain amusements of the world?

Resting on these two principles, your first determination must be a deep and unshaken resolution never to commit mortal sin, for it can only rob us of the grace and friendship of God. Such a resolution is the basis of a virtuous life. As long as the soul perseveres in it she possesses divine charity, which makes her a child of God, a member of Christ, a temple of the Holy Ghost, and gives her a right to the blessings of the Church here and the kingdom of Heaven hereafter.

In all things we distinguish substance and accidents. The latter may be changed, while the former remains the same; but if the substance fails all is lost.

Thus a house is still called a house though its ornaments are removed, but if the building is destroyed the ornaments perish with it. Now, the very substance, the life of virtue is charity. This remains, and therefore our spiritual edifice stands as long as we maintain our resolution not to commit mortal sin. If this fails, the whole structure is reduced to ruin; we cease to be God's friends; we become His enemies.

Hence the constancy with which the martyrs endured such cruel torments. Rather than be deprived of God's grace by mortal sin they submitted to be burned, to have their flesh torn with heated irons, and to suffer every torture which the cruelty of men could invent. They knew that had they sinned they could, if time were given them, repent and obtain forgiveness, as Peter did immediately after denying his Master; yet the most terrible torments were more tolerable to them than the momentary deprivation of God's favor and grace.

Holy Scripture gives us a glorious example of this constancy in the mother of the seven sons, whom she exhorted to die manfully, and whose martyrdom she heroically witnessed before she gave up her own life for the law. (Cf. *2 Mac.* 7). Equally sublime was the fortitude of Felicitas and Symphorosa, who lived in the early age of the Church, and who had also seven sons each. These intrepid soldiers of Christ were present at the martyrdom of their children, and in accents of sublime courage besought them to endure their tortures with constancy. They had the heavenly consolation of seeing them die for Christ, and then, with a heroism born only of faith, they yielded their own lives to complete the sacrifice.

In his *Life of St. Paul,* the first hermit, St. Jerome tells of a young man whom, after the tyrants had vainly used many means to force him to sin, they finally bound him in so helpless a condition that he could not escape from the wretched creature whom they brought to him to tempt him. Yet his courage failed him not, but, biting off his tongue, which they could not bind, he spat it into the face of his tempter, who fled in dismay. In this he was doubtlessly inspired by the Holy Ghost, as were so many of the saints, who by every kind of bodily suffering subdued the violence of passions which would lead them to offend God.

He who desires to walk resolutely in the same path must strive to imitate them by fixing this resolution deep in his soul. Appreciating things at their true value, he must prefer the friendship of God to all the treasures of earth; he must unhesitatingly sacrifice perishable joys for delights that will be eternal. To accomplish this must be the end of all his actions; the object of all his prayers; the fruit he seeks in frequenting the sacraments; the profit he derives from sermons and pious reading; the lesson he should learn from the beauty and harmony of the world, and from all creatures. This will be the happy result of Our Saviour's Passion and all the other works of love which He unceasingly performs. They will inspire him with a horror of offending the good Master who has done so much for him. Finally, this holy fear and firm resolution will be the mark of his progress in virtue.

Take a lesson from the carpenter, who, when he wishes to drive a large nail, is not satisfied with giving it a few strokes, but continues hammering until he is sure it is firmly fastened. You must imitate him, if you would firmly implant this resolution in your soul. Be not satisfied with renewing it from time to time, but daily take advantage of all the opportunities afforded you in meditation, in reading, in what you see or hear, to fix this horror of sin more deeply in your soul.

If all the calamities which have existed in the world since the creation, and all the sufferings of Hell, were put into one side of a scale, and but one mortal sin into the other, it would outweigh all these evils, for it is incomparably greater. This is a truth which must be strongly felt and constantly remembered. I know that the world judges differently, but the darkness which reigns in this second Egypt cannot change the real character of sin. Is it astonishing that the blind do not see an evil, however great, or that the dead do not feel the pain of a mortal wound?

We shall treat, therefore, not only of mortal but of venial sin; not that the latter destroys the life of the soul, but because it weakens us and disposes us to mortal sin, which is death. We shall first speak of the seven deadly sins, the source of all the others. These sins are not always mortal, but they can easily become so, particularly when they violate a commandment of God or of the Church, or destroy charity.

In the *Memorial of a Christian Life* we treated of this subject, and gave a number of remedies against sin in general. Our intention at present is to give special remedies applicable to particular sins, such as pride, covetousness, anger, or revenge. By this means we hope to supply each one with the medicine necessary for his infirmities, and with arms suitable for engaging in this warfare. Before entering upon this subject, it is important to observe that in this spiritual combat we have more need of eyes than of hands and feet. The eyes, which signify vigilance, are the principal weapons to be used in this war, which is waged, not against flesh and blood, but against the malice of the evil spirits.

The reason for this is because the first source of sin is error in the understanding, which is the natural guide and counselor of the will. Consequently, the chief endeavor of the devil is to darken the understanding, and thus draw the will into the same error. Thus he clothes evil with the appearance of good, and presents vice under the mask of virtue, that we may regard it as a counsel of reason rather than a temptation of the enemy. When we are tempted to pride, anger, ambition, or revenge, he strives to make us believe that our desire is just, and that not to follow it is to act against the dictates of reason. Man, therefore, must have eyes to perceive the perfidious hook which is concealed beneath the tempting bait, that he may not be misled by vain appearances.

This clearness of mental vision is also necessary to enable the Christian to appreciate the malice and hideousness of sin, and the dangers to which it will expose us. Seeing the evil, we must restrain our appetites and fear to taste the poison which will immediately cause death. We also gather this lesson from that passage in Holy Scripture (Cf. *Ezech.* 1:18) which speaks of those mysterious creatures, figures of the just, which had eyes all over their bodies, for in them we find a striking symbol of that watchful vigilance which the Christian must constantly exercise to avoid the snares of vice.

CHAPTER 30

Remedies against Pride

SECTION I
General Remedies

We have already called the deadly or capital sins the sources of all iniquity. They are the roots of the mighty tree of vice, and if we can destroy them the trunk and branches must soon decay. With them, therefore, we shall begin, following the example of Cassian and other spiritual writers, who were so firmly convinced that if they could only rout these enemies the defeat of the others would be an easy task.

St. Thomas gives us a profound reason for this. All sin, he says, proceeds from self-love, for we never commit sin without coveting some gratification for self. From self-love spring those three branches of sin mentioned by St. John: "the concupiscence of the flesh, the concupiscence of the eyes, and the pride of life" (*1 Jn.* 2:16), which are love of pleasure, love of riches, and love of honors. Three of the deadly sins, lust, gluttony, and sloth, spring from love of pleasure, pride springs from love of honors, and covetousness from love of riches. The remaining two, anger and envy, serve all these unlawful loves. Anger is aroused by any obstacle which prevents us from attaining what we desire, and envy is excited when we behold anyone possessing what our self-love claims. These are the three roots of the seven deadly sins, and consequently of all the others.

Let these chiefs be destroyed and the whole army will soon be routed. Hence we must vigorously attack these mighty giants who dispute our entrance to the promised land.

The first and most formidable of these enemies is pride, that inordinate desire of our own excellence, which spiritual writers universally regard as the father and king of all the other vices. Hence Tobias, among the numerous good counsels which he gave his son, particularly warns him against pride: "Never suffer pride to reign in thy mind or in thy words, for from it all perdition took its beginning." (*Job.* 4:14). Whenever, therefore, you are attacked by this vice, which may justly be called a pestilence, defend yourself with the following considerations:

First reflect on the terrible punishment which the angels brought upon themselves by one sin of pride. They were instantly cast from Heaven into the lowest depths of Hell. Consider how this fall transformed Lucifer, the prince of the angelic hosts, and the bright and beautiful star surpassing in splendor the sun itself. In one moment he lost all his glory, and became not only a demon but the chief of demons. If pure spirits received such punishment, what can you expect, who are but dust and ashes? God is ever the same, and there is no distinction of persons before His justice.

Pride is as odious to Him in a man as in an angel, while humility is equally pleasing to Him in both. Hence St. Augustine says, "Humility makes men angels, and pride makes angels devils." And St. Bernard tells us, "Pride precipitates man from the highest elevation to the lowest abyss, but humility raises him from the lowest abyss to the highest elevation. Through pride the angels fell from Heaven to Hell, and through humility man is raised from earth to Heaven."

After this, reflect on that astonishing example of humility given us by the Son of God, who for love of us took upon Himself a nature so infinitely beneath His own, and "became obedient unto death, even the death of the cross." (*Phil.* 2:8). Let the example of your God teach you, O man, to be obedient. Learn, O dust, to humble yourself. Learn, O clay, to appreciate your baseness. Learn from your God, O Christian, to be "meek and humble of heart." (*Matt.* 11:29). If you disdain to walk in the footsteps of men, will you refuse to follow your God, who died not only to redeem us but to teach us humility? Look upon yourself and you will find sufficient motives for humility. Consider what you were before your birth, what you are since your birth, and what you will be after death. Before your birth you were, for a time, an unformed mass; now a fair but false exterior covers what is doomed to corruption; and in a little while you will be the food of worms. Upon what do you pride yourself, O man, whose birth is ignominy, whose life is misery, whose end is corruption? If you are proud of your riches and worldly position, remember that a few years more and death will make us all equal. We are all equal at birth with regard to our natural condition; and as to the necessity of dying, we shall all be equal at death, with this important exception: that those who possessed most during life will have most to account for in the day of reckoning.

"Examine," says St. Chrysostom, "the graves of the rich and powerful of this world, and find, if you can, some trace of the luxury in which they lived, of the pleasures they so eagerly sought and so abundantly enjoyed. What remains of their magnificent retinues and costly adornments? What remains of those ingenious devices destined to gratify their senses and banish the weariness of life? What has become of that brillant society by which they were surrounded? Where are the numerous attendants who awaited their commands? Nothing remains of their sumptuous banquets. The sounds of laughter and mirth are no longer heard; a somber silence reigns in these homes of the dead. But draw nearer and see what remains of their earthly tenements, their bodies which they loved too much. Naught but dust and ashes, worms and corruption."

This is the inevitable fate of the human body, however tenderly and delicately nurtured. Ah! Would to God that the evil ended here! But more terrible still is all that follows death: the dread tribunal of God's justice; the sentence passed upon the guilty; the weeping and gnashing of teeth; the tortures of the worm that never dies; and the fire which will never be extinguished.

Consider also the danger of vainglory, the daughter of pride, which as St. Bernard says, enters lightly but wounds deeply. Therefore, when men praise you, think whether you really possess the qualities for which they commend you. If you do not, you have no reason to be proud. But if you have justly merited their praise, remember the gifts of God, and say with the Apostle, "By the grace of God I am what I am." (*1 Cor.* 15:10). Humble yourself, then, when you hear the song of praise, and refer all to the glory of God. Thus you will render yourself not unworthy of what He bestows upon you. For it is incontestable that the respect men pay you, and the good for which they honor you, are due to God. You rob Him, therefore, of all the merit which you appropriate to yourself. Can any servant be more unfaithful than one who steals his master's glory? Consider, moreover, how unreasonable it is to rate your merit by the inconstant opinion of men who today are for you, and tomorrow against you; who today honor you, and tomorrow revile you. If your merit rests upon so slight a foundation, at one time you will be great, at another base, and again nothing at all, according to the capricious variations of the minds of men.

Oh, no; do not rely upon the vain commendations of others, but upon what you really know of yourself. Though men extol you to the skies, listen to the warnings of your conscience and accept the testimony of this intimate friend rather than the blind opinion of those who can judge you only from a distance and by what they hear. Make no account of the judgments of men, but commit your glory to the care of God, whose wisdom will preserve it for you and whose fidelity will restore it to you in the sight of angels and men.

Be mindful also, O ambitious man, of the dangers to which you expose yourself by seeking to command others. How can you command when you have not yet learned to obey? How can you take upon yourself the care of others when you can hardly account for yourself? Consider what a risk you incur by adding to your own sins those of persons subject to your authority. Holy Scripture tells us that they who govern will be severely judged, and that the mighty shall be mightily tormented. (Cf. *Wis.* 6:6). Who can express the cares and troubles of one who is placed over many? We read of a certain king who, on the day of his coronation, took the crown in his hands, and, gazing upon it, exclaimed, "O crown richer in thorns than in happiness, did one truly know thee he would not stoop to pick thee up even if he found thee lying at his feet."

Again, O proud man, I would ask you to remember that your pride is displeasing to all—to God, who resists the proud and gives His grace to the humble (Cf. *James* 4:6); to the humble, who hold in horror all that savors of arrogance: and to the proud themselves, who naturally hate all who claim to be greater than they. Nor will you be pleasing to yourself. For if it ever be given to you in this world to enter into yourself and recognize the vanity and folly of your life, you will certainly be ashamed of your littleness. And if you do not correct it here, still less satisfaction will it afford you in the next world, where it will bring upon you eternal torments.

St. Bernard tells us that if we truly knew our hearts we would be displeasing to ourselves, which alone would make us pleasing to God; but because we do not know ourselves we are inflated with pride and therefore hateful in His sight. The time will come when we shall be odious to God and to ourselves—to God because of our crimes, and to ourselves because of the punishment they will bring upon us. Our pride pleases the devil only; for as it was pride which changed him from a pure and beautiful angel into a spirit of malice and deformity, he rejoices to find this evil reducing others to his unhappy state.

Another consideration which will help you acquire humility is the thought of the little you have done purely for God. How many vices assume the mask of virtue! How frequently vainglory spoils our best works! How many times actions which shine with dazzling splendor before men have no beauty before God! The judgments of God are different from those of men. A humble sinner is less displeasing in His sight than a proud just man, if one who is proud can be called just.

Nevertheless, though you have performed good works, do not forget your evil deeds, which probably far exceed your works of virtue, and which may be so full of faults and so negligently performed that you have more reason to ask to be forgiven for them than to hope for reward. Hence St. Gregory says: "Alas for the most virtuous life, if God judge it without mercy, for those things upon which we rely most may be the cause of the greatest confusion to us. Our bad actions are purely evil, but our good actions are seldom entirely good, but are frequently mixed with much that is imperfect. Your works, therefore, ought to be a subject of fear rather than confidence, after the example of holy Job, who says, 'I feared all my works, knowing that thou didst not spare the offender.'" (*Job* 9:28).

SECTION II
Particular Remedies

Since humility comes from a knowledge of ourselves, pride necessarily springs from ignorance of ourselves. Whoever, therefore, seriously desires to acquire humility must earnestly labor to know himself. How, in fact, can he be otherwise than humbled who, looking into his heart with the light of truth, finds himself filled with sins; defiled with the stains of sinful pleasures; the sport of a thousand errors, fears, and caprices; the victim of innumerable anxieties and petty cares; oppressed by the weight of a mortal body; so forward in evil and so backward in good? Study yourself, then, with serious attention, and you will find in yourself nothing of which to be proud.

But there are some who, though humbled at the sight of their failings, are nevertheless excited to pride when they examine the lives of others whom they consider less virtuous than themselves. Those who yield to this illusion ought to reflect, though they may excel their neighbors in some virtues, that in others they are inferior to them. Beware, then, lest you esteem yourself and despise your neighbor because you are more abstemious and industrious, when he is probably much more humble, more patient, and more charitable than you. Let your principal labor, therefore, be to discover what you lack, and not what you possess.

Study the virtues which adorn the soul of your neighbor rather than those with which you think yourself endowed. You will thus keep yourself in sentiments of humility, and increase in your soul a desire for perfection. But if you keep your eyes fixed on the virtues, real or imaginary, which you possess, and regard in others only their failings, you will naturally prefer yourself to them, and thus you will become satisfied with your condition and cease to make any efforts to advance.

If you find yourself inclined to take pride in a good action, carefully watch the feelings of your heart, bearing in mind that this satisfaction and vainglory will destroy all the merit of your labor. Attribute no good to yourself, but refer everything to God. Repress all suggestions of pride with the beautiful words of the great Apostle: "What hast thou that thou hast not received? And if thou hast received, why dost thou glory as if thou hadst not received it?" (*1 Cor.* 4:7). When your good works are practices of supererogation or perfection, unless your position requires you to give an example, do not let your right hand know what your left hand does, for vainglory is more easily excited by good works done in public.

When you feel sentiments of vanity or pride rising in your heart, hasten to apply a remedy immediately. One that is most efficacious consists in recalling to mind all your sins, particularly the most shameful. Like a wise physician, you will thus counteract the effect of one poison by another. Imitate the peacock, and when you feel yourself inflated with pride turn your eyes upon your greatest deformity, and your vanity will soon fall to the ground. The greater your position the greater should be your humility, for there is not much merit in being humble in poverty and obscurity. If you know how to preserve humility in the midst of honors and dignities you will acquire real merit and virtue, for humility in the midst of greatness is the grandest accompaniment of honors, the dignity of dignities, without which there is no true excellence. If you sincerely desire to acquire humility you must courageously enter the path of humiliation, for if you will not endure humiliations you will never become humble. Though many are humbled without diminishing their pride, humiliation, as St. Bernard tells us, is nevertheless the path to humility, as patience is the path to peace, and study to learning. Be not satisfied, therefore, with humbly obeying God, but be subject to all creatures for love of Him. (Cf. *1 Pet.* 2:13).

In another place St. Bernard speaks of three kinds of fear with which he would have us guard our hearts. "Fear," he says, "when you are in possession of grace, lest you may do something unworthy of it; fear when you have lost grace, because you are deprived of a strong protection; and fear when you have recovered grace, lest you should again lose it." Thus you will never trust to your own strength; the fear of God which will fill your heart will save you from presumption.

Be patient in bearing persecution, for the patient endurance of affronts is the touchstone of true humility. Never despise the poor and abject, for their misery should move us to compassion rather than contempt. Be not too eager for rich apparel, for humility is incompatible with a love of display. One who is too solicitous about his dress is a slave to the opinions of men, for he certainly would not expend so much labor upon it if he thought he would not be observed. Beware, however, of going to the other extreme and dressing in a manner unsuited to your position. While claiming to despise the approbation or notice of the world, many secretly strive for it by their singularity and exaggerated simplicity. Finally, do not disdain humble and obscure employments. Only the proud seek to avoid these, for the man of true humility deems nothing in the world beneath him.

CHAPTER 31

Remedies against Covetousness

SECTION I
Against Covetousness in General

Covetousness is an inordinate desire for riches. Hence we regard as covetous not only the man who steals, but also the man who passionately longs for another's goods or too eagerly clings to his own. With great force St. Paul condemns this vice and declares it the source of all iniquity: "They that will become rich fall into temptation and into the snare of the devil, and into many unprofitable and hurtful desires, which drown men into destruction and perdition; for the desire of money is the root of all evil." (*1 Tim.* 6:9-10).

When you are assailed by this vice, arm yourself with the following considerations: Remember that Our Lord and Saviour, at His coming into this world, disdained to possess riches, which are the object of your desires. On the contrary, He so loved poverty that He chose for His Mother not a rich and powerful queen, but a poor and humble Virgin. He willed to be born, not in a palace, but in a bleak stable, the manger of which, covered with a little straw, was His only couch.

During His life upon earth He never ceased to manifest His love for poverty and His contempt for riches. For His Apostles He chose not the princes of great houses, but poor and ignorant fishermen. What greater presumption can there be than that of a base worm coveting riches, when the Creator of the universe became so poor for love of him!

Consider, moreover, your own vileness, since you are willing for a gross and perishable interest to sacrifice your immortal soul, created to the image of God and redeemed by His Blood, compared with which the whole world is nothing. God would not give His life for this material world, but He gave it for the soul of man. How much greater, therefore, must be the value of a soul! True riches do not consist in silver, or gold, or precious stones, but in virtue, the inseparable companion of a good conscience. Set aside the vain opinions of men, and you will see that these precious metals are such only by the judgment of the world. Will you, who are a Christian, become a slave to that which even pagan philosophers despised? "He who guards his riches like a slave is their victim," says St. Jerome; "but he who throws off their yoke possesses them as their lord and master."

Consider also these words of Our Saviour: "No man can serve two masters, God and mammon." (*Matt.* 6:24). Man cannot freely rise to God and the contemplation of His beauty while he is breathless in the pursuit of riches. A heart filled with material and earthly pleasures can never know spiritual and divine joys. No; it is impossible to unite what is false with what is true; what is spiritual with what is carnal; what is temporal with what is eternal; they can never dwell together in one heart.

There is another truth of which you must not lose sight: The more worldly prosperity you enjoy, the more destitute you are likely to be of spiritual riches, for an abundance of this world's goods leads you to trust in them rather than in God. Oh! That you knew the misery which such prosperity prepares for you! The desire of more which springs from the love of riches is a torment which far exceeds the pleasure we derive from their possession. It will entangle you in a thousand temptations, fill you with cares, and under the delusive image of pleasure plunge you into renewed sin and prove an inexhaustible source of trouble and disquiet. Again, riches are acquired only at the expense of pain and labor; they are preserved only by care and anxiety; and they are never lost without bitter vexation and grief. But, worse than all this, they are rarely accumulated without offence against God; for, as the proverb says, "A rich man is either a wicked man or a wicked man's heir."

Moreover, all the riches of the world, did you possess them, would never satisfy the desires of your heart. They would only excite and increase them. However great the possessions you accumulate, there will be a continual void within you; you will never cease to long for more. In its pursuit of worldly possessions your poor heart fruitlessly exhausts itself, for it will never find content. It drinks deeply at the fountains of pleasure, yet its thirst is never appeased. Its enjoyment of the possessions it has already acquired is destroyed by an insatiable thirst for more. Marveling at the covetousness of the human heart, St. Augustine asks: "Whence is it that man is so insatiable in his desires, while brutes observe a measure in theirs? They seek their prey only when they feel the cravings of hunger, and after this is appeased they are satisfied and rest. But the covetousness of the rich knows no limit; it is never satisfied, but is perpetually seeking more."

Has not experience shown you also that where there are great riches there are many to consume, to steal, or to squander them? If you would free yourself from all the anxiety consequent on these cares, put yourself in the hands of God and fully confide in His providence, for He never forsakes those who trust in Him. Since He has subjected man to the necessity of seeking food, He will not permit him to perish from hunger. Could God, who cares for the birds of the air and clothes the lilies of the field, be indifferent to the necessities of one of His noblest creatures? Life is short; every moment brings us nearer to death. Why, then, lay up so much provision for so short a journey? Why burden yourself with so many possessions which must necessarily impede your progress?

When you will have reached the end of your earthly pilgrimage, poor in this world's goods, your wealth of real treasure will far exceed that of the covetous, whose lives have been spent in accumulating riches. How different will be the account exacted of you, and how readily you will part from the little you may have of the goods of earth, because you always esteemed them at their true value! But the rich and the covetou, in addition to the terrible account which will be required of them, will be rent with anguish at parting from that wealth which they loved and adored during life.

Besides the reflections I have suggested, I would ask: For whom are you amassing these goods? Do you not know that you must leave this world as poor and naked as you entered it? (Cf. *Job* 1:21). Think of this, says St. Jerome, and it will be easy for you to despise the riches of this world. (Cf. *Ad Paulin. in Prol. Bib.*). Beware, then, lest in the pursuit of these you lose the treasures of eternity.

Death will rob you of all your earthly possessions; your works, good and bad, will alone accompany you beyond the tomb. If this dread hour finds you unprepared, great will be your misfortune. All that remains to you will then be distributed into three portions, your body will become the food of worms; your soul the victim of demons, and your wealth the prey of eager and perhaps ungrateful or extravagant heirs. Ah! Dear Christian, follow the counsel of Our Saviour; share your wealth with the poor, that it may be borne before you into the kingdom which you hope to enjoy. What folly to leave your treasures in a place of banishment whither you will never return, instead of sending them before you to that country which is intended for your eternal home!

Again, I would remind you that God, as a wise and sovereign Ruler, has appointed some of His children the depositaries of His power and the dispensers of His benefits, to guide and maintain the others. If you are of the number of those who from their surplus possessions must contribute to the support of the poor, do you think that you are justified in expending upon yourself what has been given to you for the benefit of others? "The bread which you withhold," says St. Basil, "is the food of the poor; the garments you conceal should clothe the naked; the gold you accumulate is the portion of the needy." Therefore, you rob the poor whenever you refuse to succor them from your abundance. The riches you have received from God are meant to remedy human misery, not to be the instruments of a bad life. Therefore, do not let your prosperity cause you to forget the Author of all your blessings, and let not those blessings be a subject of vainglory. Do not, I conjure you, prefer a land of exile to your true country. Do not convert into obstacles what is meant to aid you on your journey, and do not make of the succors of life instruments of eternal death. Be content with the condition in which God has placed you, bearing in mind the words of the Apostle: "Having food and wherewith to be covered, with these we are content." (*1 Tim.* 6:8).

"A servant of God," says St. Chrysostom, "should never seek by his dress to gratify his vanity or indulge his flesh; his only object should be to comply with the necessities and requirements of his condition." "Seek ye, therefore, first the kingdom of God and His justice, and all these things shall be added unto you." (*Matt.* 6:33).

Remember also that it is not poverty but the love of poverty which is a virtue. Hence all who voluntarily forsake wealth bear a striking resemblance to Our Saviour, who, being rich with the riches of God, became poor for love of us. They who are compelled to live in poverty, but bear it with patience, never coveting the wealth which is denied them, convert their necessity into a meritorious virtue. As the poor by their poverty conform themselves to Jesus Christ, so the rich by their alms can conform their hearts to the merciful Heart of this Divine Model, who in His lowly crib received not only the shepherds with their simple tokens of affection, but also the wise and powerful men of the East, who came to lay at His feet the treasures of their gold and frankincense and myrrh.

If, then, God has given you wealth, bestow it generously on the poor, assured that it will be laid up for you as treasure in the kingdom of Heaven; but if you waste the means God has given you, you must not expect to find any before you when you leave this life. Unless such a disposition is made of your possessions, how can you call them good, since you cannot bear them with you and enjoy them in your true home? Lay up, then, by a worthy use of your worldly wealth, a store of spiritual possessions, which alone are truly good, and of which, unless you freely surrender them, not even death can deprive you.

SECTION II
Against the unjust Detention of Another's Goods

In connection with the evil of which we are treating, let us say a few words on the sin of retaining the goods of another. Theft consists not only in unjustly taking what belongs to another, but also in unlawfully retaining it against the owner's will. Our intention to restore it later will not suffice if we are able to do it at once, for we are obliged to make restitution as soon as possible. Inability to make immediate restitution justifies us in deferring it; while continued poverty, if so great as to afford us no means, excuses us entirely, for God does not require what is impossible.

We cannot better explain this doctrine than by the words of St. Gregory: "Remember that the riches you have unlawfully acquired remain in this world, but the sins you committed in obtaining them will accompany you into the next. How great is your folly, then, to leave your profit here and to take only your loss with you—to afford others gratification in this world while you endure everlasting sufferings in the world to come!" (*Epist. ad Just*).

The folly of covetousness goes still further, and causes you to sacrifice yourself, your body and your soul, to your miserable possessions. You are like a man who, to save his coat, exposes his body to be pierced with a dagger. In what does your conduct differ from that of Judas, if for a little money you will sell justice, divine grace, your soul itself? The hour of death, at the latest, will compel you to make restitution if you would save your soul. How incomprehensible, then, is the mad folly which prompts you to accumulate your unlawful gains, and, by living in sin, confessing in sin, approaching the Holy Table in sin, completely deprive yourself of spiritual treasures which are incomparably superior to all the wealth of this world! Is he not devoid of reason who acts in this manner? Endeavor, therefore, to pay what you owe, even to the smallest sum, and permit no man to suffer by your neglect. (Cf. *Deut.* 24:15). Do not detain the laborer's wages. (Cf. *Tob.* 4:15). Do not compel him to seek and plead for what justly belongs to him, that he may not have reason to say that it was more difficult to obtain his wages than to earn them.

If you have the duties of executor to fulfill, beware of defrauding departed souls of help due them, lest their expiation may be prolonged because of a neglect for which you must some day heavily atone. Pay your dependants regularly, and let your accounts be carefully kept, that they may give rise to no disputes or claims after your death. Do not wholly leave to those who survive you the execution of your last wishes, but fulfill them yourself as far as you are able; for if you are careless of your own affairs, how can you expect others to be more diligent?

Make it a point of honor to owe no man, and you will thus enjoy peaceful slumbers, a quiet conscience, a contented life, and a happy death. The means of acquiring these precious results is to control your desires and appetites and to govern your expenditure by your income, not by your caprices. Our debts proceed from our ill-regulated, uncontrolled desires more than from our necessities, and consequently moderation is more profitable than the largest revenues. Let us be convinced that the only real riches, the only real treasures, are those which the Apostle bids us seek when he tells us to fly covetousness and pursue justice, godliness, faith, charity, patience, and mildness, for godliness with contentment is great gain. (Cf. *1 Tim.* 6:6,11). Be contented with the position in which God has placed you. Man would always enjoy peace did he accept the portion which God gives him; but, seeking to gratify ambition or cupidity, which craves more than God has given him, he exposes himself to trouble and disquiet, for real happiness or success can never be known by one who strives against the will of God.

CHAPTER 32

Remedies against Lust

SECTION I
General Remedies

Lust is an inordinate desire of unlawful pleasures. It is a vice most widely spread in the world; one that is most violent in its attacks, most insatiable in its cravings. Hence St. Augustine says that the severest warfare which a Christian has to maintain is that in defense of chastity, for such combats are frequent, and victories rare.

Whenever you are assailed by this shameful vice resist it with the following considerations: Remember, first, that this disorder not only stains your soul, purified by the Blood of Christ, but defiles your body, in which the thrice Holy Body of Christ has been placed, as in a shrine. If it be a sacrilege to defile a material temple dedicated to God's service, what must it be to profane this living temple, which God has chosen for His dwelling? For this reason the Apostle tells us: "Fly fornication. Every sin that a man doth is without the body, but he that committeth fornication sinneth against his own body." (*1 Cor.* 6:18). Consider, secondly, that this deplorable vice necessarily involves scandal to numerous souls and the spiritual ruin of all who participate in your crime. This thought will cause the sinner to suffer the greatest remorse at the hour of death; for if in the Old Law God required a life for a life, an eye for an eye, a tooth for a tooth (Cf. *Ex.*

21:23-24), what satisfaction can be offered Him for the destruction of so many souls, purchased at the price of His Blood?

This treacherous vice begins in pleasure, but ends in an abyss of bitterness and remorse. There is nothing into which man is more easily drawn, but nothing from which he is with more difficulty freed. Hence the Wise Man compares an impure woman to a deep ditch, a narrow pit, to show how easily souls fall into this vice, but with what difficulty they are extricated. Man is first allured by its flattering aspect, but when he has assumed the sinful yoke, and particularly when he has cast aside all shame, it requires almost a miracle of grace to deliver him from his degrading bondage. For this reason it is justly compared to a fisherman's net, which the fish easily enter, but from which they rarely escape. Learn, too, how many sins spring from this one vice; for during this long captivity of the soul how often is God offended by thoughts, words, and desires, if not by actions?

The evils which it brings in its train are no less numerous than the sins it occasions. It robs man of his reputation—his most important possession, for there is no vice more degrading or more shameful. It rapidly undermines the strength, exhausts the energy, and withers the beauty of its victim, bringing upon him the most foul and loathsome diseases. It robs youth of its freshness, and hurries it into a premature and dishonorable old age. It penetrates even to the sanctuary of the soul, darkening the understanding, obscuring the memory, and weakening the will. It turns man from every noble and honorable work, burying him so deeply in the mire of his impurities that he can neither think nor speak of anything but what is vile.

Nor are the ravages of this vice confined only to man himself. They extend to all his possessions. There is no revenue so great that the exactions and follies of impurity will not exhaust; for it is closely allied to gluttony, and these two vices combine to ruin their victim. Men given to impurity are generally addicted to intemperance, and squander their substance in rich apparel and sumptuous living. Moreover, their impure idols are insatiable in their demands for costly jewels, rich adornments, rare perfumes, which gifts they love much better than they love the donors, their unfortunate victims. The example of the prodigal son, exhausting his inheritance in these pleasures, shows how terrible is such a passion.

Consider, further, that the more you indulge in these infamous gratifications, the more insatiable will be your desire for them, the less they will satisfy you. It is the nature of these pleasures to excite the appetite rather than appease it. If you consider how fleeting is the pleasure and how enduring its punishment, you will not for a moment's enjoyment sacrifice the unspeakable treasure of a good conscience in this life and the eternal happiness of Heaven in the next. St. Gregory, therefore, has truly said that the pleasure is momentary, but the suffering is eternal. (*Moral.* 9,44).

Consider also the nobility and the value of virginal purity, which this vice destroys. Virgins begin here below to live as angels, for the beauty of these glorious spirits is reflected in the splendor of their chastity. "Living in the flesh," says St. Bernard, "and despising its allurements is more angelic than human." (*In Nat. Virg.*).

"Virginity," says St. Jerome, "is the virtue which, amid the corruption of this mortal life, best represents the perfection of immortal glory. It brings before us the happy condition of the celestial City, where there is no marrying, and gives us a foretaste of eternal joy." (*De Virginitatis Laude*). Hence virginity is specially rewarded in Heaven. St. John tells us that virgins follow the Lamb whithersoever He goeth. (Cf. *Apoc.* 14:4). They have risen above their fellow men in their imitation of Christ. They will therefore be more closely united to Him for all eternity, and will find in the spotless purity of their bodies a source of ineffable joy.

Virginity not only renders man like unto Christ, but makes him the temple of the Holy Spirit. For this Divine Lover of purity abhors whatever is defiled, and delights to dwell in chaste souls. The Son of God, who was conceived of the Holy Ghost, so loved purity that He wrought His greatest miracle to preserve the purity of His Virgin Mother. If you have suffered the loss of this beautiful virtue, learn from the temptations which wrought the evil to guard against a second fall.

If you have not preserved the gift of chastity in the perfection in which God gave it to you, endeavor to restore the beauty of the Creator's work by giving yourself to His service with a zeal and fervor born of deep gratitude for forgiven sin, and with an ardent desire to repair the past. "It often happens," says St. Gregory, "that one who was tepid and indifferent before his fall becomes, through repentance, a strong and fervent soldier of Christ." (*Past.*, p 1). Finally, since God continued to preserve your life after you had so basely offended Him, profit by this benefit to serve Him and make reparation for your sins, lest another fall should be irremediable.

SECTION II
Particular Remedies

Besides these general remedies there are others more special, and perhaps more efficacious. The first of these is vigorously to resist the first attacks of this vice. If we do not resist it in the beginning, it rapidly acquires strength and gains an entrance to our souls. "When a taste for sinful pleasures," says St. Gregory, "takes possession of a heart, it thinks of nothing but how to gratify its inordinate desires." (*Moral.* 21,7). We must, then, struggle against it from the beginning by repelling every bad thought, for by such fuel is the flame of impurity fed. As wood nourishes fire, so our thoughts nourish our desires; and, consequently, if the former be good, charity will burn in our breast—but if they are bad, the fire of lust will certainly be kindled.

In the second place, we must carefully guard our senses, particularly the eyes, that they may not rest upon anything capable of exciting sinful desires. A man may inflict a deep wound upon his soul by inconsiderately turning his eyes upon a dangerous object. Prudently guard your eyes in your intercourse with the other sex, for such glances weaken virtue.

Hence we are told by the Holy Ghost: "Look not round about thee in the ways of the city. Turn away thy face from a woman dressed up, and gaze not upon another's beauty." (*Ecclus.* 9:7-8). Think of Job, that great servant of God, of such tried virtue, who kept so vigilant a guard over his senses that, in the expressive language of Scripture, he made a covenant with his eyes not so much as to *think* upon a virgin. (Cf. *Job* 31:1). Behold also the example of David, who, though declared by God to have been a man after His own Heart, yet fell into three grievous crimes by inconsiderately looking upon a woman.

Be no less watchful in protecting your ears from impure discourses. If unbecoming words are uttered in your presence, testify your displeasure by at least a grave and serious countenance; for what we hear with pleasure we learn to do with complacency. Guard with equal care your tongue. Let no immodest words escape you; for "evil communications," says the Apostle, "corrupt good morals." (*1 Cor.* 15:33). A man's conversation discovers his inclination, for, to quote the words of the Gospel, from the abundance of the heart the mouth speaketh.

Endeavor to keep your mind occupied with good thoughts and your body employed in some profitable exercise, "for the devil," says St. Bernard, "fills idle souls with bad thoughts, so that they may be thinking of evil if they do not actually commit it."

In all temptations, but particularly in temptations against purity, remember the presence of your guardian angel and of the devil, your accuser, for they both witness all your actions, and will render an account of them to Him who sees and judges all things. If you follow this counsel, how can you, before your accuser, your defender, and your Judge, commit a base sin, for which you would blush before the lowest of men? Remember also the terrible tribunal of God's judgment and the eternal flames of Hell; for as a greater pain makes us insensible to a less, so the thought of the inexhaustible fire of Hell will render us insensible to the fire of concupiscence.

In addition to all this, be very guarded in your intercourse with women, and beware of continuing alone with one for any length of time; for, according to St. Chrysostom, the enemy attacks men and women more vigorously when he finds them alone. He is bolder when there are no witnesses present to thwart his artifices. Avoid the society of women who are not above suspicion, for their words inflame the heart, their glances wound the soul, and everything about them is a snare to those who visit them with imprudent familiarity. Be mindful of the example of the elders (Cf. *Dan.* 13), and let not old age render you less prudent. Do not trust to your own strength; and let not a habit of virtue inspire you with presumptuous confidence. Let there be no improper interchange of presents, visits, or letters, for these are so many snares which entangle us and reawaken dangerous affections. If you experience any friendship for a virtuous woman let your intercourse be marked by grave respect, and avoid seeing her too often or conversing too familiarly with her. But, as one of the most important remedies is avoiding dangerous occasions, we shall give an example from the *Dialogues* of St. Gregory to show you with what prudence holy souls guard this angelic virtue.

There lived in the province of Mysia a holy priest who was filled with the fear of God, and who governed his church with zeal and wisdom. A very virtuous woman had charge of the altar and church furniture. This holy soul the priest loved as a sister, but he was as guarded in his intercourse with her as if she were his enemy. He never permitted her to approach him or converse familiarly with him, or enter his dwelling, thus removing all occasions of familiarity; for the saints not only reject unlawful gratifications, but forbid themselves even innocent pleasures when there is the slightest indication of danger to the soul. For this reason the good priest would never allow her to minister to him, even in his extreme necessities.

At an advanced age, after he had been 40 years in the sacred ministry, he fell gravely ill, and was soon almost at the point of death. As he lay in this condition, the good woman, wishing to discover whether he still lived, bent over him and put her ear to his mouth to listen to his breathing. The dying man, perceiving her, indignantly exclaimed, "Get thee hence, woman! Get thee hence! The fire still glows in the embers. Beware of kindling it with straw!" As she withdrew he seemed to gain new strength, and raising his eyes, he cried out with a loud voice, "Oh! Happy hour! Welcome, my lords, welcome! I thank you for deigning to visit so poor a servant. I come! I come!" He repeated these words several times, and when they who were present asked him to whom he spoke, he said with astonishment, "Do you not see the glorious Apostles St. Peter and St. Paul?" And, raising his eyes, he again cried,

"I come! I come!" and as he uttered these words he gave up his soul to God.

An end so glorious was the result of a prudent vigilance which cannot be too highly extolled; and such confidence at the hour of death seemed a fitting reward for one who during life had been filled with a holy fear of God. (*Dial.* 4,11).

CHAPTER 33

Remedies against Envy

Envy consists in grieving at another's good or repining at another's happiness. The envious man looks with hatred upon his superiors who excel him, upon his equals who compete with him, upon his inferiors who strive to equal him. Saul's envy of David and the Pharisees' envy of Christ could only be satisfied by death; for it is the character of this cruel vice to stop at nothing until it has compassed its end. Of its nature it is a mortal sin, because, like hatred, it is directly opposed to charity. However, in this, as in other sins, there are degrees which do not con- stitute a mortal sin, as, for example, when hatred or envy is not grave, or when the will does not fully consent.

Envy is a most powerful, a most injurious vice. It is spread all over the world, but predominates particularly in the courts of kings and in the society of the rich and powerful. Who, then, can be free from its attacks? Who is so fortunate as to be neither the slave nor the object of envy? From the beginning of the world history abounds with examples of this fatal vice. It was the cause of the first fratricide which stained the earth, when Cain killed Abel. (Cf. *Gen*. 4). It existed between the brothers Romulus and Remus, the founders of Rome, and the latter fell a victim to the envy of the former. Behold its effects in the brothers of Joseph, who sold him as a slave. (Cf. *Gen*. 37); in Aaron and Mary, the brother and sister of Moses.

(Cf. *Num.* 12). Even the disciples of Our Lord, before the coming of the Holy Ghost, were not wholly free from it.

Ah! When we see such examples, what must we expect to find among worldlings, who are far from possessing such sanctity, and who are seldom bound to one another by any ties? Nothing can give us an idea of the power of this vice or the ravages it effects. Good men are its natural prey, for it attacks with its poisoned dart all virtue and all talent. Hence Solomon says that all the labors and industries of men are exposed to the envy of their neighbors. (Cf. *Eccles.* 4:4).

Therefore, you must diligently arm yourself against the attacks of such an enemy, and unceasingly ask God to deliver you from it. Let your efforts against it be firm and constant. If it persevere in its attacks, continue to oppose an obstinate resistance, and make little account of the unworthy sentiments it suggests. If your neighbor enjoys a prosperity which is denied you, thank God for it, persuaded that you have not merited it or that it would not be salutary for you. Remember, moreover, that envying the prosperity of others does not alleviate your own misery, but rather increases it.

To strengthen your aversion to this vice, make use of the following reflections: Consider, first, what a resemblance the envious man bears to the devils, who look with rage upon our good works and the heavenly reward we are to receive for them. They have no hope of the happiness of which they would deprive us, for they know that they have irretrievably lost it; but they are unwilling that beings created out of dust should enjoy honors of which they have been dispossessed. For this reason St. Augustine says, "May God preserve from this vice not only the hearts of all Christians, but of all men, for it is the special vice of devils, and one which causes them the most hopeless suffering." The crime of Satan is not theft or impurity, but enviously seeking, after his fall, to make man imitate his rebellion. This is truly the feeling which actuates the envious.

Oftentimes the prosperity of others is no prejudice to them; they could not profit by what they strive to take from their neighbor; but they would have all equally miserable with themselves. If, then, the possessions which you envy in another could not be yours were he dispossessed of them, why should they be a cause of grief to you? When you envy the virtue of another you are your own greatest enemy; for if you continue in a state of grace, united to your neighbor through charity, you have a share in all his good works, and the more he merits the richer you become. So far, therefore, from envying his virtue, you should find it a source of consolation. Alas! Because your neighbor is advancing, will you fall back? Ah! If you would love in him the virtues which you do not find in yourself, you would share in them through charity; the profit of his labors would also become yours.

Consider, moreover, how envy corrodes the heart, weakens the understanding, destroys all peace of soul, and condemns us to a melancholy and intolerable existence. Like the worm which eats the wood in which it is engendered, it preys upon the heart in which it was given birth. Its ravages extend even to the countenance, whose paleness testifies to the passion which rages within. This vice is itself the severest judge against its victim, for the envious man is subjected to its severest tortures. Hence certain authors have termed it a *just* vice, not meaning that it is good, for it is a most heinous sin, but meaning that it is its own greatest punishment.

Consider, again, how opposed is the sin of envy to charity, which is God, and to the common good, which everyone should promote to the best of his ability; for when we envy another's good, when we hate those to whom God unceasingly manifests His love, when we persecute those whom He created and redeemed, do we not, at least in desire, strive to undo the work of God?

But a more efficacious remedy against this vice is to love humility and abhor pride, which is the father of envy. A proud man, who cannot brook a superior or an equal, naturally envies all who appear to excel him, persuading himself that he descends in proportion as another rises. Hence the Apostle says, "Let us not be desirous of vain glory, provoking one another, envying one another." (*Gal.* 5:26). In other words, let us destroy the root of envy, which is vainglory.

Let us wean our hearts from worldly honors and possessions, and seek only spiritual riches, for such treasures are not diminished when enjoyed by numbers, but, on the contrary, are increased. It is otherwise with the goods of the earth, which must decrease in proportion to the numbers who share them. For this reason envy finds easy access to the soul which covets the riches of this life, where one necessarily loses what another gains.

Do not be satisfied with feeling no grief at the prosperity of your neighbor, but endeavor to benefit him all you can, and the good you cannot give him ask God to grant him. Hate no man. Love your friends in God, and your enemies for God. He so loved you while you were still His enemy that He shed the last drop of His Blood to save you from the tyranny of your sins.

Your neighbor may be wicked, but that is no reason for hating him. In such a case imitate the example of a wise physician, who loves his patient, but hates his disease. We must abhor sin, which is the work of man, but we must always love our neighbor, who is the work of God. Never say in your heart: "What is my neighbor to me? I owe him nothing. We are bound by no ties of blood or interest. He has never done me a favor, but has probably injured me."

Reflect rather on the benefits which God unceasingly bestows upon you, and remember that all He asks in return is that you be charitable and generous, not to Him, for He has no need of you or your possessions, but to your neighbor, whom He has recommended to your love.

CHAPTER 34

Remedies against Gluttony

Gluttony is an inordinate love of eating and drinking. Our Saviour warns us against this vice, saying, "Take heed to yourselves lest your hearts be overcharged with surfeiting and drunkenness, and the cares of this life." (*Lk.* 21:34).

When you feel the promptings of this shameful disorder, subdue them by the following considerations: Call to mind that it was a sin of gluttony which brought death into the world, and that it is the first and most important passion to be conquered, for upon the subjugation of this vice depends your victory over all others. We cannot successfully battle with enemies abroad when the forces within us are in a state of rebellion. Thus we see that the devil first tempted Our Saviour to gluttony, wishing to make himself master of the avenue through which all other vices find an easy entrance.

Consider also Our Saviour's extraordinary fast in the desert and the many other rigorous mortifications which He imposed upon His Sacred Body, not only to expiate our excesses, but to give us a salutary example. How, then, can you call yourself a follower of Christ, if, when He fasts, you abandon yourself to the gross pleasures of the table? He refuses no labor, no suffering, to redeem you, and you will do nothing for your own salvation!

If you find abstinence difficult, think of the gall and

vinegar which were given to Our Saviour on the cross; for as St. Bernard tells us, there is no food so unpleasant that it may not be made palatable by mingling it with this bitter draught. Frequently reflect upon the terrible austerities and wonderful fasts observed by the Fathers of the desert; how they fled from the world to remote solitude, where, after the example of Christ, they crucified their flesh with all its irregular appetites, and, sustained by God's grace, subsisted for many years on no other food but roots and herbs. Behold how these men imitated their Divine Model; behold what they thought necessary to reach Heaven. How can you gain this same Heaven by the path of gross and sensual pleasures? Think of the innumerable poor who are in need of bread; and at the sight of God's liberality to you, blush to make the gifts of His bounty instruments of gluttony. Consider, again, how often the Sacred Host has rested upon your tongue, and do not permit death to enter by that gate through which life is conveyed to your soul.

We may say of gluttony what we have said of impurity, that its pleasures are equally restricted and fleeting. Yet earth, sea, and air seem unable to gratify this passion, for many crimes are perpetrated, the poor are defrauded and oppressed, and little ones compelled to suffer hunger, to satisfy the sensuality of the great. It is deplorable to think that for the gratification of one sense man condemns himself body and soul to eternal suffering. What incomprehensible folly to flatter with such delicate care a body which is destined to be the food of worms! For this miserable body you neglect your soul, which will appear before the tribunal of God as poor in virtues as its earthly companion is rich in sensual pleasures. Nor will the body escape the punishment to which the soul will be condemned. Having been created for the soul, it will share its sufferings. Thus by neglecting the nobler part of your being to devote yourself to the inferior, you lose both and become your own executioner.

To excite in your heart a salutary fear of this vice, recall to mind what is related in the Gospel of Lazarus, of his poverty, of his hunger which craved the crumbs which fell from the rich man's table, and how he was carried by angels to Abraham's bosom; while the rich man, who fed upon delicacies and was clothed in purple and fine linen, was buried in the depths of Hell. Moderation and gluttony, temperance and excess, will not reap the same fruit in the next world. To patient suffering will succeed ineffable happiness, and sensual pleasures will be followed by eternal misery. What remains to you now of the pleasures of your guilty excesses? Nothing but remorse of conscience, which will be the principal torture of the life to come. All that you have lavished upon your ungoverned appetite you have irrevocably lost, but that which you have given away to the poor is still yours, for its merit is laid up in the kingdom of Heaven.

That you may not be deceived by the snares of this vice disguised as necessities, govern your appetite by reason, not by inclination. Remember that your soul can never rule the flesh, if it be not itself submissive to God. This submission will be the rule and foundation of its empire. Let God command our reason; let reason direct the soul, and the soul will be able to govern the body. By observing this wise order decreed by the Creator, the whole man will be reformed. But when the soul rebels against reason, and reason against God, the body will soon rebel against the soul.

If tempted by gluttony, remember that you have already tasted its pleasures and that they endured but a moment. They passed like a dream, except that while the light of day dispels the images of the night, the remorse for gluttony remains long after its pleasure has departed. But overcome this enemy, and you will experience consolation and peace. Therefore, the following wise saying has justly become celebrated: "If you find difficulty in the performance of a virtuous action, the trouble is soon past and the virtue remains; but if you take pleasure in committing a base action, its pleasure disappears, but its shame continues with you." (Aul. Gel., *Noct. Attic.* 8,15).

CHAPTER 35

Remedies against Anger and Hatred

Anger is an inordinate desire of revenge. Against this vice the Apostle strongly speaks: "Let all bitterness and anger, and indignation and clamor, and blasphemy be put away from you, with all malice. And be ye kind one to another, merciful, forgiving one another, even as God hath forgiven you in Christ." (*Eph.* 4:31-32). And Our Saviour Himself tells us: "Whosoever is angry with his brother shall be in danger of the judgment. And whosoever shall say, thou fool, shall be in danger of hell fire." (*Matt.* 5:22).

When this furious enemy assails you, let the following considerations help you overcome its movements: Consider, first, that even beasts live at peace with their kind. Elephants do not war upon one another; sheep live peaceably in one fold; and cattle go together in herds. We see the cranes taking by turns the place of guard at night. Storks, stags, dolphins, and other creatures do the same. Who does not know of the friendship between the ants and the bees? Even the wildest animals live united among themselves. One lion is rarely known to attack another, neither will a tiger devour one of his kind. Yes, even the infernal spirits, the first authors of all discord, are united in a common purpose—the perversion of mankind. Man alone, for whom peace is most fitting, lives at enmity with his fellow men and indulges in implacable hatred. All animals are born with weapons for combat. The bull has horns; the boar has tusks;

the bird has a beak and claws; the bee has a sting, and even the tiny fly or other insect has power to bite. But man, destined to live at peace with his fellow creatures, comes into the world naked and unarmed. Reflect, then, how contrary to your rightful nature it is to seek to be revenged upon one of your kind, to return evil for evil, particularly by making use of weapons which nature has denied you.

In the second place, a thirst for vengeance is a vice which befits only savage beasts. You belie your origin, you disgrace your descent, when you indulge in ungovernable rage, worthy only of a wild animal. AElian tells of a lion that had been wounded by an African in a mountain defile. A year after, when this man passed the same way in the suite of King Juba, the lion, recognizing him, rushed among the royal guards, and, before he could be restrained, fell upon his enemy and tore him to pieces. Such is the model of the angry, vindictive man. Instead of calming his fierce rage by the power of reason, that noble gift which he shares with the angels, he abandons himself to the blind impulse of passions which he possesses in common with the brutes.

If it be hard to subdue your anger, excited by an injury from one of your fellow creatures, consider how much more God has borne from you and how much He has endured for you. Were you not His enemy when He shed the last drop of His Blood for you? And behold with what sweetness and patience He bears with your daily offenses against Him, and with what mercy and tenderness He receives you when you return to Him.

If anger urges that your enemy does not deserve forgiveness, ask yourself how far you have merited God's pardon. Will you have God exercise only mercy toward you, when you pursue your neighbor with implacable hatred? And if it be true that your enemy does not deserve pardon from you, it will be equally true that you do not deserve pardon from God. Remember that the pardon which man has not merited for himself, Christ has superabundantly merited for him. For love of Him, therefore, forgive all who have offended you.

Be assured, moreover, that as long as hatred predominates in your heart you can make no offering which will be acceptable to God, who has said: "If thou offer thy gift at the altar, and there thou remember that thy brother hath anything against thee, leave there thy offering before the altar, and go first to be reconciled to thy brother, and then coming thou shalt offer thy gift." (*Matt.* 5:23-24). Hence you can realize how grievous is the sin of enmity among men, since it causes an enmity between God and us, and destroys the merit of all our good works. "We gain no merit from good works," says St. Gregory, "if we have not learned to endure injuries with patience." (*Moral.* 21:16).

Consider also that the fellow creature whom you hate is either a just man or a sinner. If a just man, it is certainly a great misfortune to be the declared enemy of a friend of God. If a sinner, it is no less deplorable that you should undertake to punish the malice of another by plunging your own soul into sin. And if your neighbor in his turn seeks vengeance for the injury you inflict upon him, where will your enmities end? Will there be any peace on the earth?

The Apostle teaches us a more noble revenge when he tells us "not to be overcome by evil, but to overcome evil by good" (*Rom.* 12:21)—that is, to triumph by our virtues over the vices of our brethren. In endeavoring to be revenged upon a fellow creature you are often disappointed and vanquished by anger itself. But if you overcome your passion, you gain a more glorious victory than he who conquers a city. Our noblest triumph is won by subduing ourselves, by subjecting our passions to the empire of reason.

Besides these, reflect on the fatal blindness into which this passion leads man. Under the cover of justice or right, how often does it drive him to excesses which cause him a lifelong remorse!

The most efficacious, the sovereign remedy against this vice is to pluck from your heart inordinate love of self and of everything that pertains to you. Otherwise the slightest word or action directed against you or your interests will move you to anger. The more you are inclined to this vice the more persevering you should be in the practice of patience. Accustom yourself, as far as you can, calmly to face the contradictions and disappointments you are likely to encounter, and their effect upon you will thus be greatly diminished.

Make a firm resolution never to speak or act under the influence of anger, nor to heed any suggestions, however plausible, which your heart may urge at such moments. Never act until your anger has subsided, or until you have once or twice repeated the Our Father or some other prayer. Plutarch tells of a wise man who, on taking leave of a monarch, advised him never to speak or act in anger, but to wait until he had repeated to himself the letters of the alphabet. Learn a lesson from this, and avoid the evil consequences of acting from the impulse of anger.

Though there is no time more unfavorable for action, yet there is no time in which we feel ourselves more strongly impelled to act than when in anger. This is an additional reason for opposing, with all our strength, the suggestions of this passion. For as a man intoxicated with wine is incapable of acting according to reason, and afterwards repents of what he has done in such a condition, so a man beside himself with passion, intoxicated with anger, is incapable of any action of which he will not repent in his calmer moments. Anger, wine, and sensuality are evil counselors. "Wine and women," says Solomon, "make wise men fall off." (*Ecclus.* 19:2). By wine he means not only the liquor which stupefies the intellect, but all violent passion which blinds the judgment. Bear in mind also that you are held responsible for sins committed in such a state.

Another very salutary remedy is to turn your thoughts to other things when excited to anger, and to endeavor to banish from your mind the subject which irritates you; for if you take away the fuel of a fire the flame soon expires. Endeavor also to love him with whom you are forced to be forbearing, for patience which is not accompanied with love, being only exterior, is often changed into hatred. Hence, when the Apostle tells us that charity is patient, he immediately adds that it is kind (Cf. *1 Cor.* 13:4); for true charity loves those whom it patiently endures. Finally, if you have excited the anger of your neighbor, quietly withdraw until his passion has subsided, or at least answer him with mildness, for "a mild answer breaketh wrath." (*Prov.* 15:1).

CHAPTER 36

Remedies against Sloth

Sloth is a reluctance to attend to duty, and, according to Cassian, it is especially a weariness or distate for spiritual things. The peril to which this vice exposes us is clearly set forth in these words of Our Saviour: "Every tree that bringeth not forth good fruit shall be cut down and shall be cast into the fire." (*Matt.* 7:19). Against its evil effects He again warned His disciples when, exhorting them to diligence, the opposite of sloth, He told them to watch and pray, for they knew not when the Lord of the house would come. (Cf. *Mk.* 13:35).

Therefore, if this shameful vice attack you, banish it by the thoughts we are about to suggest.

First call to mind the extraordinary labors which Our Lord endured for you; the many sleepless nights He spent in prayer for you; His weary journeys from city to city, healing the sick, comforting the sorrowful, and raising the dead. How ardently, how unceasingly He devoted Himself to the work of our redemption! Consider particularly how, at the time of His Passion, He bore upon His bruised and bleeding shoulders the heavy weight of His cross for love of you. If the God of majesty labored thus to deliver you, will you refuse to cooperate in your own salvation? When this tender Lamb endured such rude labors to free you from your sins, will you endure nothing to expiate them? Remember, too, the weary labors of the Apostles, who preached the Gospel

297

to the whole world. Think of the sufferings endured by the martyrs, confessors, virgins, anchorites, and by all who are now reigning with Christ. It was by their teaching and their toil that the Faith of Christ spread through the known world and that the Church has been perpetuated to the present day.

Turn your eyes towards nature, and you will find nothing idle. The heavens, by their perpetual motion, unceasingly proclaim the glory of their Creator. The sun, moon, and stars, with all the brilliant planets which people almost infinite space, daily follow their courses for the benefit of man. The growth of plants and trees is continual until they have attained their appointed strength and proportions. Behold the untiring energy with which the ant labors for its winter's food; with which the bees toil in building their hives and storing them with honey. These industrious little creatures will not allow an idler to exist among them; the drones are all killed. Throughout nature you find the same lesson.

Will not man, therefore, blush for a vice which the instinct of irrational creatures teaches them to avoid? To what labor do not men condemn themselves for the acquisition of perishable riches, the preservation of which, when they are obtained, is an ever-increasing source of care and anxiety! You are striving for the kingdom of Heaven. Will you show less energy, will you be less diligent, in toiling for spiritual treasures, which can never be taken from you?

If you will not profit by time and strength to labor now, a day will come when you will vainly seek these present opportunities. Sad experience tells us how many have thus been disappointed. Life is short, and obstacles to good abound. Do not, therefore, let the promptings of sloth cause you to lose advantages which will never return, for "the night cometh when no man can work." (*Jn.* 9:4).

The number and enormity of your sins demand a proportionate penance and fervor to satisfy for them. St. Peter denied his Master three times, but never ceased to weep for his sin, though he knew it had been pardoned. St. Mary Magdalen to the end of her life likewise bewailed the disorders of her youth, though she heard from Our Saviour's lips these sweet words: "Thy sins are forgiven thee." Numerous are the examples of those who, returning to God, continued during life to do penance for their sins, though many of them had offended God far less grievously than you.

You daily heap up your sins; and can you consider any labor too severe to expiate them? Oh! Profit by this time of grace and mercy to bring forth fruits worthy of penance, and by the labors of this life to purchase the eternal repose of the next. Our works in themselves are paltry and insignificant, but united to the merits of Christ they acquire infinite value in the sight of God. The labor endures but a short time; the reward will continue for eternity. We are told of a saint who was wont to exclaim at the striking of the clock: "O my God! Another hour has flown—one of those hours sent me in which to work out my salvation, and for which I must render an account to Thee." Let his example inspire us with a determination to profit by the time which is given us to lay up works for eternal life.

If overwhelmed with labors, remember that we must enter Heaven by the way of tribulation, and that he only will be crowned who strives lawfully. (Cf. *2 Tim.* 2:5). If tempted to abandon the struggle, remember that it is written: "He that shall persevere unto the end, he shall be saved." (*Matt.* 10:22). Without this perseverance, our labor will neither bear fruit nor merit reward. Our Saviour would not descend from the cross when asked by the Jews, for the work of our redemption was not yet accomplished. If, then, we desire to follow in the footsteps of our Divine Model, let us labor to the end with unwearied zeal. Is not the reward which awaits us eternal? Let us continue to do penance; let us carry our cross after Christ. What will it avail us to have weathered the storms and triumphed over the perils of the sea of life, if we suffer shipwrecks as we are about to enter the port of eternal rest?

Let not the duration or difficulty of the labors alarm you. God, who calls you to combat, will give you victory. He sees your weakness; He will support you when you falter, and He will reward you when you conquer. Reanimate your failing courage, not by comparing the difficulties of virtue with the pleasures of vice, but by comparing the labor which precedes virtue with the trouble which surely follows vice. Place side by side the fleeting pleasure of sin and the eternal happiness of virtue, and you will see how preferable is God's service to the fatal repose to which sloth allures you.

Yet do not allow victory to render you indolent, for success often lulls us into a dangerous confidence. Never abandon your arms; for your enemies never sleep, and life without temptations is as impossible as a sea of perpetual calm. A man is usually tempted most at the beginning of a good life, for the devil has no need to tempt those who have abandoned themselves to his control. But he is unceasing in his efforts against those who have resolved to give themselves to God. Therefore, let him never find you unprepared, but, like a soldier in an enemy's country, be always ready for combat.

If you are sometimes wounded, beware of throwing away your arms and surrendering in dismay. Rather, imitate those brave warriors whom the shame of defeat spurs to more heroic resistance and greater deeds of valor. Thus you will rise from a fall with new strength. You will see the enemy to whom you were formerly submitted now flying before you. And if, as it may happen in battle, you are repeatedly wounded, do not lose heart, but remember that the valor of a soldier does not consist in escaping wounds, but in never surrendering. We do not call a combatant de-feated when he is covered with wounds, but when he loses courage and abandons the field. And when you are wounded lose no time in applying a remedy; for one wound is more easily cured than two, and a fresh wound more quickly than one that has been inflamed by neglect. Do not be satisfied with resisting temptation, but gather from it greater incentives to virtue, and with the assistance of God's grace you will reap profit rather than harm from the attacks of the enemy.

If you are tempted to gluttony or sensuality, retrench something from your usual repasts, even though they in no way exceed the limits of sobriety, and give yourself with more fervor to fasting and other practices of devotion. If you are assailed by avarice, increase the amount of your alms and the number of your good works. If you feel the promptings of vainglory, lose no opportunity of accepting humiliations. Then, perhaps, the devil may fear to tempt you, seeing that you convert his snares into occasions of vir-tue, and that he only affords you opportunities of greater good. Above all things fly idleness. Even in your hours of relaxation do not be wholly unoccupied. And, on the other hand, do not be so absorbed in your labors that you cannot from time to time raise your heart to God and treat with Him in prayer.

CHAPTER 37

Other Sins to be avoided

SECTION I
On Taking the Name of God in Vain

Besides the seven capital sins of which we have been treating, there are others which a good Christian should avoid with equal diligence.

The first is taking God's name in vain. This sin directly attacks the majesty of God and is more grievous than any of which we could be guilty against our neighbor. And this is true not only when we swear by God's holy name, but when we swear by the cross, by the saints, or by our own salvation. Any of these oaths, if taken falsely, is a mortal sin. Holy Scripture frequently speaks of the heinousness of such offenses against God. It is true that if one swears inadvertently to what is false the offense is not a mortal sin, which requires the full knowledge of the intellect and the full assent of the will. But this restriction does not apply to those who have a habit of confirming their statements by careless oaths without making any effort to correct themselves. Those who swear in this way, without weighing the import of their words, are culpable for this very negligence. Nor will it avail them to urge that the intention of swearing to what is false was furthest from their thoughts. They persevere in a bad habit without any attempt to overcome it, and therefore they must bear its consequences.

A Christian, if he would not constantly expose himself to

the guilt of mortal sin, should earnestly endeavor to conquer a habit so pernicious. To this end let him follow the counsel given us by Our Saviour, and which St. James repeats in these words: "Above all things, my brethren, swear not, neither by heaven, nor by the earth, nor by any other oath. But let your speech be, yea, yea; no, no; that you fall not under judgment." (*James* 5:12). By these words we are taught the danger of contracting a habit of careless swearing which may eventually lead us to swear falsely, and so to fall under the sentence of eternal death. Swearing in "truth, judgment, and justice" (*Jer.* 4:2), as the prophet declares, is the only swearing that is justifiable. That is, we should swear only to what is true in a just cause, and with deliberation.

But we should not be satisfied with merely shunning the vice of taking God's name in vain; we should excite a horror of it in our children and servants, and reprove it whenever we encounter it. If at times we inadvertently fall into it, we should impose upon ourselves some penance of a prayer, or an alms, not only to punish ourselves, but to impress on our minds the determination of avoiding it in the future.

All that has been said applies especially to blasphemy and perjury. Beware also of that vice known as cursing. The Name at whose mention "every knee in heaven, on earth, and in hell should bow down" in reverence (*Phil.* 2:10) should be used only with devotion and affection. Strive, therefore, to speak with piety of the holy Name of God, and do what you can by your prayers, your exhortations, and your example to banish the terrible evil of which we have been speaking.

SECTION II
On Detraction and Raillery

The abominable sin of detraction is so prevalent at the present day that there is scarcely a society, a family, an individual not guilty of it. There are some persons so perversely inclined that they cannot bear to hear any good of another, but are always alive to their neighbor's faults, always ready to tear his character to pieces.

To excite in your heart a salutary hatred of this detestable and dangerous vice, consider the three great evils which it involves. First, it always borders upon mortal sin, even when it is not actually such. From criticisms and censures, with which people generally begin, we easily fall into detraction or calumny. Detraction is committed when we tell another's real faults; calumny, when the fault we mention is not real, but the invention of our malicious lies. Thus, though we may not be guilty of calumny, how often does it happen that a person, from criticizing the failings of others which are generally known, is gradually led to mention some hidden and grave sin which robs him of his reputation and his honor! That the fault revealed is true in no manner saves the detractor from the guilt of mortal sin.

The descent to such a crime is easy; for when the tongue of the detractor is started, and a desire to embellish his story seizes him, it is as difficult to restrain him as to extinguish a fire fanned by a high wind, or to stop a horse when he has taken the bit in his teeth and is dashing madly on. It is the fear of this evil which led the author of Ecclesiasticus to cry out: "Who will set a guard before my mouth and a sure seal upon my lips, that I fall not by them, and that my tongue destroy me not?" (*Ecclus.* 22:33). He keenly realized the difficulties in the way, knowing, as Solomon says, that "it is the part of man to prepare the soul, and of the Lord to govern the tongue." (*Prov.* 16:1).

The second evil of this vice consists in the threefold injury which it inflicts—namely, on the one who speaks, on him who listens with approval, and on the victim who is assailed in his absence.

In addition to this, the person who complacently listens to detraction is frequently a talebearer. To ingratiate himself with the victims of the detraction he carries to them all that has been said against them, and thus excites enmities which are seldom extinguished, and which sometimes end even in bloodshed. "The whisperer and the double-tongued is accursed," we are told in the Sacred Scriptures, "for he hath troubled many that were at peace." (*Ecclus.* 28:15).

To teach us the baneful effects of this insidious vice, the Holy Ghost compares it at one time to the swift blow of a "sharp razor" (*Ps.* 51:4); at another time to the bite of the poisonous asp, (Cf. *Ps.* 13:3), which disappears, but leaves its venom in the wound. With reason, then, did the author of Ecclesiasticus say: "The stroke of a whip maketh a blue mark, but the stroke of the tongue will break the bones." (*Ecclus.* 28:21).

The third evil of this vice is the horror it inspires and the infamy which it brings upon us. Men fly from a detractor as naturally as they would from a venomous serpent. "A man full of tongue," says Holy Scripture, "is terrible in his city, and he that is rash in his word shall be hateful." (*Ecclus.* 9:25). Are not these evils sufficient to make you abhor a vice so injurious and so unprofitable? Why will you make yourself odious in the sight of God and men for a sin from which you can reap no advantage? Remember, moreover, that in no other vice do we so quickly form a habit, for every time we speak with others we expose ourselves to the danger of relapsing.

Henceforward consider your neighbor's character as a forbidden tree which you cannot touch. Be no less slow in praising yourself than in censuring others, for the first indicates vanity and the second a want of charity. Speak of the virtues of your neighbor, but be silent as to his faults. Let nothing that you say lead others to think that he is aught but a man of virtue and honor. You will thus avoid innumerable sins and much remorse of conscience; you will be pleasing to God and men; and you will be respected by all as you respect others. Put a bridle upon your tongue and learn to withhold an angry word when your heart is moved. Believe me, there is no control more difficult and at the same time more noble and advantageous than that which a wise man exercises over his tongue. Do not think yourself guiltless because you artfully mingle your malicious insinuations with words of praise. In this respect the detractor is like the surgeon, who soothingly passes his hand over the vein before piercing it with the lancet: "His words are smoother than oil, and the same are darts." (*Ps.* 54:22).

To refrain from speaking ill of others is always a virtue, but it is a still greater virtue to refrain from reviling those who have injured us; for the greater the injured feeling which prompts us to speak, the greater is our generosity in resisting it.

Nor is it sufficient not to indulge in detraction; you must also endeavor to avoid hearing it. Be faithful to the counsel of the Holy Spirit, who tells you to "hedge in thy ears with thorns, and hear not a wicked tongue." (*Ecclus.* 28:28). Observe that you are not told to hedge in your ears with cotton, but with thorns, that you may not only repel the words of the detractor, but that you may pierce him, and, by showing him a grave countenance, teach him how displeasing to you is his conduct.

"The north wind driveth away rain," says Solomon, "as doth a sad countenance a backbiting tongue." (*Prov.* 25:23). Impose silence, therefore, upon the detractor, if he be your inferior or one whom you can reprove without offense. If you cannot do this, prudently endeavor to turn

the conversation, or show by the severity of your countenance that his conversation is not pleasing to you. Beware
of hearing the detractor with smiling attention, for you thus
encourage him, and consequently share in his guilt. It is a
grievous offense to set fire to a house, but it is scarcely less
culpable to stand idly by witnessing its destruction instead
of aiding in extinguishing the flames.

But of all detractions, that which is directed against virtuous persons is the most sinful. It not only injures the person assailed, but tends to discourage others who are beginners in virtue, while it confirms the cowardice of those who
will not risk our censures by striving to do good. For what
would be no scandal or stumbling block to the strong may
prove an insurmountable obstacle to the weak. If you would
appreciate the evil of this kind of scandal, reflect upon these
words of Our Saviour: "He that shall scandalize one of
these little ones that believe in me, it were better for him
that a millstone should be hanged about his neck, and that
he should be drowned in the depth of the sea." (*Matt.* 18:6).
Avoid, therefore, as you would a sacrilege, all scandalous
reflections upon persons consecrated to God. If their conduct furnish matter for censure, nevertheless continue to
respect the sacred character with which they are invested,
for it is of them that Our Saviour has said: "He that
toucheth you, toucheth the apple of my eye." (*Zach.* 2:8).

All that we have said of detraction applies with still more
reason to those who make others the object of derision and
raillery; for this vice, besides having all the evil consequences of the first two, presupposes pride, presumption,
and contempt for one's neighbor. In the Old Law God
especially warns us against it: "Thou shalt not be a detractor, nor a whisperer among the people." (*Lev.* 19:16). We
have no need to insist upon the enormity of this vice; what
we have said on the subject of detraction is sufficient.

SECTION III
On Rash Judgments

Those who are addicted to detraction and raillery do not confine themselves to what they know, but indulge in suppositions and rash judgments. When they no longer find matter to censure they invent evil intentions, misinterpret good actions, forgetting that Our Saviour has said: "Judge not, that you may not be judged; for with what judgment you judge you shall be judged." (*Matt.* 7:1-2). Here also the offense may frequently be a mortal sin, particularly when we venture to judge in a matter of grave importance upon very slight evidence. If it be only a suspicion, not a real judgment, it may be only a venial sin, because the act has not been completed. Even by suspicion, however, a mortal sin can be committed by suspecting virtuous persons of enormous crimes.

SECTION IV
On the Commandments of the Church

Besides these sins against the Commandments of God there are those against the commandments of the Church, which also impose upon us a grave obligation. Such are the precepts to hear Mass on Sundays and holy days of obligation; to confess our sins at least once a year, and to receive the Holy Eucharist at Easter or thereabouts; to pay tithes to our pastor, and to observe the days of fasting and abstinence prescribed by the Church. The precept of fasting is binding from the age of 21 and upwards; that of abstinence obliges all who have attained the age of reason. The sick, the convalescent, nursing women, women in pregnancy, those whose labors are severe, and those who are too poor to afford one full meal a day, are exempt from the law of fasting. There may be other lawful reasons for dispensation, for which the faithful ought to apply to their pastor or confessor, and not take it upon themselves to set aside the law of the Church.

The difference between abstinence and fasting should be remembered. By fasting we mean eating only one full meal in the day, with a slight collation in the evening. By abstinence we mean giving up the use of flesh-meat. It should be borne in mind, therefore, on Ember days and at other times of fast, that the law is not fulfilled by simply abstaining from meat. Unless you are excused by some of the reasons given above or by dispensation, you must observe the fast by eating only one full meal, with the collation in the evening, and a warm drink, with a cracker or small piece of bread, in the morning.

In regard to hearing Mass, we must endeavor to be present at the Holy Sacrifice not only in body but in mind, with silence and recollection, having our thoughts fixed upon the mystery of the altar, or upon some other pious subject. The recital of devout prayers, especially the Rosary, is an excellent means of keeping ourselves united with God. If we are at the head of a house we must be careful to see that all under our charge hear Mass, not only on Sundays, but also on holy days. Too much laxity regarding holy days is apt to prevail among those who earn their bread by the sweat of their brow. They should remember that the obligation to hear Mass on a holy day is the same as the obligation to hear it on Sunday. Consequently, they must make serious and sincere efforts to comply with this duty. To attend an early Mass may involve the loss of a little sleep, but they should remember that these holy days occur but seldom, and that they must do something to atone for their sins and to merit the kingdom of Heaven. Parents and employers will have a severe account to render to God if they cause or permit those confided to their care to neglect this sacred duty. When there is a just reason, such as the care of the sick or any other pressing necessity which prevents our hearing Mass, we are released from the obligation.

CHAPTER 38

Venial Sins

Though the sins of which we have been treating are those which we should avoid with most care, yet do not think that you are dispensed from vigilance in regard to venial sins. I conjure you not to be one of those ungenerous Christians who make no scruple of committing a sin because it is venial. Remember these words of Holy Scripture: "He that contemneth small things shall fall by little and little." (*Ecclus.* 19:1). "Do not despise venial sins because they appear trifling," says St. Augustine, "but fear them because they are numerous. Small animals in large numbers can kill a man. Grains of sand are very small, yet, if accumulated, they can sink a ship. Drops of water are very small, yet how often they become a mighty river, a raging torrent, sweeping everything before them!"

The holy Doctor goes on to observe that though no number of venial sins can constitute a mortal sin, yet these slighter failings predispose us to greater faults, which often become mortal. St. Gregory observes with equal truth that slight faults are sometimes more dangerous than greater ones, for the latter, when we behold their hideousness, awaken remorse and resolutions of amendment; but the former make less impression on us, and thus, by easily relapsing into them, we soon contract a strong habit.

Finally, venial sin, however slight, is always prejudicial to the soul. It weakens our devotion, troubles the peace of our conscience, diminishes the fervor of charity, exhausts the strength of our spiritual life, and obstructs the work of the Holy Ghost in our souls. I pray you then to do all in your power to avoid these sins, for there is no enemy too weak to harm us if we make no resistance. Slight anger, gluttony, vanity, idle words and thoughts, immoderate laughter, loss of time, too much sleeping, trivial lies or flatteries—such are the sins against which I would particularly warn you. Great vigilance is required against offenses of this kind, for occasions of venial sin abound.

CHAPTER 39

*Shorter Remedies against Sins, particularly
the Seven Deadly Sins*

The means we have already suggested will suffice to strengthen you in virtue and arm you against vice. The following short considerations, however, you can use with advantage at the moment of temptation. They were found among the writings of a man of great sanctity, who had himself experienced their efficacy.

In temptations to pride he would say: When I reflect upon the depth of humility to which the Son of God, the second Person of the Blessed Trinity, descended for love of me, I feel that, however profound a contempt men may have for me, I yet deserve to be still more humbled and despised.

When attacked by covetousness he would think: Having once understood that nothing but God can satisfy the heart, I am convinced of the folly of seeking anything but this supreme Good.

In assaults against purity he would reflect: To what a dignity has my body been raised by the reception of the Holy Eucharist! I tremble, therefore, at the sacrilege I would commit by profaning with carnal pleasures this temple in which God has chosen to dwell.

Against anger he would defend himself by saying: No injury should be capable of moving me to anger when I reflect upon the outrages I have offered my God.

When assailed by temptations to hatred he would answer the enemy: Knowing the mercy with which God has received me and pardoned my sins, I cannot refuse to forgive my greatest enemy.

When attacked by gluttony he would say: I call to mind the vinegar and gall which were offered to Our Saviour on the cross, and shall I not blush if I do not deny my appetite or endure something for the expiation of my sins?

In temptations to sloth he would arouse himself by the thought: Eternal happiness can be purchased by a few years of labor here below; shall I, then, shrink from any toil for so great a reward?

In a word which some attribute to St. Augustine, and others to St. Leo, we find similar remedies which are equally efficacious. The author shows us on one side the allurements with which each vice solicits us, and on the other the arguments with which we must resist it.

Pride is the first to address us, in the following deceitful language: You certainly excel others in learning, eloquence, wealth, rank, and many other things. Being so superior, therefore, you have every reason to look down upon them. Humility answers: Remember that you are but dust and ashes, destined, as rottenness and corruption, to become the food of worms; and were you all that you imagine, the greater your dignity the greater should be your humility if you would escape a miserable fall. Does your power equal that of the angels who fell? Do you shine upon earth as Lucifer shone in Heaven? If pride thrust him from such a height of glory to such an abyss of misery, how can you, a slave to the same pride, expect to rise from your wretchedness to the honor from which he fell?

Vainglory speaks thus: Yes, do all the good you can, but publish it, so that the world may regard you as a man of great virtue and treat you with consideration and respect. Fear of God answers: It is great folly to devote to the acquisition of temporal renown that which can obtain for you eternal glory. Endeavor to hide your good actions, and if they appear in spite of your efforts to conceal them it will not be accounted vanity in you when you have no desire to display them.

Hypocrisy counsels: Assume the good qualities you do not possess, and make men think you better than you are, that you may not excite their contempt. Sincerity answers: It is better to be virtuous than to try to appear so. By attempting to deceive others you will only cause your own ruin.

Rebellion and Disobedience argue: Why should you be subject to those who are your inferiors? It is your place to command and theirs to obey, for they are inferior to you in wisdom and virtue. It suffices to obey the laws of God; you have no need to be bound by the commands of man. Submission and Obedience answer: The law of God obliges you to submit to the authority of man. For has not God said, "He that heareth you heareth me, and he that despiseth you despiseth me" (*Lk.* 10:16)? Nor can you urge that this injunction is only to be observed when he who commands is wise and virtuous, for the Apostle says, "There is no power but from God; and those that are, are ordained of God." (*Rom.* 13:1). Therefore, your duty is not to criticize those in authority, but to obey them.

Envy whispers: In what are you inferior to such men whom others extol? Why should you not enjoy the same and even greater consideration, for you excel them in many things? It is unjust that they should be ranked as your equals; with much less reason should they be placed above you. Brotherly Love answers: If your virtue exceeds that of others it is safer in obscurity, for the greater the elevation to which a man is raised, the greater is the danger of his fall. If the possessions of others equal or exceed yours, in what does it prejudice you? Remember that by envying others you only liken yourself to him of whom it is written: "By the envy of the devil death came into the world; and they follow him that are of his side." (*Wis.* 2:24-25).

Hatred says: God cannot oblige you to love one who contradicts and opposes you, who continually speaks ill of you, ridicules you, reproaches you with your past failings, and thwarts you in everything, for he would not thus persecute you if he did not hate you. True Charity answers: We must not, because of these deplorable faults, cease to love the image of God in our fellow creatures.

Did not Jesus Christ love His enemies who nailed Him to the cross? And did not this Divine Master, before leaving the world, exhort us to imitate His example? Drive, then, from your heart the bitterness of hatred and yield to the sweetness of fraternal charity. Independently of your eternal interests, which impose this duty upon you, there is nothing sweeter than love, and nothing more bitter than hatred, which preys like a cancer on the heart of its victim, where it was first engendered.

Detraction exclaims: It is impossible to be silent any longer about the faults of such a one. Is not concealment condoning them and rendering ourselves partakers of them? Charity, which appreciates the duty of fraternal correction, answers: You must neither publish your neighbor's sins nor be accessory to them; but reprove him with mildness and patiently bear with him. Moreover, it is the part of wisdom sometimes to ignore the faults of another until a favorable opportunity occurs for warning him against them.

Anger cries out: How can you bear such affronts? It does not become you to submit calmly to such injuries. If you do not resent them you will be insulted with impunity. Patience answers: Reflect upon the ignominy Our Saviour endured for you, and there is no wrong which you will not bear with meekness. Remember also these words of St. Peter: "Christ suffered for us, leaving you an example that you should follow his steps. Who, when he was reviled, did not revile; when he suffered, he threatened not." (*1 Pet.* 2:21,23).

Consider also how trifling are our sufferings compared to the torments He endured for us. He was buffeted, scourged, spat upon, crowned with thorns, covered with ignominy, and nailed to a cross. And, though all these were borne for us, yet how quickly we are enraged by a trifling word or a slight incivility!

Hardness-of-heart urges: It profits nothing to speak kindly to stupid, ignorant men who will probably presume upon your kindness and become insolent. Meekness answers: Do not hearken to such thoughts, but heed the words of the Apostle: "The servant of the Lord must not wrangle, but be mild towards all men." (*2 Tim.* 2:24). Inferiors should endeavor with no less care to bear themselves with meekness and respect towards their superiors, and beware of presuming, as many do, upon the kindness and gentleness of those in authority.

Presumption and Imprudence argue thus: God witnesses your actions; what do you care, then, how they affect others? Prudence answers: You owe a duty of edification to your neighbor, and your actions should furnish him no reason to suspect evil. Beware, therefore, of scandalizing another, even in acts that are good but misunderstood. If the reproofs of your neighbor are well-founded, humbly acknowledge your fault; if you are guiltless, avow your innocence with no less sincere humility.

Sloth and Indolence suggest: If you apply yourself to study, prayer, meditation, and tears you will injure your eyes. If you prolong your vigils and fasts you will weaken your body and unfit yourself for spiritual exercises. Industry and Zeal answer: Who has assured you many years for the performance of these good works? Are you sure of tomorrow, or even of the present moment? Have you forgotten these words of Our Saviour: "Watch ye, therefore, because you know not the day nor the hour" (*Matt.* 25:13)? Arise, then, and cast aside this indolence which has seized you, for the kingdom of Heaven, which suffers violence, is not for the slothful, but for the violent who will bear it away. (Cf. *Matt.* 11:12).

Covetousness insinuates: Do not give any of your possessions to strangers, but keep them for yourself and your own. Mercy answers: Remember the lesson of the covetous rich man of the Gospel who was clothed in purple and fine linen; he was not condemned for taking what did not belong to him, but for not giving from his abundance. (Cf. *Lk.* 16:22). From the depth of Hell he begged for a drop of water to quench his thirst; but it was denied him, because he had refused to the poor man at his gate even the crumbs which fell from his table.

Gluttony urges: God created all these things for us, and he who refuses them despises the benefits of God. Temperance answers: True, God created these things for our maintenance, but He willed that we should use them with moderation, for He has also imposed upon us the duty of sobriety and temperance. It was principally a disregard of these virtues which brought destruction upon the city of Sodom. (Cf. *Ezech.* 16:49). Therefore, a man, even when enjoying good health, should consult necessity rather than pleasure in the choice of his food. He has perfectly triumphed over this vice who not only limits the quantity of his food, but who denies himself delicacies except when necessity, charity, or politeness prompts him to accept them.

Loquacity tells us: It is no sin to talk much if you say no evil, as, on the contrary, it does not free you from fault to allege that your words are few if what you have said is bad. Discreet Reserve answers: That is true; but great talkers seldom fail to offend with the tongue. Hence the Wise Man says, "In the multitude of words there shall not want sin."

(*Prov.* 10:19). And if you are so fortunate as to avoid injurious words against your neighbor, you will hardly avoid idle words, for which, however, you must render an account on the last day. Be reserved and moderate, therefore, in your speech, that a multiplicity of words may not entangle you in sin.

Impurity counsels thus: Profit now by the pleasures life offers you, for you know not what may happen tomorrow; it is unreasonable to restrict the pleasures of youth, which passes like a dream. If God had not willed us the enjoyment of these pleasures, He never would have created us as we are. Chastity answers: Be not deceived by such illusions. Consider what is prepared for you. If you live pure lives on earth you will be rewarded hereafter with ineffable and eternal joys. But if you abandon yourself to your impure desires you will be punished by torments equally unspeakable and eternal. The more sensible you are of the fleeting nature of these pleasures, the more earnestly you should endeavor to live chastely; for wretched indeed is that hour of gratification which is purchased at the expense of endless suffering.

All that we have said in the preceding pages will furnish you with spiritual arms to triumph over your enemies. If you follow these counsels you will take the first step in virtue; that is, you will extirpate your vices. Thus will you defend your soul, the citadel which God has confided to your care, and in which He wills to take up His abode. If you defend it resolutely and faithfully you will enjoy the presence of this heavenly Guest, for the Apostle tells us that "God is charity, and he that abideth in charity abideth in God, and God in him." (*1 Jn.* 4:16). Now, he abides in charity who does nothing to destroy this virtue, which perishes only by mortal sin, against which the preceding considerations may be applied as a preventive or remedy.

CHAPTER 40

*The Three Kinds of Virtues in which the
Fullness of Justice Consists; and first, Man's
Duty to Himself*

SECTION I
Our Threefold Obligation to Virtue

Having spoken at length of the sins which profane and
degrade the soul, let us now turn to the virtues which ele-
vate and adorn it with the spiritual treasures of justice. It
belongs to justice to render to everyone his due: to God, to
our neighbor, and to ourselves. If we faithfully acquit ourselves of these duties to God, to our neighbor, and to ourselves, we fulfill the obligations of justice and thus become
truly virtuous.

To accomplish this great work let your heart be that of a
son towards God, that of a brother towards your neighbor,
and that of a judge towards yourself. In this, the prophet
tells us, the virtue of man consists: "I will show thee, O
man, what is good and what the Lord requireth of thee:
Verily, to do judgment, and to love mercy, and to walk
solicitous with thy God." (*Mich.* 6:8). The duty of judgment
is what man owes to himself; the duty of mercy what he
owes to his neighbor; and to walk carefully before God is
the duty he owes to his Creator.

Section II
The Reformation of the Body

Charity, it is truly said, begins at home. Let us, therefore, begin with the first obligation mentioned by the prophet—the duty of judgment which man must exercise towards himself. Every just judge must enforce order and discipline in the district over which he exercises jurisdiction. Now, the kingdom over which man rules is divided into two distinct parts: the body with all its organs and senses, and the soul with all its affections and powers. Over all these he must establish the empire of virtue, if he would faithfully perform his duty to himself.

To reform the body and bring it under the dominion of virtue, the first thing to be acquired is a modest and decorous bearing. "Let there be nothing in your carriage, your deportment, or your dress," says St. Augustine, "capable of scandalizing your neighbor, but let everything about you be conformable to the purity and sanctity of your profession." Hence a servant of God should bear himself with gravity, humility, and sweetness, that all who approach him may profit by his example and be edified by his virtues. The great Apostle would have us, like fragrant plants, giving forth the sweet perfume of piety and filling all about us with the odor of Jesus Christ. (Cf. *2 Cor.* 2:15).

Such, indeed, should be the effect of the words, the actions, and the bearing of those who serve God, so that none who draw near to them can resist the sweet attraction of sanctity. This is one of the principal fruits of a modest and recollected deportment. It is a mute but eloquent teaching, which draws men to the love of virtue and the service of God. Thus do we fulfill the precept of Our Saviour: "So let your light shine before men that they may see your good works, and glorify your Father who is in heaven." (*Matt.* 5:16). The prophet Isaias also tells us that God's servants should be plants bearing fruits of righteousness and virtue, the beauty of which will lead men to extol the power of their Creator. (Cf. *Is.* 61:3). This does not mean that our good works must be done to gain the applause of men, for, as St. Gregory tells us, "a good work may be public only while its intention remains a secret between God and the soul. The example we thus afford our brethren destroys neither the merit of humility nor the desire to please only God." (*Moral.* 29,18).

Another fruit which we derive from this exterior modesty is a greater facility in preserving the recollection, devotion, and purity of the soul. The interior and the exterior man are so closely united that good or evil in one is quickly communicated to the other. If order reign in the soul, its effect is experienced in the body; and the body, if disturbed, renders the soul likewise restless. Each may in all respects be considered a mirror of the other, for the actions of one are faithfully represented in the other. For this reason a composed and modest bearing must contribute to interior recollection and modesty, while a restless exterior must be incompatible with peace of soul. Hence the Wise Man tells us: "He that is hasty with his feet shall stumble." (*Prov.* 19:2). Thus would he teach us that he whose exterior is wanting in that calm gravity which is the distinctive mark of God's servants must inevitably stumble and frequently fall.

A third effect of the virtue we are considering is to communicate to man a composure and gravity befitting any office he may fill. We behold an example of this in Job, who tells us that the light (the dignity) of his countenance never fell to the earth. (Cf. *Job* 29:24). And speaking of the authority of his bearing, he says: "The young men saw me and hid themselves, and the old men rose up and stood. The princes ceased to speak, and laid the finger on their mouth. The rulers held their peace, and their tongue cleaved to their throat." (*Job* 29:8-10). But the gravity and dignity of this holy man were mingled with so much sweetness and mercy that, as he tells us, when seated as a king with his army about him he was a comforter to them that mourned. (Cf. *Job* 25).

Wise men condemn this want of modest gravity less as a fault in itself than as a mark of levity; for, as we have already observed, an unreserved and frivolous exterior indicates an uncontrolled and ill-regulated interior. Hence the author of Ecclesiasticus says: "The attire of the body, and the laughter of the teeth, and the gait of the man show what he is." (*Ecclus.* 19:27). "As the faces of them that look therein shine in the water," says Solomon, "so the hearts of men are laid open to the wise" by their exterior acts. (*Prov.* 27:19).

Such are the benefits which result from a grave and modest deportment. We cannot but deplore the conduct of those who, through human respect, laugh and jest with a freedom unbecoming their profession, and allow themselves indulgences which deprive them of many of the fruits of virtue. "A religious," says St. John Climachus, "should not abandon his fasts through fear of falling into the sin of vainglory." Neither should fear of the world's displeasure cause us to lose the advantages of gravity and modesty in our conduct; for it is as unreasonable to sacrifice a virtue through fear of offending men as it would be to seek to overcome one vice by another.

The preceding remarks apply to our manners in general. We shall next treat of the modesty and sobriety which we should observe at table.

SECTION III
Temperance

The first thing to be done for the reformation of the body is to put a rigorous curb on the appetites and to refrain from immoderate indulgence of any of the senses. As myrrh, which is an exceedingly bitter substance, preserves the body from corruption after death, so mortification preserves it during life from the corruption of vice. For this reason we shall consider the efficacy of sobriety, or temperance—a virtue upon which all the others depend, but which is very difficult to attain because of the resistance of our corrupt nature.

Read, then, the words in which the Holy Spirit deigns to instruct us in this respect: "Use as a frugal man the things that are set before thee, lest if thou eatest much thou be hated. Leave off first for manners' sake, and exceed not lest thou offend. And if thou sittest among many, reach not thy hand out first of all, and be not the first to ask for drink." (*Ecclus.* 31:19-21). Here are rules worthy of the Sovereign Master, who wills that we should imitate in our actions the decorum and order which reign in all His works. St. Bernard teaches us the same lesson in these words: "In regard to eating there are four things to be regulated: the time, the manner, the quantity, and the quality. The time should be limited to the usual hours of our repast; the manner should be free from that eagerness which makes us appear absorbed in what is set before us; the quantity and quality should not exceed what is granted others, except when a condition of health manifestly requires delicacies." (Ep. ad *Fratres de Monte Dei.*).

In forcible words, supported by appropriate examples, St. Gregory declares the same sentiments: "It belongs to abstinence not to anticipate the ordinary time of meals, as Jonathan did when he ate the honeycomb (Cf. *1 Kg.* 14:27); not to desire the greatest delicacies, as the Israelites did in the desert when they longed for the fleshpots of Egypt (Cf. *Exod.* 16:3); not to wish for the choicest preparation of food, as the people of Sodom (Cf. *Gen.* 19); and not to yield to greediness, as Esau did (Cf. *Gen.* 25:33) when he sold his birthright for a mess of pottage." (*Moral.* 30,27).

Hugh of St. Victor tells us we must be very attentive to our deportment at table, always observing a certain modesty of the eyes and a reserve of speech. There are some, he says, who are no sooner seated at table than their uncontrolled appetite is manifested by their bearing: Their eyes eagerly scan the whole board; they rudely help themselves before others, and seize upon the nearest dish, regardless of all save self. They approach the table as a general approaches a fort which he is to assail, as if they were considering how they can most quickly consume all that lies before them. (*Discip. Monast.*). Control these disgraceful indications of a degrading vice, and overcome the vice itself by restricting the quantity and quality of your food. Bear these wise counsels in mind at all times, but particularly when the appetite is stimulated by hunger, or by rare and sumptuous viands which prove strong incentives to gluttony.

Beware of the illusions of this vice, which St. John Climachus tells us is most deceptive. At the beginning of a repast it is so clamorous that it would seem that no amount could satisfy our hunger; but if we are firm in resisting its unruly demands, we shall see that a moderate portion is sufficient for nature.

An excellent remedy against gluttony is to bear in mind when we go to table that there are, as a pagan philosopher says, two guests to be provided for: the body, to which we must furnish the food which its necessity craves; and our soul, which we must maintain by the virtues of self-denial and temperance. A no less efficacious remedy is to compare the happy fruits of abstinence with the gross pleasures of gluttony, which will enable us to appreciate the folly of sacrificing such lasting advantages for such pernicious and fleeting gratifications.

Remember, moreover, that of all the pleasures of the

senses those of taste and feeling are the lowest. We have them in common with all animals, even the most imperfect, while there are many which lack the other three, seeing, hearing, and smelling. These former senses, tasting and feeling, are not only the basest, but their pleasures are the least enduring, for they vanish with the object which produced them.

Add to these considerations the thought of the sufferings of the martyrs, and the fasts and mortifications of the saints. Think, too, of your many sins which must be expiated; of the pains of Purgatory; of the torments of Hell. Each of these things will tell you how necessary it is to take up the cross, to overcome your appetites, and to do penance for the sinful gratifications of the past. Remember, then, the duty of self-denial; prepare for your necessary meals with such reflections before your mind, and you will see how easy it will be to observe the rules of moderation and sobriety.

Though this great prudence is necessary in eating, how much more is required in drinking! There is nothing more injurious to chastity than the excessive use of wine, in which, as the Apostle says, there is luxury. (Cf. *Eph.* 5:18). It is at all times the capital enemy of this angelic virtue; but it is particularly in youth that such indulgence is most fatal. Hence St. Jerome says that wine and youth are two incentives to impurity. *(Ad Eustoch, de Cust. Virg.).* Wine is to youth what fuel is to fire. As oil poured upon the flames only increases their intensity, so wine, like a violent conflagration, heats the blood, enkindling and exciting the passions to the highest pitch of folly and madness. Witness the excesses into which man is led by hatred, love, revenge, and other passions, when stimulated by intoxicating liquors. The natural effect of this fatal indulgence is to counteract all the results of the moral virtues. These subdue and control the baser passions, but wine excites and urges them to the wildest licentiousness. Judge, therefore, with what vigilance you should guard against the attacks of such an enemy.

Remember, too, that by wine is meant every kind of drink capable of robbing man of the use of his reason or his senses. A philosopher has wisely said that the vine bears three kinds of grapes: one for necessity, one for pleasure, and one for folly. In other words, wine taken with moderation supports our weakness; beyond this limit it only flatters the senses; and drunk to excess it produces a species of madness. Heed no inspiration or thought which you have reason to think is excited by wine, the worst of evil counselors.

Avoid with equal care all disputes or arguments at table, for they are often the beginning of grave quarrels. Be no less moderate in speech than in the indulgence of your appetite; for, as Holy Scripture tells us, "there is no secret where drunkenness reigneth." (*Prov.* 31:4). We shall find rather unbridled tongues, immoderate laughter, vulgar jokes, violent disputes, the revelation of secrets, and many other unhappy consequences of intemperance.

Another evil against which I would warn you is dwelling upon the merits of certain dishes, and condemning others because they are not so delicate. How unworthy it is of man to fix his mind and heart on eating and drinking with such eagerness that the burden of his conversation is on the excellent fish of such a river, the luscious fruit of such a country, and the fine wines of such a region! This is a clear proof that he has lost sight of the true end of eating, which is to support nature, and that, instead of devoting to this work the senses destined for it, he debases his heart and his intelligence to make them also slaves of his gluttony.

Avoid with especial care all attacks upon your neighbor's character. The malicious rapacity which prompts us to tear our neighbor's reputation in pieces was justly condemned by St. John Chrysostom as a species of cannibalism: "Will

you not be satisfied with eating the flesh of animals? Must
you devour human flesh by robbing another of his good
name?" St. Augustine had so great a horror for this vice,
from which so few tables are free, that he inscribed on the
walls of his dining room the following lines:

> "This board allows no vile detractor place
> Whose tongue will charge the absent with disgrace."
> —*Vita Aug*; c. 22

Still another point to which I wish to direct your attention
is the warning given by St. Jerome, that it is better to eat
moderately every day than to fast for several days and then
to eat to excess. A gentle rain, he says, in proper season
benefits the earth, but violent floods only devastate it. (*Ep.
7 ad Loec.*).

Finally, let necessity, not pleasure, govern you in eating
and drinking. I do not say that you must allow your body to
want for nourishment. Oh, no; like any animal destined for
the service of man, your body must be supported. All that is
required is to control it, and never to eat solely for pleasure.
We must conquer, not destroy, the flesh, says St. Bernard;
we must keep it in subjection, that it may not grow proud,
for it belongs to it to obey, not to govern. (*Ep. ad FF, de
Monte Dei.*).

This will suffice to show the importance of this virtue.
But he who would learn more of the happy fruits of temperance, and its salutary effects not only upon the soul but
even upon health, life, honor, and happiness, may read a
special treatise on this subject which we have added to our
book on meditation and prayer.

SECTION IV
The Government of the Senses

The next step in the reformation of the body is the government of the senses. These are the avenues which a Christian should guard with special care, particularly the eyes, which, in the language of Holy Scripture, are the windows through which death enters to rob us of life. Persons desirous of making progress in prayer should be very vigilant in guarding this sense, for this watchfulness not only promotes recollection, but is a most efficacious means of preserving chastity. Without this guard they are a prey to all the vanities which surround them, and which take such possession of the imagination that it is impossible to banish them during prayer. This is the reason of the modesty of the eyes which devout souls observe. Not only do they avoid images which could tarnish the purity of their hearts, but they resolutely turn their eyes from curious objects and worldly vanities, that their mind and heart may be free to converse with God without distraction, and to advance in the knowledge of spiritual things. Prayer is so delicate an exercise that it is impeded not only by sinful images, but also by the representation of objects otherwise harmless in themselves.

The sense of hearing requires a no less vigilant guard, for through it we learn a multitude of things which weary, distract, and even defile the soul. We should protect our ears not only from evil words, but from frivolous conversations, worldly gossip, and idle discourses. During meditation we suffer from a want of vigilance in this respect, for these things are great obstacles to recollection, and persistently interpose between God and the soul in time of prayer.

Little need be said of the sense of smell, for an inordinate love of perfumes and sweet essences is so sensual and so effeminate that most men are ashamed of it, for this is a gratification in which few but women indulge.

Here is a subject upon which there is much to be said, for we are told in Holy Scripture that "death and life are in the power of the tongue." (*Prov.* 18:21). From this we can understand that the happiness or misery of every man depends upon the use he makes of this organ.

St. James asserts this truth no less strongly when he says, "If any man offend not in word, the same is a perfect man. He is able also with a bridle to lead about the whole body. We put bits into the mouths of horses that they may obey us, and we turn about their whole body. Behold also ships, whereas they are great and are driven by strong winds, yet are they turned about with a small helm whithersoever the force of the governor willeth. So the tongue also is, indeed, a little member and boasteth great things. Behold how small a fire kindleth a great wood. And the tongue is a fire, a world of iniquity." (*James* 3:2-6). To govern this great instrument for good we must bear in mind, when we speak, four things: of what we speak, how we speak, the time we speak, and the object for which we speak.

In regard to the first point, what we speak, remember the counsel of the Apostle: "Let no evil speech proceed from your mouth, but that which is good to the edification of faith, that it may administer grace to the hearers. All uncleanness, or covetousness, let it not be so much as named among you, as becometh saints, or obscenity, or foolish talking, or scurrility." (*Eph.* 4:29 and 5:3-4). As the sailor always bears with him a chart indicating the shoals and rocks which could wreck his vessel, so should the Christian bear with him these counsels of the Apostle indicating the shoals of speech which could wreck him in his voyage to eternity. Be no less careful in guarding a secret which has been confided to you, for the betrayal of a trust is one of the vilest faults into which the tongue can lead us.

In regard to the second point, how we are to speak, let us observe a just medium between silence and talkativeness, between timidity and self-sufficiency, between frivolity and pomposity; always speaking with becoming gravity, moderation, sweetness, and simplicity. Beware of haughtily asserting and obstinately persisting in your statements, for this fault gives rise to disputes which wound charity and destroy the peace of the soul. It is the part of a generous nature to yield in such contentions, and a prudent man will follow the counsel of the inspired writer: "In many things be as if thou wert ignorant, and hear in silence and withal seeking." (*Ecclus*. 32:12).

Consider also the necessity of observing when you speak, and always endeavor to select a suitable time: "A parable coming out of a fool's mouth shall be rejected, for he doth not speak it in due season." (*Ecclus*. 20:22).

Finally, we must consider the end for which we speak. There are some whose only purpose is to appear learned. Others desire to parade their wit and conversational powers. The first are thus led into hypocrisy and deceit, and the second become the sport of self-love and vanity. It does not suffice, therefore, that our conversation be good in itself—it must be directed to some good end, such as the glory of God or the profit of our neighbor.

In addition to this we must also consider the persons to whom we speak. For example, it does not become the young to engross the conversation in the presence of their elders, nor the ignorant in the presence of the learned, nor lay persons in the presence of ecclesiastics or religious. When you have reason to think that your words may be untimely or presumptuous, be silent. All persons are not capable of judging correctly in these points, and therefore, in doubt, the wisest course is a prudent silence. We shall thus conform to all the rules we have been considering; for, as the Wise Man says, "Even a fool, if he will hold his peace, shall be counted wise; and if he close his lips, a man of understanding." (*Prov.* 17:28).

SECTION VI
The Mortification of the Passions

Having thus regulated the body and all its senses, the most important reformation still remains to be effected, which is that of the soul with all its powers. Here the first to present itself is the sensitive appetite which comprises all our natural affections: love, hatred, joy, sorrow, fear, hope, anger, and other sentiments of a like nature. This appetite is the inferior part of the soul, which gives us our strongest resemblance to irrational animals, because, like them, it is guided solely by inclination. Nothing degrades us more or leads us further from God. Hence St. Bernard says that if we take away self-love, by which he understands all the movements of the sensitive appetite, there will be no longer any reason for the existence of Hell. (*De Resurrectione Dni.,* Serm. 3).

The sensitive appetite is the arsenal which supplies sin with its most dangerous arms. It is the vulnerable part of the soul, a second Eve, frail and inconstant, heeding the wiles of the old serpent and dragging with her in her fall the unhappy Adam—that is, the superior part of the soul, the seat of the will and the understanding. Original sin is here manifested in all its power. Here the malignity of its poison is concentrated. Here is the field of man's combats, defeats, and victories. Here is the school in which virtue is exercised and trained, for all our courage, all our merit consists in overcoming the blind passions which spring from the sensitive appetite.

This is why our soul is represented sometimes as a vine needing the careful pruning of the husbandman; sometimes as a garden from which the gardener must diligently uproot the weeds of vice to give place to the plants of virtues. It should be the principal occupation of our lives, therefore, to cultivate this garden, ruthlessly plucking from our soul all that can choke the growth of good. We shall thus become true children of God, guided by the motions of the Holy Ghost. We shall thus live as spiritual men, following the guidance of grace and the dictates of reason, and not as those carnal men who, following the irrational animals, obey only the impulse of passion. This subjection of the sensitive appetite is the mortification so much commended in Scripture; the death to which the Apostle so frequently exhorts us; the practice of justice and truth so constantly ex-tolled by David and the other prophets. Therefore, let it be the object of all our labors, all our prayers, and all our pious exercises.

Each one should carefully study his own disposition and inclinations, in order to place the most vigilant guard on the weakest side of his nature. We must wage constant war against all our appetites, but it is particularly necessary to combat the desire of honors, of riches, and of pleasures, for these are the roots of all evil.

Beware, too, of that pride which bears with no opposition. It is a fault which prevails among persons of elevated station accustomed to command, and to deny themselves no caprice. To conquer it, learn to deny yourself innocent grat-ifications, that you may more easily sacrifice those which are unlawful. Learn to bear contradictions with a dignity and patience worthy of a creature who was not made for the things of this world, but who aspires to immortality. Such exercises will render us skillful in the use of spiritual weap-ons, which require no less practice than is necessary for the proper management of material arms. Much more important, however, is a skillful use of the former, for a victory over self, over pride, or over any passion far outweighs all the conquests of the world. Humble yourself, then, in the performance of lowly and obscure works, regardless of the world's opinion; for what can it take from us, or what can it give us, when our inheritance is God Himself?

SECTION VII
The Reformation of the Will

One of the most efficacious means of effecting this reformation is to strengthen and adorn the superior will—that is, the rational appetite—with humility of heart, poverty of spirit, and a holy hatred of self. If we possess these, the labor of mortification is easily accomplished. Humility, according to the definition of St. Bernard, is contempt of self founded on a true knowledge of our baseness. The effect of this virtue is to pluck from our heart all the roots of pride as well as all love of earthly honors and dignities. It inspires us to seek the lowest place, persuading us that had another received the graces we enjoy he would have been more grateful and would have used them more profitably for the glory of God. It is not sufficient that man cherish these sentiments in his heart; they should also be evident in his deportment and surroundings, which, regardless of the world's opinion, should be as humble and simple as his position will admit. And while he maintains the dignity due to his station his heart should ever be ready to submit not only to superiors and equals, but even to inferiors for the love of God.

The second disposition required to strengthen and adorn the will is poverty of spirit, which consists in a voluntary contempt for the things of this world, and in a perfect contentment in the position in which God has placed us, however poor and lowly it may be. This virtue effectually destroys cupidity, and affords us so great a peace and contentment that Seneca did not hesitate to affirm that he who closed his heart to the claims of unruly desires was not inferior in wealth or happiness to Jupiter himself. By this he signified that as man's misery springs from unfulfilled desires, he may be said to be very near the summit of happiness who has learned to subdue his desires so that they cannot disturb him.

The third disposition is a holy hatred of ourselves. "He that loveth his life shall lose it," says Our Saviour, "and he that hateth his life in this world keepeth it unto life eternal." (*Jn.* 12:25). By this hatred of self Our Lord did not mean that wicked hatred in which they indulge who yield to despair, but that aversion which the saints experienced for their flesh, which they regarded as the source of many evils and as a great obstacle to good. Hence they subjected it to the empire of reason, and denied its inordinate desires, that it might continue a humble servant and willing helper of the soul.

If we treat it otherwise we shall realize these words of the Wise Man: "He that nourisheth his servant delicately from his childhood, afterwards shall find him stubborn." (*Prov.* 29:21). This hatred of self is our chief instrument in the work of salvation. It enables us to uproot and cast from us all our evil inclinations, however much nature may rebel. Without it how could we strike rude blows, penetrate to the quick with the knife of mortification, and tear from our hearts objects upon which our affections are centered? Yes, the arm of mortification, which draws its force as much from hatred of self as from love of God, enables us to treat our failings with the firmness of a skillful physician, and relentlessly to cut and burn with no other thought than to rid the soul of every evil tendency. Having developed this subject in the *Memorial of a Christian Life*, we shall not here speak of it at greater length.

SECTION VIII
The Government of the Imagination

Besides these two faculties of the sensitive appetite there are two others, imagination and understanding, which belong to the intellect. The imagination, a less elevated power than the understanding, is of all the faculties the one in which the effects of original sin are most evident, and which is least under the control of reason. It continually escapes our vigilance, and like a restless child runs hither and thither, sometimes flying to the remotest corners of the world before we are aware of its ramblings. It seizes with avidity upon objects which allure it, persistently returning after we have withdrawn it from them. If, therefore, instead of controlling this restless faculty, we treat it like a spoiled child, indulging all its caprices, we strengthen its evil tendencies, and in time of prayer we shall vainly seek to restrain it. Unaccustomed to pious objects, it will rebel against us.

Knowing the dangerous propensities of this power, we should vigilantly guard it and cut off from it all unprofitable reflections. To do this effectually we must carefully examine the thoughts presented to our minds, that we may see which we shall admit and which we shall reject. If we are careless in this respect, ideas and sentiments will penetrate our hearts and not only weaken devotion and diminish fervor, but destroy charity, which is the life of the soul.

We read in Holy Scripture that while his doorkeeper, who should have been cleansing wheat, fell asleep, assassins entered the house of Isboseth, son of Saul, and slew him. (Cf. *2 Kg.* 4). A like fate will be ours if we permit sleep to overcome our judgment, which should be employed in separating the chaff from the grain—that is, good thoughts from evil thoughts. While unprotected, bad desires, the assassins of the soul, in this manner are able to enter and rob us of the life of grace.

But this vigilance not only serves to preserve the life of the soul, but most efficaciously promotes recollection in prayer; for as a wandering and uncontrolled imagination is a source of much trouble in prayer, so a subdued imagination accustomed to pious subjects sweetens our conversation with God.

SECTION IX
The Government of the Understanding

We have now come to the greatest and noblest of the faculties, the understanding, which raises man above all visible creatures, and in which he most resembles his Creator. The beauty of this power depends upon that rare virtue, prudence, which excels all others. In the spiritual life prudence is to the soul what the eyes are to the body, what a pilot is to a vessel, what a head is to a commonwealth. For this reason the great St. Anthony, in a conference with several holy monks on the excellence of the virtues, gave the first place to prudence, which guides and controls all the others.

Let him, therefore, who desires to practice the other virtues with profit earnestly endeavor to be guided by prudence in all things. Not limited to any special duty, it enters into the fulfillment of all duties, into the practice of all virtues, and preserves order and harmony among them. Having the foundation of faith and charity, it first belongs to prudence to direct all our actions to God, who is our last end. As self-love, according to a holy writer, seeks self in all things, even the holiest, prudence is ever ready to examine what are the motives of our actions, whether we have God or self as the end of what we do.

Prudence also guides us in our intercourse with our neighbor, that we may afford him edification and not give him scandal. To this end it teaches us to observe the condition and character of those about us, that we may more wisely benefit them, patiently bearing with their failings and closing our eyes to infirmities which we cannot cure. "A wise man," says Aristotle, "should not expect the same degree of certainty in all things, for some are more susceptible of proof than others. Nor should he expect the same degree of perfection in all creatures, for some are capable of a perfection which is impossible in others. Whoever, therefore, would force all lives to the same standard of virtue would do more harm than good."

Prudence also teaches us to know ourselves, our inclinations, our failings, and our evil tendencies, that we may not presume upon our strength, but recognizing our enemies, perseveringly combat them. It is this virtue also which enables us wisely to govern the tongue by the rules which we have already given, teaching us when to be silent and when to speak. Prudence likewise guards us against the error of opening our minds to all whom we may meet, or of making confidants of others without due reflection. By putting a just restraint upon our words, it saves us from too freely expressing our opinion and thereby committing many faults.

Thus we are kept constantly reminded of the words of Solomon: "A fool uttereth all his mind; a wise man deferreth and keepeth it till afterwards." (*Prov.* 29:11). Prudence also forearms us against dangers, and strengthens us by prayer and meditation to meet all the accidents of life. This is the advice of the sacred writer: "Before sickness take a medicine." (*Ecclus.* 18:20).

Whenever, therefore, you expect to participate in entertainments, or to transact business with men who are easily angered, or to encounter any danger, endeavor to foresee the perils of the occasion and arm yourself against them. Prudence guides us in the treatment of our bodies, causing us to observe a just medium between excessive rigor and immoderate indulgence, so that we may neither unduly weaken the flesh nor so strengthen it that it will rule the spirit.

It is also the duty of prudence to introduce moderation into all our works, even the holiest, and to preserve us from exhausting the spirit by indiscreet labor. We read in the rules of St. Francis that the spirit must rule our occupations, not be ruled by them. Our exterior labors should never cause us to lose sight of interior duties, nor should devotion to our neighbor make us forget what we owe to God. If the Apostles, who possessed such abundant grace, deemed it expedient to renounce the care of temporal things in order to devote themselves to the great work of preaching and other spiritual functions (Cf. *Acts* 6:2-4), it is presumption in us to suppose that we have strength and virtue capable of undertaking many arduous labors at one time.

Finally, prudence enlightens us concerning the snares of the enemy, counseling us, in the words of the Apostles, "to try spirits if they be of God," "for Satan transformeth himself into an angel of light." (*1 Jn.* 4:1 and *2 Cor.* 11:14). There is no temptation more to be feared than one which presents itself under the mask of virtue, and there is none which the devil more frequently employs to deceive pious souls. Inspired and guided by prudence, we shall recognize these snares; we shall be restrained by a salutary fear from going where there is danger, but animated by a holy courage to conquer in every struggle; we shall avoid extremes; we shall endeavor to prevent our neighbor from suffering scandal, but yet we shall not be daunted by every groundless fear; we shall learn to despise the opinions of the world, and not to fear its outcries against virtue, remembering, with the Apostle, that if we please men we cannot be the servants of Jesus Christ. (Cf. *Gal.* 1:10).

SECTION X
Prudence in Temporal Affairs

The virtue of prudence is no less efficacious in the direction of temporal affairs. It preserves us from serious, and sometimes from irremediable, errors which not unfrequently destroy both our material and spiritual welfare. To escape this double misfortune, here are the counsels which prudence suggests: The first is that of the Wise Man, who says: "Let thy eyes look straight on, and let thy eyelids go before thy steps." (*Prov.* 4:25). In other words, look at the enterprise you are about to undertake, and do not rashly enter upon it. First recommend it to God; then weigh all its circumstances, and the consequences which are likely to follow from it; seek counsel of just minds concerning it; deliberate upon the advice you receive, and reflect upon your resolution before acting upon it.

In a word, beware of the four great enemies of prudence: precipitation, passion, obstinate persistence in our own opinions, and vanity. Precipitation admits no reasoning; passion blinds us; obstinancy turns a deaf ear to all counsel; and vanity ruins everything.

It also belongs to prudence to observe a just medium in all things, for extremes are no less opposed to virtue than to truth. Let not the faults of a few lead you to condemn the multitude, nor should the virtues of a few lead you to suppose that all are pious. Follow the guidance of reason in all things, and do not allow yourself to be hurried to extremes by passion or prejudice. This latter failing is apt, moreover, to dispose us favorably towards what is old, and give us a dislike for what is new. Prudence guards us against this, for age can no more justify what is bad than novelty can condemn what is good. Let us esteem things not for their age, but for their merit. A vice of long standing is only more difficult to eradicate, and a virtue of recent growth has only the fault of being unknown.

Beware also of appearances. There are few who have not been taught by experience how deceptive these often are.

Finally, let us be thoroughly convinced that as reflection and gravity are the inseparable companions of prudence, so rashness and levity ever accompany folly. Therefore, we must guard against these two faults at all times, but particularly in the following cases: in believing everything that is reported, for this indicates levity of mind; in making promises, in which we often bind ourselves beyond our means; in giving, in which liberality often makes us forget justice; in forming resolutions which from want of consideration often lead us into errors; in conversation, in which so many faults may be committed; and in temptations to anger, which shows the folly of man. "He that is patient," says Solomon, "is governed with much wisdom, but he that is impatient exalteth his folly." (*Prov.* 14:29).

SECTION XI

Means of Acquiring this Virtue

Not the least important means of acquiring this virtue is the experience of our own failures and the success of others, from which we may gather wise lessons of prudence. For this reason the past is said to be a wise counselor, for today learns from yesterday. "What is it that hath been? The same thing that shall be. What is it that hath been done? The same that shall be done." (*Eccles.* 1:9). But a still more efficacious means of becoming prudent is humility, for pride is the greatest obstacle to this virtue. "Where pride is, there also shall be reproach," the Holy Ghost tells us; "but where humility is, there also is wisdom." (*Prov.* 11:2). And throughout the Scriptures we are frequently reminded that God instructs the humble and reveals His secrets to the lowly.

Humility, however, does not require us to yield blindly to all opinions or indiscreetly to follow every counsel. This is not humility, but weakness and instability, against which the author of Ecclesiasticus warns us: "Be not lowly in thy wisdom, lest being humbled thou be deceived into folly." (*Ecclus.* 13:11). By this we should understand that a man must resolutely maintain the truth and vigorously support justice, not allowing himself to be carried away by contrary opinions.

Finally, devout and humble prayer will afford us powerful aid in acquiring the virtue of prudence. For the principal office of the Holy Ghost being to enlighten the understanding with the gifts of knowledge, wisdom, and counsel, the greater the humility and devotion with which we present ourselves before this Divine Spirit, the greater will be the grace we shall receive.

CHAPTER 41

Man's Duty to his Neighbor

Man's duty towards his neighbor is embraced in the practice of charity and mercy. Read Holy Scriptures and you will appreciate the importance of these virtues. The writings of the prophets, Apostles, and evangelists abound with counsels concerning them.

God teaches us in Isaias that one of the duties of justice is charity to our neighbor. Thus when the Jews exclaimed: "Why have we fasted, and thou hast not regarded; have we humbled our souls, and thou hast not taken notice?" God answers: "In the day of your fast your own will is found, and you exact of all your debtors. You fast for debates and strife, and strike with the fist wickedly. Is this such a fast as I have chosen? Is not this rather the fast that I have chosen—loose the bands of wickedness; undo the bundles that oppress; let them that are broken go free; and break asunder every burden. Deal thy bread to the hungry, and bring the needy and harborless into thy house. When thou shalt see one naked, cover him, and despise not thy own flesh. Then shalt thou call, and the Lord shall hear, and give thee rest continually, and fill thy soul with brightness." (*Is.* 58). The prophet continues to the end of the chapter to declare the blessings with which God will reward this charity to our neighbor.

Behold how highly the great Apostle extols the virtue of charity; how strongly he recommends it; how minutely he enumerates its advantages. He gives it the first place among the virtues, and tells us that it is the bond of perfection, the end of the commandments, and the fulfillment of the law. (Cf. *1 Cor.* 13:13; *Col.* 3:14; *1 Tim.* 1:5; *Rom.* 13:8; *Gal.* 5:14).

It would be difficult to say more in praise of charity. Certainly these words of the Apostle must suffice to make you love and practice this virtue, if you desire to be pleasing to God.

Charity was also a favorite virtue with the beloved disciple. He frequently mentions it in his epistles, with the highest praise and commendation. And not only in his writings but in his discourse did he display the same devotedness to this virtue. So frequently did he repeat to his disciples the touching words, "My little children, love one another," that at last, as St. Jerome tells us, they became somewhat weary of always hearing the same, and asked him: Good master, why do you always give us this one command? His answer, says St. Jerome, was worthy of John: "Because it is the command of the Lord; and if you do this alone it will suffice." (*De Scriptoribus Eccles.*). Without doubt, therefore, he who desires to please God must fulfill this great precept of charity, not only in word but also in deed. "He that hath the substance of this world," says St. John, "and shall see his brother in need, and shall shut up his bowels from him, how doth the charity of God abide in him? My little children, let us not love in word nor in tongue, but in deed and in truth." (*1 Jn.* 3:17-18).

Among the works comprised in charity to our neighbor the following are the most important: advice, counsel, succor, forbearance, pardon, edification. These are so strongly linked with charity that the practice of them indicates the progress we have made in the practice of charity.

There are Christians who pretend to love their neighbor, but their charity goes no further than words. Others are willing to give advice, but no more substantial proof of their charity. Others will perform both these duties, but will not refrain from resenting an injury, or will refuse to bear with the infirmities of their neighbor, forgetting that the Apostle tells us: "Bear ye one another's burdens, and so you shall fulfill the law of Christ." (*Gal.* 6:2).

Others, again, while not resenting an injury, continue to harbor it in their hearts and will not freely pardon it. Finally, many fulfill all these obligations, yet in their words or conduct they fail to give their neighbor that edification which is the most important duty of charity. Let us diligently examine our hearts and our actions, and learn how far we fulfill the precepts of this virtue.

It may be said that he who simply loves his neighbor possesses the first degree of charity; he who gives him good counsel possesses the second; he who assists him in poverty or distress possesses the third; he who patiently bears an injury possesses the fourth; he who freely pardons it, the fifth; and he who in addition to all these fulfills the duty of edification to his neighbor has attained the highest degree of charity.

The works of which we have just been treating are what are called positive acts of charity, which teach us what we ought to do for our neighbor. Besides these there are others, called negative duties, which indicate what we must avoid in our intercourse with our neighbor. Such are judging rashly, speaking evil, using abusive or insulting language, injuring his honor or reputation, and giving scandal by words or evil counsel. If you would fulfill the law of charity, avoid all these.

To reduce to practice what we have said, let your love for your neighbor be like that of a mother for her child. See with what devotion a good mother cares for her child; how prudently she counsels him in danger; how faithfully she assists him in his necessities; how ingenious she is in regard to his faults, sometimes patiently bearing them, at other times justly punishing them, or again prudently ignoring them. How earnestly she rejoices in his prosperity; how deeply she grieves at his misfortune as if it were her own! How zealous she is for his honor and advancement; how fervently she prays for him; how cheerfully she denies herself to give to him; how utterly she forgets herself in her care of him! Your charity would be perfect did it resemble this. Though you may not attain this degree, you must nevertheless aspire to it, for the higher you aim the more noble will be your conduct.

You will doubtless urge that you cannot feel such affection for one who is a stranger to you. But you should not regard your neighbor as a stranger. Behold in him rather the image of God, the work of His divine hands, and a living member of Christ. (Cf. *Rom.* 12:5). Hence St. Paul tells us that when we sin against our neighbor we sin against Christ. (Cf. *1 Cor.* 8:12). Look on your neighbor, therefore, not as a man but as Christ Himself, or one of His living members; for though he is not so in body, he is truly so by participation in the spirit of Christ, and by the reward which is promised to us, for Christ assures us that He will consider as done to Himself all that we do to our neighbor.

Think of the affection which ties of blood establish between creatures, and blush to let nature influence you more powerfully than grace. You will doubtless urge that your relatives are descended with you from the same ancestor, and that the same blood flows in your veins. Remember, however, that there are closer and stronger bonds uniting us as brethren in Christ. In God we have one Father; in the Church one mother; and in Jesus Christ one Lord and Saviour. One faith springs from the same source which enlightens all Christians and distinguishes them from the rest of men.

The object of our hope is the same kingdom, where we

shall have but one heart and one soul. Baptism has made us children of the same Father, brothers and heirs of the same inheritance. Our souls are nourished with the same Food, the adorable Body of our Lord Jesus Christ, who makes us one with Himself. Finally, we are united in a participation of the same Holy Spirit, who dwells in us by faith alone or by the union of faith and grace, communicating to us life and strength. Behold the union which exists between the members of the same body, however diverse their functions, because they are animated by one soul! How much greater should be the union between the faithful who are animated by the same Divine Spirit, the Holy Ghost Himself!

But, above all, ever keep before your eyes the incomparable example of Our Saviour's love for us. Why did He love us with so much tenderness, devotion, and generosity, if not to encourage us by His example, and oblige us by His benefits faithfully to fulfill the precept which He has imposed upon us? "A new commandment I give unto you," were His parting words to His Apostles on the night before He suffered; "that you love one another, as I have loved you." (*Jn.* 13:34). Having treated this subject at greater length in a work on *Prayer and Meditation,* I would refer the reader to it for a more complete development of this virtue.

CHAPTER 42

Man's Duty to God

SECTION I
Man's Duties in General

The third and noblest obligation of justice comprises man's duty to God, which includes the practice of the three theological virtues, faith, hope, and charity, and of that virtue called religion, which has for its object the worship due to God.

To love God with the affection of a dutiful son is the most secure way of fulfilling this obligation, as the most effective means of discharging the other duties of justice is to be to ourselves an upright judge, and to our neighbor a kind and watchful mother.

Consider, then, how a good son manifests his love for his father. How great is his devotion, his fear, his reverence for him! How faithfully he obeys him; how zealously and disinterestedly he serves him! With what confidence he goes to him in all his necessities! With what submission he accepts his corrections! How patiently he bears his reproofs! Only serve God with such a heart, and you will faithfully fulfill this obligation of justice.

But to attain these dispositions the following virtues seem to me indispensable: love, holy fear, confidence, zeal for the glory of God, purity of intention, the spirit of prayer, gratitude, conformity to the will of God, humility, and patience in tribulation.

SECTION II
The Love of God

Our first duty is to love God, as He has commanded us, with our whole heart, with our whole soul, and with our whole strength. (Cf. *Deut.* 6:5). All our faculties must cooperate in loving and serving this great Master: the understanding by frequently thinking of Him; the will by loving Him; the passions by turning their strength to His service; the senses and members by zealously executing whatever His love prescribes.

As the *Memorial of a Christian Life* contains a treatise on this subject, we refer the reader to it for a more complete discussion of this virtue.

SECTION III
The Fear of God

After love comes fear, which in fact springs from love. For the greater our love for another, the greater is our fear not only of losing him but of offending him. See how carefully a good son avoids anything that could displease his father, or a loving wife all that could displease her husband. This fear is the guardian of innocence, and for this reason we should deeply engrave it in our souls, praying with David that the Lord may pierce our flesh with His holy fear. (Cf. *Ps.* 118:120). This pious monarch desired that even his flesh should be penetrated with this salutary fear, that, piercing his heart like a thorn, it might unceasingly warn him against all that could lead him to offend God, the object of his love and fear. It was for this reason that the inspired author wrote, "The fear of the Lord driveth out sin." (*Ecclus.* 1:27).

The effect of this fear is not only to make us avoid actions that are positively sinful, but even those that may lead us into evil or endanger our virtue. These words of Job, "I feared all my works, knowing that thou didst not spare the offender" (*Job* 9:28), testify how deeply this sentiment was imprinted in his soul.

If we are penetrated with this salutary fear it will be manifest in our bearing when we enter God's house, and particularly in the presence of the Blessed Sacrament. We shall beware of irreverently talking or gazing about us as if we were unconscious of the dread Majesty in whose temple we are.

The love of God, as we have already said, is the first source of this fear. Servile fear, however, which is the fear, not of a son, but of a slave, is, in a measure, profitable, for it introduces filial fear as the needle introduces the thread. But we shall strengthen and confirm this sentiment of holy fear by reflecting upon the incomprehensible majesty of God, the severity of His judgments, the rigor of His justice, the multitude of our sins, and particularly our resistance to divine inspirations.

SECTION IV
Confidence in God

To fear we must also join confidence. Like a child who fears no danger in his father's protecting arms, we must cast ourselves into the arms of our Heavenly Father, confident that those Hands which sustain the heavens are all powerful to supply our necessities, to uphold us in temptation, and to turn all things to our profit. And why should we not have confidence in God? Is He not the most powerful as well as the most tender of fathers? If your want of merit and the number of your sins alarm and discourage you, fix your thoughts upon the goodness of God, upon His adorable Son, our Redeemer and Mediator, who died to expiate our sins.

When you are crossing a rapid stream, and the turbulence of the waters makes you dizzy, instead of looking down at the torrent you look above, and your steadiness is restored. Do likewise when disturbed by the fears we have mentioned. Do not dwell upon your unworthiness or your failings, but raise your eyes to God and consider the infinite goodness and mercy with which He deigns to apply a remedy to all our miseries. Reflect upon the truth of His words, for He has promised to help and comfort all who humbly and confidently invoke His sacred name. Consider also the innumerable benefits which you have hitherto received from His paternal hand, and let His bounty in the past inspire you to trust the future to Him with renewed hope.

Above all, consider the merits and sufferings of Christ, which are our principal title to God's grace and mercy, and which form the treasure whence the Church supplies the necessities of her children. It was from a confidence inspired by such motives that the saints drew that strength which rendered them as firm as Mount Sion, and established them in the holy city whence they never could be moved. (Cf. *Ps.* 124:1). Yet, notwithstanding these powerful reasons for hope, it is deplorable that this virtue should still be so weak in us. We lose heart at the first appearance of danger, and go down into Egypt hoping for help from Pharaoh (Cf. *Is.* 30:2)—that is, we turn to creatures instead of God. There are many servants of God who zealously devote themselves to fasting, prayer, and almsgiving, but few who possess the confidence with which the virtuous Susanna was animated, even when condemned to death and led to execution. (Cf. *Dan.* 13). Read the Holy Scriptures, particularly the Psalms and the writings of the prophets, and you will find abundant motives for unfailing hope in God.

Section V
Zeal for the Glory of God

Zeal consists in promoting the honor of God and striving to advance the fulfillment of His will on earth, even as it is accomplished in Heaven. If we love God we cannot but be pierced with grief to behold so many not only neglecting to obey His holy will, but even acting in a manner directly opposed to it. Full of this zeal was David when he cried out, "The zeal of thy house hath eaten me up." (*Ps.* 68:10). Strive to imitate him, doing what you can by word and example, as well as by prayer, to increase the honor of God through the salvation of souls. Thus may you hope to receive that mark, mentioned by the prophet, which will sign you as one of the elect of God. (Cf. *Ezech.* 9:4).

Section VI
Purity of Intention

This virtue, which is intimately connected with zeal, enables us to forget ourselves in all things, and to seek first the glory of God and the accomplishment of His good pleasure, persuaded that the more we sacrifice our own interests in His service, the greater advantage and blessing we shall reap. For this reason we must examine the motives of all our actions, that we may labor purely for God, since nothing is more subtle than self-love, which insinuates itself into every work, unless we maintain a constant guard. Many who now seem rich in good works will be found very poor at the day of judgment for lack of this pure intention. This is the virtue which Our Lord symbolized when He said: "The light of thy body is thy eye. If thy eye be single thy whole body shall be lightsome. But if thy eye be evil thy whole body shall be darksome." (*Matt.* 6:22-23).

We often see men in high positions lead irreproachable

lives, carefully avoiding anything unbecoming the dignity of their station; but, in many cases, what is the motive which animates them? They see that virtue befits their position, and consequently they practice it, in order to discharge the duties of their office in a manner that will seem becoming, or to secure promotion to still greater dignities. Thus the principle of their actions is not the fear or the love of God, or obedience to His divine will, but their own interest. Such virtue may deceive men, but in the eyes of God it is as smoke; it is only the shadow of justice.

The practice of the moral virtues and the most severe mortifications are meritorious before God only inasmuch as they are animated by His Divine Spirit.

The temple of Jerusalem contained nothing which was not either of gold or covered with gold. It is no less fitting that in our souls, the living temples of the Divinity, there should be nothing that is not charity or animated by it. Let us bear in mind that God values the intention more than the action, and that the simplest work becomes noble when performed with a noble intention, while the greatest will be of little value if performed from an indifferent motive.

By endeavoring to acquire this purity of intention we shall follow the example and counsel of Our Saviour, who tells us to love as He has loved (Cf. *Jn.* 13:34)—that is, purely and disinterestedly. Happy is he who imitates this noblest characteristic of the divine love. Rapid will be his growth in the likeness of God, and consequently in His love, for resemblance usually begets love. Let us rid ourselves of human respect, and, keeping God ever before our eyes, let us not suffer selfish or worldly motives to mar the merit of our good works and rob us of their reward, which is Heaven and the possession of God Himself.

As it is a difficult undertaking to acquire this virtue, we must earnestly ask it of God, especially in the Lord's Prayer, frequently repeating with fervor, "Thy will be done on earth, as it is in Heaven." Beg of Him to grant you grace to imitate on earth the purity and devotion with which the heavenly choirs bless and fulfill His adorable will.

Section VII
Prayer

Having in another work treated more fully of this subject, I would here only urge you to turn to God in childlike prayer whenever afflictions or temptations come upon you. Strive, moreover, to maintain the spirit of prayer, and thus you will preserve a continual recollection of God. You will live in His presence, and His love will abide in your heart. Finally, prayer will enable you most faithfully and frequently to testify your filial reverence and love for your Heavenly Father.

Section VIII
Gratitude

Gratitude, which should be in our hearts and on our lips, is a virtue which excites us to praise God unceasingly for all His benefits: "I will bless the Lord at all times; his praise shall be always in my mouth. Let my mouth be filled with praise, that I may sing thy glory, thy greatness all the day long." (*Ps.* 33:1 and 70:8). Since God not only gives us life, but continues to preserve it, protecting us, lavishing blessings on us, and causing all creatures to serve our necessities and desires, is it not just that we should continually praise Him?

Thanksgiving, therefore, should be the first of all our exercises, and, according to St. Basil, it should form the beginning of all our prayers. Morning and evening, and at all times, we should render thanks to God for His many benefits, general and particular, of nature and of grace; but, above all, for the incomprehensible benefits of Redemption and the Blessed Sacrament of the altar. Let us bear in mind that in all these blessings He sought only our welfare. He could expect nothing; He desired nothing from us. Out of pure love for us He gave us all.

SECTION IX
Obedience

Obedience is a virtue which renders us most pleasing to God, for it embraces the perfection of justice. We distinguish in this virtue three degrees: The first is obedience to the commandments of God, the second to His counsels, the third to His inspirations. The first is absolutely necessary for salvation; the second facilitates the observance of the commandments, for if we neglect the counsels, as far as our state permits, we risk violating the precepts. If, for instance, you avoid needlessly affirming the truth with an oath, you will more easily escape perjury. If you avoid all contentions you will assuredly secure peace and charity. If you renounce your own worldly possessions, you will not be tempted to covet those of your neighbor. If you return good for evil, you will be saved from the passion of revenge. Thus we see that the counsels form the bulwarks which guard the commandments.

If you would make your salvation secure do not be satisfied with observing the commandments only, but add the practice of the counsels as far as your state will admit. In traversing a rapid river you do not cross it in a direct line, for if you did so you would be borne beyond the place at which you wished to land. Rather, you go higher up the stream to have the advantage of the tide, and thus secure a safe passage to the point at which you desire to embark. Do likewise in spiritual things. Aim higher than is necessary, so that if you fail you may at least reach the mark of what is indispensable for salvation.

The third degree of obedience, as we have said, consists in fidelity to divine inspirations. Good servants do not confine their obedience to the formal commands of their master, but promptly execute the least indication of his will. So should we act towards God. This is a subject, however, in which we are exposed to grave illusions by mistaking the whisperings of self-love or the suggestions of the devil for divine inspirations. Hence we must follow the counsel of St. John and "believe not every spirit, but try the spirits if they be of God." (*1 Jn.* 4:1).

We have for our guidance in this respect, besides Holy Scripture and the teaching of the saints, this general rule: The service of God embraces two kinds of acts, one of which is of our own choice, the other of obligation. However meritorious works of our own choice may be, we must always select what is of obligation in preference to them.

This is the teaching of the Holy Spirit: "Obedience is better than sacrifices." (*1 Kg.* 15:22). God first requires of us the faithful fulfillment of His word. When our obedience in this respect is perfect, we may follow the guidance of pious inspirations.

This fidelity to the word of God comprises, first, obedience to the commandments, without which there is no salvation; secondly, obedience to our lawful superiors, for the Apostle tells us, "He that resisteth the power, resisteth the ordinance of God" (*Rom.* 13:2); thirdly, obedience to the laws of our state, whether it be the priesthood, religion, or marriage; and, fourthly, fidelity to practices which, though not of precept, greatly facilitate the observance of the commandments.

For example, if you find, by daily reflecting upon your faults and by asking God to inspire you with the most efficacious means of correcting them, that you lead a more regular life, that you acquire more control over your passions, and that your heart becomes more inclined to virtue; while, on the other hand, your neglect of these precautions weakens your virtue, throws you back into many failings, and exposes you to the danger of relapsing into former evil habits, you cannot doubt that God calls you to these pious exercises. Experience has taught you that they are the means which He has chosen to enable you to overcome your sins and to prevent you from committing them again. God does not, it is true, formally command these practices, but He strongly exhorts you to embrace them if you would faithfully fulfill what He does command.

Again, if you find that you are self-indulgent and opposed to everything which disturbs you, and that this love of comfort hinders your spiritual progress and leads you to neglect good works because they are laborious and painful, while you indulge in culpable actions because they are attractive and pleasant, you must conclude that God calls you to practice mortification and to overcome your appetite for pleasure by penance and austerities. Examine all your propensities in this way, and you will easily discern what will be most profitable to you. Be always guided, however, in this respect, by the counsels of your superiors.

Thus we see that we are not always to choose what is best in itself, but what is best for us. Hence there are many excellent practices from which we would derive no advantage, either because they are above our strength or because God does not call us to embrace them. Then let us not soar above our state; let us aspire to what will strengthen us, not to what will overwhelm us. "Lift not up thy eyes to riches which thou canst not have," says Holy Scripture, "because they shall make themselves wings like those of an eagle, and shall fly towards heaven." (*Prov.* 23:5).

Among those acts which we are free to do or not to do, some are performed in public, others in secret. The former procure us temporal pleasure or advantage, while the latter bring no such reward. In general, prefer what is done in secret without any temporal recompense. You will thus preserve yourself from the snares of self-love, which, as we have already said, insinuates itself into the holiest actions. For this reason a certain man remarkable for his piety was accustomed to say, "Do you know where God is? He is where you are not." By this he meant that where self-interest has not penetrated, there only can God be sought and found.

We do not counsel you to follow this rule so rigidly as to exclude good deeds that are public or profitable. Oh, no; that would be a reprehensible extreme, for very often there is great merit in overcoming the promptings of self-love to which these deeds expose us. Our intention is only to warn you against the artifices of self-love, that you may ever distrust it, particularly when it presents itself under the mask of virtue.

These three degrees which constitute the perfection of obedience seem to be indicated in these words of the Apostle: "Be not conformed to this world, but be reformed in the newness of your mind, that you may prove what is the good, and the acceptable, and the perfect will of God." (*Rom.* 12:2). The observance of the commandments is *good;* the practice of the counsels is *acceptable;* and fidelity to divine inspirations is *perfect.* When one has learned to practice these three degrees he has attained the perfection of obedience.

Another virtue, which may be considered a fourth degree of obedience, is conformity to the divine will in all things. This enables us to accept from the hands of God, with equal submission, honor or ignominy, obscurity or renown, stripes or caresses, health or sickness, life or death; for we look, not at our chastisements, but at Him who inflicts them through love of us. An earthly father loves his child when he corrects him no less than when he caresses him. Does his love bear any comparison to the love of the Heavenly Father? Let us realize, then, that all that comes from His hand is for our welfare, and we shall become so firmly established in submission to His holy will that He may mold us according to His good pleasure, as clay in the hands of the potter.

Thus we shall no longer live for ourselves, but for God. We shall be happy only in accomplishing His divine will, in doing all things, in bearing all things for His glory, and acting at all times as His submissive servants. Such were the sentiments of David when he said, "I am become as a beast before thee, and I am always with thee." (*Ps.* 72:23). A beast of burden goes not where he wills, nor rests when he pleases, but lives in complete obedience to his master. A Christian should live in like submission to the will of His Heavenly Father.

Let us not forget, however, that this submission to God, and this promptness in obeying Him, must ever be accompanied by prudence and judgment, so that we may not mistake our own will for that of God. In most cases let us distrust what flatters our own inclinations, and proceed with more confidence when we are acting contrary to our personal interests.

This is the most pleasing sacrifice we can make to God. In other sacrifices we offer Him only our possessions. In this we immolate ourselves. St. Augustine says that though God is the Lord of all that exists, yet it is not everyone who can say with the Psalmist, "O Lord! I am thy servant" (*Ps.* 115:16), but those only who have renounced their own will and consecrated themselves to His service. There is, moreover, no better disposition for attaining the perfection of a Christian life.

As God in His infinite goodness is ever ready to overwhelm us with His graces when we offer no obstacle to His merciful designs, whoever is perfectly confined to His will can justly expect an abundance of His favors. Yes, God will treat him with great liberality, and will make him, like another David, a man after His own Heart.

SECTION X
Patience in Afflictions

To arrive at perfect obedience to God's will, there is no more efficacious means than patience under sufferings of every kind. "My son," says Solomon, "reject not the correction of the Lord, and do not faint when thou art chastised by him; for whom the Lord loveth he chastiseth, and as a father in the son he pleaseth himself." (*Prov.* 3:11-12).

St. Paul quotes these words and develops them at considerable length in his Epistle to the Hebrews: "Persevere," he says, "under discipline. God dealeth with you as with his sons, for what son is there whom the father doth not correct? But if you be without chastisement, whereof all are made partakers, then are you bastards, and not sons. Moreover, we have had fathers of our flesh for instructors, and we reverenced them. Shall we not much more obey the Father of spirits, and live?" (*Heb.* 12:7-9).

Since, then, it is the duty of a good father to correct and reprove his children, it is the duty of a good son patiently to endure the correction and accept it as a proof of love. This is the lesson which the Son of the Eternal Father taught when He said to St. Peter, "The chalice which my Father hath given me, shall I not drink it?" (*Jn.* 18:11). Were the chalice of suffering offered us by another hand we might with reason refuse it; but the knowledge that it is sent by the wisest and tenderest of Fathers should suffice to make us accept it without hesitation. Nevertheless there are Christians, perfectly conformed to the divine will in prosperity, whose submission vanishes at the approach of adversity.

They are like cowards, who vaunt their courage in time of peace, but throw down their arms and fly at the first sound of battle. Life is full of combats and trials. Strengthen your soul, therefore, by salutary reflections, that in the hour of conflict you may be perfectly submissive to the divine will.

Remember that the sufferings of this life bear no proportion to the rewards of the next. The happiness of Heaven is so great, so unspeakable, that we would gladly purchase one hour of its enjoyment by the sacrifice of all earthly pleasures and by the endurance of all earthly sorrows. But we have not to buy it even at this rate, for, as the Apostle says, "that which is at present momentary and light of our tribulation worketh for us above measure exceedingly an eternal weight of glory." (*2 Cor.* 4:17).

Consider also the different effects of prosperity and adversity. The former inflates us with pride; the latter humbles and purifies us. In prosperity we often forget to whom we owe all that we are; but adversity usually brings us to the feet of our Creator. Prosperity often causes us to lose the fruits of our best actions; but adversity enables us to expiate our past failings, and preserves us against future relapses. If you are afflicted by sickness, consider that God has doubtless permitted this to preserve you from the abuse you might have made of your health; for it is better to languish under bodily sufferings than gradually to destroy the life of the soul by sin.

Certainly God, who is so merciful, takes no pleasure in our afflictions, but in His love He sends us these necessary remedies to cure our infirmities. Thus suffering purifies the stains of sinful pleasures, and the privation of innocent gratifications expiates unlawful indulgence. He punishes us in this world, that He may reward us in the next; He treats us with merciful rigor here to save us from His wrath in eternity. Hence St. Jerome says that God's anger against sinners is never more terrible than when He seems to forget them during life. It was through fear of such a misfortune that St. Augustine prayed, "Here, O Lord, burn, here cut, that Thou mayst spare me in eternity."

Behold how carefully God guards you, that you may not abandon yourself to your evil inclinations. When a physician finds the condition of his patient hopeless he indulges him in all his caprices, but while there is any hope of recovery he rigidly restricts him to a certain diet and forbids him all that could aggravate his malady. In like manner, parents refuse their children the money they have accumulated only for them when they find they are squandering it in play and riotous living. Thus are we treated by God, the sovereign Physician and most loving Father of us all, when He sends us trials and privations.

Consider also the sufferings which Our Saviour endured from creatures. He was bruised, and buffeted, and spat upon. With what patience He bore the mockery of the multitude! With what resignation he drank the bitter draught of vinegar and gall! How willingly He embraced the death of the cross to deliver us from eternal death! How, then, can you, a vile worm of the earth, presume to complain of sufferings which you have justly merited by your sins—those sins for which the spotless Lamb of God was immolated? He would teach us by His example that unless we strive for the mastery legitimately—that is, courageously and perseveringly—we shall not be crowned. (Cf. *2 Tim.* 2:5).

Moreover, let me appeal to your self-interest. Will you not at least make a virtue out of necessity? You must suffer. You cannot escape it, for it is a law of your nature. Can you resist the almighty power of God when He is pleased to send you afflictions? Knowing these truths, and knowing that your sins deserve more than you can bear, why will you struggle against your trials? Why not bear them patiently, and thus atone for your sins and merit many graces? Is it not madness to try to escape them, and thereby lose the blessings they can give, receiving instead a weight of impatience and misery which only adds to the load you must carry? Stand prepared, then, for tribulations, for what can you expect from a corrupt world, from a frail flesh, from the envy of devils, and from the malice of men, but contradictions and persecutions?

Act, therefore, as a prudent man, and arm yourself against such attacks, proceeding with as much caution as if you were in an enemy's country, and you will thus gain two important advantages: First, the trials against which you are forearmed will be easier to bear, for "a blow which we have anticipated," says Seneca, "falls less heavily." And this agrees with the counsel of Wisdom: "Before sickness take a medicine." (*Ecclus.* 18:20).

Secondly, by anticipating in a spirit of resignation the afflictions which God may send you, you offer a sacrifice like that of Abraham, about to immolate his son. Nothing, in fact, is more pleasing to God, nothing is more meritorious for us, than the resignation with which we prepare ourselves to accept all the trials that may come upon us, either from the hand of God or the wickedness of men. Though these sufferings may never reach us, yet our good intention will be rewarded in the same way as if we had borne them. Thus was Abraham rewarded as if he had really sacrificed his son, because he was ready to do so in obedience to God.

Be not afraid, therefore, of tribulations, for unto these are you called. (Cf. *1 Pet.* 3:9,14). Remember that you are as a rock in the midst of the ocean. The winds and waves of the world will beat against you, but you remain unshaken. To do good and to suffer are, according to St. Bernard, the duties of the Christian life. The latter is the more difficult. Prepare yourself, then, to fulfill it with courage.

Let us observe, in conclusion, that theologians distinguish three degrees in this virtue. The first consists in patiently bearing afflictions; the second in desiring to suffer for the love of God; and the third in rejoicing to suffer for the same motive. In the patience of Job we find an example of the first degree. The ardent desire of the martyrs to suffer for Christ affords us proof of the second. The joy which filled the hearts of the Apostles because they were accounted worthy to suffer reproach for the name of Christ is a bright example of the third. (Cf. *Acts* 5:41). St. Paul had attained this sublime height when he gloried in his tribulations. (Cf. *Rom.* 5:3). In this he was nobly followed by many of the early Christians, as we learn from his Epistle to the Corinthians, whom he tells of the grace given to the Macedonians which caused them to experience abundance of joy in much tribulation. (Cf. *2 Cor.* 8:2). This is the highest degree of virtue, but it is not commanded us.

A faithful servant of Christ will not, however, rest satisfied with the first degree, but will strive unceasingly to reach the second and even the third.

What we have said on this subject must not be interpreted to mean that we should rejoice at the sufferings of others. Oh, no; charity requires us to sympathize with others in affliction, especially with our kindred and with the Church. The mortifications we impose on ourselves must not be extended to others, but should render us even more considerate towards them.

CHAPTER 43

The Obligations of our State

We shall here briefly consider the importance of fidelity to the duties of our state, which vary according to our position. The duties of one who governs, for example, are very different from those of one in subjection; the duties of a religious are very different from those of the father of a family.

According to the Apostle, those who govern must be vigilant in labor and in all things. (Cf. *2 Tim.* 4:5). This watchfulness is generally proportioned to the value of the object and to the danger which surrounds it. Now, there is nothing of greater value, and at the same time nothing more exposed to danger, than a soul. Consequently nothing requires greater vigilance than the care which must be bestowed by one who is charged with so important a trust.

The principal duty of a subordinate is to behold God in his superiors and to pay them prompt and entire obedience. If a monarch order me to obey his minister, do I not obey the monarch by obeying the minister? In like manner, when God orders me to obey my superiors do I not obey Him by submitting to them? This is the teaching of St. Paul: "Servants, be obedient to them that are your lords, as to Christ." (*Ephes.* 6:5).

There are three degrees in this virtue. The first consists in simply doing what we are commanded, the second in doing it willingly, and the third in submitting our judgment to that of our superiors by "bringing into captivity our understanding unto the obedience of Christ." (*2 Cor.* 10:5). Many fulfill the commands of a superior, but with reluctance. Others obey, but murmur and disapprove the command. Others, in fine, cheerfully obey and heartily approve whatever order they receive.

Endeavor that such may be your obedience, bearing in mind the words of Our Saviour: "He that heareth you heareth me, and he that despiseth you despiseth me." (*Lk.* 10:16). Refrain from all murmuring against superiors, that you may not deserve the reproach addressed by Moses to the Israelites: "Your murmuring is not against us, but against the Lord." (*Exod.* 16:8). Beware of despising those in authority, lest God should say to them, as He did to Samuel: "They have not rejected thee, but me, that I should not reign over them." (*1 Kg.* 8:7). Serve them with truth and sincerity, that you may never hear the terrible words of the Apostle: "Thou hast not lied to men, but to God" (*Acts* 5:4), and that you may never incur the malediction which fell upon Ananias and Saphira for their duplicity.

Let married women faithfully acquit themselves of the duties of their household, discharging all their obligations to their husband and children, that they may thus be free to attend to practices of piety without neglecting what they owe their family. That would be a worthless devotion which would occupy the time which should be given to domestic affairs.

Let fathers of families reflect upon the terrible affliction which the high priest Heli drew upon himself by neglecting to chastise his children. Sudden death came upon himself and his sons, and the priesthood was withdrawn from his family forever. (Cf. *1 Kg.* 4). As the sins of children are to a certain degree attributable to parents, the perdition of a child not infrequently involves the condemnation of the parents. How can he be called a true father who, having begotten his son for this world, fails to train him for the kingdom of Heaven? Therefore, advise and correct your children. Guard them from evil associates. Give them wise and virtuous masters. Teach them to love virtue, and let them, like Tobias, be inspired from their infancy with the fear of God. (Cf. *Tob.* 2:13).

Do not gratify their whims, but curb their wills that they may become truly submissive. Be no less solicitous in providing for their spiritual than their corporal wants; for it is unreasonable to suppose that the duty of parents extends no further than that of birds and beasts, whose only care is to feed and nourish their young. Fulfill the duties of a father in a manner becoming a Christian, a true servant of God, and thus you will bring up your children heirs to Heaven, and not slaves of Hell.

Heads of families with servants to govern should bear in mind these words of the Apostle: "If any man have not care of his own, and especially of those of his house, he hath denied the faith and is worse than an infidel." (*1 Tim.* 5:8). The members of their household form the sheep of the flock which has been confided to them, and for which they must one day render an account. Precious are they in the sight of the Lord, because they have been redeemed by the Passion of His Divine Son, through whose Blood every human being has received a nobility higher than all the honors of earth.

A good master, therefore, will carefully endeavor to abolish among his servants all public vices, such as quarreling, gambling, swearing, and especially sins of impurity. He will see that they are instructed in the principles of their faith, and that they are enabled to observe the commandments of God and of the Church, particularly the precepts to hear Mass on Sundays and holy days of obligation, and to keep the fasts and abstinence prescribed by the Church, unless they are lawfully dispensed or excused.

CHAPTER 44

*The Relative Importance and Values of the
Virtues*

A merchant about to purchase precious stones should
learn something of their relative value, if he would make a
wise selection. In like manner, a Christian should have
some knowledge of the intrinsic merit of each virtue to aid
him in making a proper choice.

The virtues of which we have been treating may be
divided into two classes, the first of which includes the more
interior and spiritual virtues, the other those which are exterior or sensible.

To the first belong the three theological virtues, which
have God for their immediate object; and the virtues which
facilitate the accomplishment of our duty to God, such as
humility, chastity, mercy, patience, prudence, devotion,
poverty of spirit, contempt of the world, denial of our own
will, love of the cross and mortification, with many others
to which we here give the name of virtue in the broadest ac-
ceptation of the term. These are called interior and
spiritual, because their action is chiefly within the soul.
Nevertheless they are often manifested to the world, as we
see, for instance, in the virtues of charity and religion,
which produce a number of exterior works to the praise and
glory of God.

The exterior virtues are fasting, mortification, pious
reading, vocal prayer, chanting of the Psalms, pilgrimages,

hearing Mass, assisting at the offices of the Church, with all the outward ceremonies and practices of a Christian or religious life. Though these virtues, like the others, have their seat in the soul, yet their action is always exterior, while the acts of the spiritual virtues, faith, hope, charity, humility, contemplation, contrition, or repentance, are often entirely within.

There is no doubt that the virtues of the first class are more meritorious and pleasing to God than those of the second. "Woman, believe me," said Our Saviour to the woman at the well, that "the hour cometh, and now is, when the true adorers shall adore the Father in spirit and in truth. For the Father also seeketh such to adore him. God is a spirit, and they that adore him must adore him in spirit and in truth." (*Jn.* 4:21,23-24).

For this reason David, describing the beauty of the Church and that of a soul in the state of grace, says that all her glory is within in golden borders, clothed round about with variety. (Cf. *Ps.* 44:14). And the great Apostle, writing to Timothy, says: "Exercise thyself unto godliness, for bodily exercise is profitable to little; but godliness is profitable to all things, having promise of the life that now is, and of that which is to come." (*1 Tim.* 4:7-8). According to St. Thomas, godliness here signifies the worship of God and charity to our neighbor, while bodily exercise means fasting and other austerities.

This is a truth of which even the pagan philosophers were not ignorant. Aristotle has written very little of God, yet in one of his works he expresses himself thus: "If the gods take any interest in human things, as we have reason to believe they do, there is no doubt that they take most pleasure in what bears most resemblance to themselves—that is, in man's spirit or mind; hence they who adorn their minds with a knowledge of truth, and their souls with the beauty and harmony of virtue, must be most pleasing to them."

The celebrated physician Galen expresses the same thought. Writing upon the structure of the human frame, and the different relations and functions of its various parts, in which the wisdom and power of the Sovereign Artisan are particularly manifest, he is overcome with admiration, and, abandoning the language of science for that of religion, he exclaims, "Let others honor the gods with offerings of hecatombs. [Sacrifices of 100 oxen or cattle offered by the pagans to their deities.] As for me, I shall honor them by proclaiming the greatness of their power, which so readily executes all that their wisdom ordains; and their infinite goodness, which refuses nothing to their creatures, but abundantly provides for all their needs."

Such are the words of a pagan philosopher. Let us refer them to the true God; and what more can a Christian say? The great Galen unconsciously repeats the words of God's prophet: "I desired mercy, and not sacrifice; and the knowledge of God more than holocausts." (*Osee* 6:6). The hecatomb of the pagan may be considered as the imitation of the holocaust of the Jew.

From the praise bestowed upon the interior virtues we must not conclude that the others are of little value. Though not so noble as the former, they are nevertheless most efficacious in acquiring and preserving them. For example, retreat and solitude guard us from innumerable sights and sounds which endanger the peace of our conscience, and imperil our chastity. We are all sensible of the importance of silence in preserving devotion, and avoiding those faults into which we are led by excessive conversation. "In the multitude of words," says Solomon, "there shall not want sin." (*Prov.* 10:19). Fasting, when performed in a state of grace, besides being a meritorious act of the virtue of temperance, as it is at all times, also expiates our sins; subdues the inclinations of the flesh; repels our enemy; disposes us for prayer, pious reading, and meditation; and preserves us from the excesses, quarrels, and passions awakened by inordinate indulgence. As for pious reading, the recitation of the Psalms, assisting at the divine office, and hearing sermons, it is evident that these acts of the virtue of religion are most efficacious in enlightening the understanding and inflaming the will with a desire for spiritual things.

To acquire and preserve this precious virtue of devotion, which of itself disposes us for the practice of all other virtues, we must watch over ourselves with special vigilance. So little suffices to make us lose this delicate virtue. Frivolous conversations, excessive mirth, immoderate indulgence at table, slight anger, unnecessary disputes, curiosity and eagerness to see and hear what does not concern us, besides many similar faults, while not grave in themselves, weaken, and sometimes destroy, the spirit of devotion. To preserve the intense heat communicated to it by the fire, iron must be kept continually in the furnace— or, at least, it must seldom be withdrawn. Otherwise it will quickly resume its former temperature. In like manner, if we would keep our hearts inflamed with the fire of devotion, we must remain closely united to God by the practices we have mentioned.

These reflections will show us the importance of the second class of virtues, and the relation which they bear to the others. The virtues of the first class form the end; the virtues of the second are the means to attain this end. The first may be said to be the health of the body; the second, the medicine to obtain it. The first may be regarded as the spirit of religion, the second as its body—though absolutely necessary for its welfare.

By observing the counsels we have here laid down you will avoid two equally lamentable errors. One was that of the Pharisees in the time of Christ, and the other is that of certain heretics of the present day. The Pharisees, carnal and ambitious men, accustomed to the literal observance of a law then framed for a carnal people, disregarded true justice and interior virtues, and were satisfied, according to the expression of the Apostle, with "an appearance of godliness." (*2 Tim.* 3:5). Under a virtuous exterior they concealed a corrupt and wicked heart.

The heretics of our day, endeavoring to avoid this error, fell into the opposite extreme and preached contempt for exterior practices. But the Catholic Church preserves a happy medium between both, and, while maintaining the superiority of the interior virtues, recognizes the merit and advantage of those that are exterior, just as in a well-governed commonwealth each one enjoys the merit and prerogatives which belong to him.

CHAPTER 45

Four Important Corollaries of the preceding Doctrine

SECTION I
The Necessity of Exterior as well as Interior Virtues

From the preceding principles we can deduce four consequences of great importance in the spiritual life. The first is that a true servant of God must not be content to seek interior virtues only, though they are the noblest, but must also add the practice of exterior virtues, both to preserve the first, and perfectly to fulfill the obligations of justice. Neither the soul without the body nor the body without the soul constitutes man. In like manner, true Christianity is neither wholly interior nor wholly exterior. The union of both classes of virtues is as necessary to the perfection of the spiritual life as the union of soul and body is to the perfection of the natural life. For as the body receives its life and dignity from the soul, so the exterior virtues receive their life and merit from our interior dispositions, particularly from charity. Therefore, he who would become a perfect Christian must remember that the interior and exterior virtues are as inseparable as soul and body, the treasure and the chest, the vine and its support—that is, the spiritual virtues and their defenses, the exterior works of piety. Otherwise he will lose the first, without which he can reap no profit from the second. Let him ever bear in mind these words of Holy Scripture: "He that feareth God neglecteth nothing, and he that contemneth small things shall fall little by little." (*Eccles.* 7:19 and *Ecclus.* 19:1). The plague of gnats in Egypt was succeeded by that of flies. Beware, then, lest in despising the sting of gnats—that is, of small faults—you may fall a victim to flies—that is, to mortal sin. (Cf. *Ex.* 8).

SECTION II
Discernment in the Pursuit of Virtue

As men will sacrifice more for the purchase of gold than silver, and will do more to preserve an eye than a finger, so we, guided by the spirit of discernment, should make more effort to acquire the greater virtues than those that are of less importance. If we invert this order, we introduce confusion into the kingdom of our soul. Therefore, while recommending the exterior virtues of recollection, modesty, silence, and fasting, we would exhort you with no less zeal to the practice of the interior virtues of humility, charity, prayer, devotion, and love of your neighbor.

Exterior faults being evident to others, we consider them of greater moment than interior defects, and pay more attention to their amendment. Moreover, the exterior virtues, besides attracting more attention, excite more esteem than the practice of hope, charity, humility, fear of God or contempt for the world, though these interior virtues are more pleasing in the sight of God. "For man seeth those things that appear, but the Lord beholdeth the heart." (*1 Kg.* 16:7). Therefore, as love of praise is one of the strongest and most subtle passions, beware lest it cause you to seek the virtues which are most esteemed by men, to the neglect of the interior virtues, which are more acceptable to God.

SECTION III
Virtues that are Less must sometimes yield to those that are Greater

When we are obliged to choose between two command-ments, we should follow the more important. Observe the same rule with regard to the virtues. Whenever you are in doubt as to which you should adopt, the lesser must give place to the greater, if you would avoid confusion. The holy Fathers, says St. Bernard, have established many practices proper to preserve and increase charity. While these prac-tices attain this end they should be rigidly observed, but if at any time they conflict with charity, it is only just that they should be modified, or omitted by proper authority, for others which will more efficaciously promote this virtue. It would certainly be most unreasonable to observe, through a motive of charity, practices which charity itself condemned. Let such practices, therefore, be faithfully observed as long as they promote charity, but no longer. (*De Proecepto et Dispen., c.*4). In support of this doctrine the great Doctor cites two pontifical decrees, one of Pope Gelasius and the other of Pope Leo.

SECTION IV
True and False Justice

A fourth consequence worthy of note is that there are two kinds of justice, one false and the other true. True justice is that which embraces both the interior and the exterior vir-tues. False justice is that which is satisfied with a few ex-terior practices, while neglecting the interior virtues, such as love of God, humility, and devotion. This was the justice of the Pharisees, to whom Our Saviour addressed these ter-rible words of reproach and condemnation: "Woe to you, scribes and Pharisees, hypocrites; because you tithe mint, and anise, and cummin, and have left the weightier things of the law; judgment, and mercy, and faith . . . Woe to you, scribes and Pharisees, hypocrites; because you make clean the outside of the cup and of the dish, but within you are full of rapine and uncleanness . . . Woe to you, scribes and Pharisees, hypocrites; because you are like to whited sepulchres, which outwardly appear to men beautiful, but within are full of dead men's bones, and of all filthiness." (*Matt.* 23:23,25,27). Such is the justice so frequently condemned in the Scriptures. Speaking in God's name, Isaias says: "This people glorify me with their lips, but their heart is far from me, and they have feared me with the commandment and doctrines of men." (Cf. *Is.* 29:13). And again: "Offer sacrifice no more in vain: incense is an abomination to me . . . My soul hateth your new moons, and your solemnities . . . I am weary of bearing them." (*Is.* 1:13-14).

What is the meaning of these words? Does God condemn acts which He Himself commanded under the severest penalties? Does He condemn the practices of that beautiful virtue, religion, the object of which is to honor and worship Him? Assuredly not; but He condemns the insincerity of His people who content themselves with the exterior observance of the law to the neglect of true justice. This He declares, for, after reproaching them with the mockery of their hollow ceremonies and practices, He tells them, "Wash yourselves, be clean, take away the evil of your devices from my eyes: cease to do perversely. Learn to do well . . . relieve the oppressed, judge for the fatherless, defend the widow . . . and if your sins be as scarlet, they shall be made as white as snow; and if they be red as crimson, they shall be white as wool." (*Is.* 1:16-18).

In still stronger language the prophet again denounces exterior practices that are not actuated by interior virtue: "He that sacrificeth an ox, is as if he slew a man; he that killeth a sheep in sacrifice, as if he should brain a dog; he that offereth an oblation, as if he should offer swine's blood; he that remembereth incense, as if he should bless an idol." (*Is.* 66:3).

Why, O Lord, these terrible words? Why didst Thou repute as abominable those sacrifices which Thou hadst formerly commanded? "All these things," I hear Thee say, "have they chosen in their ways, and their soul is delighted in their abominations." (*Is.* 66:3).

Behold the nothingness of exterior practices which are not animated by an interior spirit of virtue, but which are done solely according to the ways of men. "Take away from me the tumult of thy songs," God says by the prophet Amos, "and I will not hear the canticles of thy harp." (*Amos* 5:23). Even more strongly does He reject these works, speaking though Malachias: "I will scatter upon your face the dung of your solemnities." (*Mal.* 2:3). Do not these suffice to show us how little value exterior virtues have when not animated by the love and fear of God, and by hatred of sin, which are the foundations of true justice?

Still another reason which causes God to repel these external observances, comparing sacrifice to murder, incense to idolatry, chanting to discordant noise, solemn feasts to dung, is not only the want of merit in these practices when devoid of an interior spirit, but the fact that they frequently inflate us with pride, excite in us contempt for others, and inspire us with a false security, a fatal confidence, which effectually hinders all amendment for one who is satisfied with his condition and does not desire a change.

The prayer, or rather boasting, of the Pharisee, is a proof of this: "O God, I give thee thanks that I am not as the rest of men, extortioners, unjust, adulterers, as also is this publican. I fast twice in the week; I give tithes of all that I possess." (*Lk.* 18:11-12). Does not this so-called prayer illustrate the three dangers against which we warned you? His pride and presumption exclaim: "I am not as the rest of men"; his contempt of others says: "I am not as this publican"; and his false security shows itself in the thanks which he gives to God for the life he leads, and in which he believes himself safe from all evil.

Besides that gross hypocrisy which is the pretence of virtue made by those who know they are wicked, but who strive to conceal their vices, there is a more refined and more dangerous hypocrisy, which affects many who deceive themselves as well as others by a false show of justice. Like the Pharisee, they imagine they are virtuous, but they are far from true holiness.

Such hypocrisy is the result of that miserable piety which consists of external practices only. Solomon condemned it when he said, "There is a way which seemeth just to a man, but the ends thereof lead to death." (*Prov.* 14:12). Further on he includes this vice among the four evils which he says exist in the world: "There is a generation that curseth their father, and doth not bless their mother. A generation that are pure in their own eyes, and yet are not washed from their filthiness. A generation whose eyes are lofty, and their eyelids lifted up on high. A generation that for teeth hath swords, and grindeth with their jaw teeth, to devour the needy from off the earth, and the poor from among men." (*Prov.* 30:11-14).

You cannot fail to recognize among these the unhappy victims of self-deception, who, like the Pharisees, believe themselves pure when they are filled with corruption.

This false confidence is so dangerous that there is much more hope for a hardened sinner who recognizes his condition than for one who thus deceives himself. Acknowledging our failings is the first step towards amendment. But how can a sick man be cured who maintains that he is well, and therefore refuses all remedies? For this reason Our Saviour declares to the Pharisees that publicans and sinners shall go before them into the kingdom of Heaven. (Cf. *Matt.*

21:31). And He utters the same truth still more forcibly in the Apocalypse: "I would thou wert cold or hot. But because thou art lukewarm, and neither cold nor hot, I will begin to vomit thee out of my mouth." (*Apoc.* 3:15-16).

You marvel, doubtless, why a soul that is cold should be less displeasing to God than one that is lukewarm. The reason for this is that coldness, or the state of the sinner devoid of all virtues, is more easily cured than lukewarmness, which represents the man of few virtues, and these only exterior practices without the life of charity. The man who is loaded with sins can be brought to realize his malady, and so induced to take the proper remedies. But the man who is lukewarm rests on that false security which, as was the case with the Pharisee, leads him to believe that he possesses all the treasures of virtue. Though these soulless practices avail him naught, he will not realize his sad state, and consequently will take no measures for amendment.

To know that this is the true meaning of the text, read what follows: "Thou sayest, I am rich and made wealthy, and I have need of nothing; and thou knowest not that thou art wretched, and miserable, and poor, and blind, and naked." (*Apoc.* 3:17). Do not these words again describe the Pharisee, who thanks God for his spiritual riches when he is poor, destitute of all virtue, inflated with pride, and blind to his own failings?

There is nothing in Holy Scripture more frequently extolled than this true justice, nothing more frequently condemned than this pharisaical justice. Hence we have dwelt at some length on the excellence of the first and the danger of the second. For human nature is the same today as it was in the time of the prophets and the Apostles, whose teachings on this subject are contained in the Scriptures. We have the same inclinations, the same inheritance of original sin, and consequently our vices and failings must be the same, for like causes produce like effects.

The carnal Jews believed that they fulfilled their duty to God by a literal observance of fasts and ceremonies. Many Christians of the present day resemble them, for they hear Mass on Sundays, assist at sermons and the divine offices, daily recite a number of vocal prayers, and even fast on Saturdays in honor of the Blessed Virgin; and yet they are no less eager in the pursuit of worldly honors and in gratifying their passions. They are no less subject to anger than others who observe none of these practices. They forget the obligations of their state; they are careless of the salvation of their children and servants; they readily yield to feelings of hatred and revenge; they harbor resentment for trifling offenses, and refuse to speak to their neighbor; they withhold the wages of their servants and defraud their creditors. If their honor or interest be touched, the hollowness of their virtue will soon be apparent. Many of them are profuse in prayers, but very sparing in alms.

Others could never be persuaded to forego the observance of abstinence on Wednesdays and days of devotion; but yet they indulge with impunity in detraction and calumny. They scruple to eat the flesh of animals which God does not prohibit them, but they do not hesitate to prey upon the honor and reputation of their neighbor, which God wishes to be sacred to every Christian. These and similar inconsistencies are frequent in our day among persons of every class.

That you may profit by the preceding counsels, let each one study his own spiritual condition, that he may learn the remedies which will profit him most. There are general directions which apply to all, such as those pertaining to charity, humility, patience, or obedience. Others, again, are special and apply only to certain classes and certain conditions. For example, it is necessary to recommend to a scrupulous person greater freedom of conscience; to one who is lax, greater restraint. With a timid soul, inclined to discouragement, we must treat of the divine mercy, while a presumptuous soul should be led to reflect on the divine justice.

Those who give themselves wholly to exterior practices should be made to cultivate interior virtues, while those who are entirely devoted to the latter should be taught the value of the former when animated by the proper dispositions. They will thus learn to appreciate the merit of both kinds of virtue, and therefore to avoid the extremes into which many fall who devote themselves so closely to one as to neglect the other.

The interior virtues, however, especially the fear of God and a hatred of sin, must be particularly cultivated. Happy is he in whose soul these virtues are deeply engraved. He may build without fear upon such a foundation, for these virtues are the beginning of true justice. But without them he is a blind and miserable soul, however numerous his exterior practices of piety.

CHAPTER 46

The Different Vocations in the Church

The virtues of the Christian life being very numerous, a good Christian does not necessarily give himself to all with the same ardor. Some prefer to cultivate the virtues which have God for their direct object, and therefore embrace a contemplative life. Others prefer the virtues which enable them to be most useful to their neighbor, and consequently choose an active life. Others, in fine, prefer the virtues which more directly benefit their own souls, and therefore enter the monastic life. Again, as all virtues are means of acquiring grace, different persons adopt different means. Many seek to obtain it by fasting and like austerities; others by almsgiving and works of mercy, and others by prayer and meditation. Of this latter exercise there are also different methods, which vary according to the character of souls or the subjects chosen. The best kind of meditation is always that from which one derives most profit and devotion.

In this matter beware of a grave error into which pious persons sometimes fall. Deriving much profit from certain means, many imagine that there are no others which lead to God. Consequently they would enforce the same methods upon everyone, and think all in error who follow a different path. Thus, one who gives himself wholly to prayer thinks it the only means of salvation. Another, given to fasting and corporal mortification, sees no merit in any other practices of piety. Those who lead contemplative lives imagine that all who are engaged in an active life are in great danger, and even go so far as to hold exterior virtues in contempt.

The followers of the active life, having no experience of all that passes between God and the soul in the sweet calm of contemplation, do not sufficiently appreciate its value, and approve it only as far as it includes the practice of exterior works. One who gives himself exclusively to mental prayer is very apt to think any other form of prayer unprofitable; and, on the contrary, he who has devoted himself to vocal prayer will often argue that it is more meritorious because it is more laborious.

Thus each one, impelled by ignorance or unconscious pride, extols himself by commending the practices to which he is most given. Just as a savant will praise the science which is the object of his study, and depreciate the merit of all others, so many extol one virtue at the expense of all the rest. The orator will tell you that there is nothing comparable to eloquence; the astronomer, that there is nothing superior to the study of the heavenly bodies. In fact, the theologian, the linguist, the philosopher, the commentator, will each in his turn offer good reasons to prove the preeminence and incontestable superiority of the science he professes.

Similar, though less open, is the struggle between the advocates of the different virtues; each one would have his method prevail over that of others, believing that as it has proved profitable to him, it must prove so to all. Hence arise unfavorable judgments upon the lives of others, divisions and disputes among brethren. Such was the error of the Corinthians in the early ages of the Church. They had been favored with different graces, and each one extolled his own above the rest. The gifts of prophecy, of tongues, of interpreting the Scripture, of working miracles, were each preferred by those who had received them. (Cf. *1 Cor.* 12).

There is no more efficacious argument against this illusion than that of the Apostle, who declares that all graces and gifts are equal as to their source, for they proceed from the same Holy Spirit, though they differ in their object. "In one Spirit were we all baptized into one body" (*1 Cor.* 12:13), says the Apostle. Belonging thus to the same Head, we all partake of His dignity and glory, and in this we are equally His members, though there is a diversity of gifts and duties among us.

This diversity should not cause us to look with disfavor on those who seem less gifted, for each has his value as a member of Christ. Thus the members of the human body have not the same duties, but yet each has its own peculiar power that another does not possess. All are important, because all are necessary for the general good. "If the foot should say: Because I am not the hand, I am not of the body; is it therefore not of the body? And if the ear should say: Because I am not the eye, I am not of the body; is it therefore not of the body?" (*1 Cor.* 12:15-16). In this manner the Apostle speaks to the Corinthians, and continues his comparison to prove that we must not be misled by our preferences to judge that whoever differs from us is not right, or that gifts differing from ours have not an important place in the designs of God.

This diversity is due partly to nature and partly to grace. We say that it is due partly to nature; for though grace is the principle of every spiritual being, yet it is shaped according to the condition of the soul in which it dwells, just as water takes the form of the vessel into which it is poured. Thus, calm, peaceful temperaments are more naturally suited to a contemplative life; those of an ardent, energetic nature are better fitted for an active life; while persons of strong, robust health find more profit in a laborious life of penance. Thus is the marvelous goodness of God made manifest. Desiring to communicate Himself to all, He has willed that the ways which lead to Him should be proportioned to the diversities in the characters and conditions of men.

Grace is the second cause of this variety which the Holy Spirit, the Author of all grace, has created for the greater beauty and perfection of His Church. As the different senses and members are requisite for the beauty and perfection of the human body, so a diversity of graces is necessary for the complete harmony and beauty of the Church. If the faithful all practiced the same virtues, how could they be called a body, which necessarily consists of different members? "If the whole body," says the Apostle, "were the eye, where would be the hearing? If the whole were hearing, where would be the smelling? And if they all were one member, where would be the body." (*1 Cor.* 12:17,19).

We find the same beautiful variety in the works of nature, where the Sovereign Creator wisely apportions all gifts or qualities so that the lack of one perfection is compensated by the possession of another. The peacock, which has a most discordant note, possesses a beautiful plumage; the nightingale delights the ear, but has no charms for the eye; the horse bears us where we will and is valuable in camp and field, but is rarely used for food; the ox is useful for farm and table, but has scarcely any other qualities to recommend him; fruit trees give us food, but have little value for building; forest trees yield no fruit, but afford us the necessary material for erecting our dwellings. Thus we do not find all qualities or all perfections united in one creature, but that variety among them which constitutes the beauty of nature and binds them to one another by a mutual and necessary dependence.

God has willed that the order and beauty which we admire in nature should exist in the works of grace. For this reason He has endowed His Church with that variety of virtues which form a most symmetrical body, a most beautiful world, the most perfect harmony. Hence some of the members of this great body give themselves to a life of contemplation; others to an active life, to obedience or penance, to religious studies, to the service of the sick and the poor, or to other works of mercy.

We find the same variety in the religious orders of the Church; all aspire to the same end but pursue different paths. Some follow the way of penance; others that of poverty. Some choose a contemplative life; others an active life. Some labor in the midst of the world; others seek obscurity and solitude. The rules of one prescribe a certain revenue; those of another the strictest poverty. Nevertheless they are all animated by the same spirit, all pursue the same end. This variety extends even to the members of the same order; for while certain religious are engaged in the choir, others study in their cells; others devote themselves to manual labor; others hear confessions; while others are engaged in the temporal affairs of the community.

What, then, are all these but the several members of one body, the different notes of one grand harmony, the various elements which contribute to the beauty and perfection of the Church? Why has the lute several chords, the organ numerous pipes, but to produce greater variety and harmony? For this reason the patriarch Jacob gave his son Joseph the coat of many colors (Cf. *Gen.* 37:3), and God commanded that the curtains of the tabernacle should be of violet, purple, and scarlet twice dyed, diversified with embroidery. (Cf. *Ex.* 26:1). In both of these objects we behold an image of that beautiful variety which prevails in the Church.

Let us, then, beware of judging others because their virtues are not ours, or of expecting all to follow the same path. This would be destroying the body of the Church, rending the coat of Joseph. It would be exacting the duty of the eyes, or the hands, or the feet, from all the members of the body. In the words of the Apostle, if the whole body were the eye, where would be the hearing; or if it were the ear, where would be the eyes? Can the eyes reproach the feet for being blind, or the feet reproach the eyes for not bearing the burden of the body? No; it is necessary that the feet toil on the ground, and that the eyes be above them, protected from all that could fatigue or sully them. Nor is the duty of the eyes, notwithstanding their repose, less important than that of the feet.

The work of the pilot who stands at the helm is no less necessary than that of the sailors who manage the ropes and sails. We must not judge of an action by the labor it requires, but by its value and the effects it produces. Thus, you would not say that the work of a laborer is more important in a commonwealth than that of the statesman who wisely directs the government.

If we seriously weigh these considerations, we shall learn to respect all vocations. We shall not reproach the hand for not being the foot, nor the foot for not being the hand. We shall understand the truth of the Apostle's words when he tells us that the beauty and perfection of the body result from the diversity of its members.

CHAPTER 47

The Vigilance and Care necessary in the Practice of Virtue

Since the rule of life which we have proposed includes so many counsels and so many virtues, and since our intelligence is incapable of embracing a multitude of things at one time, it will be well to apply ourselves to the practice of one virtue which, in a measure, comprehends the rest, or supplies for all that may be wanting to them. Such is the virtue of continual vigilance in all our words and actions.

An ambassador about to address a king studies not only what he will say, but how he will say it, and strives to regulate his gestures and his whole bearing so that he may present himself to the monarch in the most becoming manner. With more reason a Christian, who is the subject of the King of kings, must watch over himself at all times, whether he speaks or is silent, at prayer or at table, at home or abroad. He must measure all his actions, all his words, by the law of his Divine Master.

We find this virtue of vigilance frequently recommended in the sacred Scriptures. "Keep thyself and thy soul carefully." (*Deut.* 4:9). "Walk solicitous with thy God." (*Mich.* 6:8). That is, be careful to avoid everything contrary to His will. The many eyes of the mysterious creatures mentioned in Ezechiel also represent the vigilance with which we must guard our soul. (Cf. *Ezech.* 1-18).

Besides the many dangers to which we are exposed, the

difficulty and delicacy of the work of salvation render this vigilance indispensable, particularly for one who aspires to the perfection of the spiritual life. For to live in union with God, to abide in the flesh and yet to be free from its corruption, and to preserve one's self from the snares of the world "without offense unto the day of Christ" (*Phil.* 1:10) require not only the assistance of grace but the greatest vigilance over ourselves. Follow in this respect the wise counsel of Seneca: "Always imagine yourself in the presence of one for whom you entertain the greatest respect, and refrain from all that you would not do in His presence." (*Epist.* 25).

A no less salutary practice is to live as if each day were the last of our lives, and the evening were to bring us before the tribunal of God to render an account of all our actions. But the most efficacious means of all is to walk continually in the presence of God, who is everywhere, and to act in all things with obedience due to so great a Master, who is the Witness and the Judge of all our works. Frequently implore the grace to avoid all that would render us unworthy of His divine presence.

Thus the vigilance which we here counsel has two ends: First, to fix the eyes of our soul upon God, and unceasingly to offer Him on the altar of our hearts a sacrifice of adoration, respect, praise, devotion, thanksgiving, and love; secondly, to watch over all our thoughts, words, and actions, that we may in all things follow the guidance of His will. Though this vigilance is not easily acquired, nevertheless we must endeavor to practice it as uninterruptedly as possible. Corporal exercises are no obstacle to it, for with fidelity to the practice of it the heart will always be free to withdraw from them for awhile, and seek its repose in the wounds of Jesus Christ.

CHAPTER 48

The Courage necessary in the Practice of Virtue

SECTION I
The Necessity of Courage

The preceding chapter furnishes us with eyes to discern our duty, and this chapter will furnish us with arms or courage to perform it.

There are two obstacles to virtue which vigilance and courage will overcome. The first is the difficulty of discerning what is good from what is evil; and the second is the labor of embracing the former and overcoming the latter. Vigilance meets the first difficulty; fortitude the second. These two virtues are indispensable, for without vigilance we are blind, without courage we are helpless.

The courage of which we are here treating is not the cardinal virtue of fortitude which calms our fears and strengthens us in affliction, but is rather a disposition of the soul which enables us to triumph over all obstacles to good. For this reason it ever accompanies virtue, sword in hand to vanquish all her foes.

As the blacksmith requires a hammer to beat the hard iron and shape it according to his will, so do we need courage, the spiritual hammer, with which we overcome the difficulties in the road to virtue and fashion our souls after our divine Model. Without this quality we can no more pursue virtue than a blacksmith can work without his hammer.

For what virtue is there that can be acquired without effort? Consider them one after another: prayer, fasting, temperance, obedience, poverty of spirit, chastity, humility— and you will find that all present some difficulty springing from self-love, the world, or the devil.

Therefore, if you sincerely desire to advance in virtue, consider the words spoken to Moses, by the God of all virtue and strength, as directly addressed to you: "Take this rod in thy hand, wherewith thou shalt do the signs" that will deliver My people. (Cf. *Ex.* 4:17). Be assured that as the rod of Moses enabled him to effect the glorious deliverance of the children of Israel, so the rod of courage will enable you to work no less striking wonders, and to free yourself from your enemies: the world, the flesh, and the devil. Keep this rod, therefore, ever in your hand, for without it you will be utterly helpless.

Avoid, too, an illusion into which beginners in the spiritual life frequently fall. Having read in certain books of the ineffable consolations of the Holy Spirit, and the joys of God's service, they persuade themselves that the path of virtue is filled with delights, and therefore, instead of entering it armed to meet their enemies, they set out as if for a festival. Truly the love of God is full of sweetness, but the way which leads to it contains much that is bitter, for self-love must first be conquered, and there is nothing harder to nature than to fight against it and all that it claims. This is the lesson we should learn from the prophet, who says, "Shake thyself from the dust, arise, sit up, O Jerusalem." (*Is.* 52:2). Shake thyself from the dust of earthly affections; arise and combat before thou canst sit and rest.

It is also true that God favors with ineffable consolations souls who faithfully labor for Him, and renounce the pleasures of the world for those of Heaven. But this absolute renunciation is necessary, for while we refuse to sacrifice the joys of this life we shall seek in vain for the joys of the Holy Spirit. The manna was given to the children of Israel only when they had consumed the food which they brought with them from Egypt.

If, then, we do not arm ourselves with courage, our pursuit of virtue will be fruitless. Rest is attained only through labor; victory only through combat; joy only through tears; and the sweetness of God's love only through hatred of self. For this reason the Holy Spirit, throughout the Proverbs of Solomon, so frequently condemns sloth and negligence and so strongly commends vigilance and courage as the safeguards of virtue.

SECTION II
Means of acquiring Courage

Solomon had reason to exclaim: "Who shall find a valiant woman? Far and from the uttermost coasts is the price of her." (*Prov.* 31:10). What, then, shall we do to acquire courage, which is of such importance and which is no less difficult than the other virtues?

We must first reflect upon the priceless merit of courage, for a quality which helps us acquire all virtues must be inestimable in value.

Men are chiefly driven from the practice of virtue by the difficulties it presents. "The slothful man saith: There is a lion in the way, and a lioness in the roads. The fool foldeth his hands together, and eateth his own flesh, saying: Better is a handful with rest than both hands full with labor and vexation of mind." (*Prov.* 26:13 and *Eccles.* 4:5-6). If, therefore, the obstacles to virtue discourage us and turn us from good, what is more necessary for us than courage? And who will regret any effort to acquire an aid which will strengthen him to conquer the kingdom of virtue, and, after it, the kingdom of Heaven? "From the days of John the Baptist until now the kingdom of heaven suffereth violence, and the violent bear it away." (*Matt.* 11:12). Finally, courage conquers self-love, which gives place to the love of God, or rather God Himself, "for he that abideth in charity abideth in God, and God in him." (*1 Jn.* 4:16).

Stimulate your courage, moreover, by contemplating the fortitude of so many Christians who cheerfully embraced poverty, mortification, humiliations, for love of Christ. Many of them so loved suffering that they sought it as eagerly as the worldling seeks pleasure, or as the merchant seeks gain, preferring poverty to riches, hunger to abundance, labors and the cross to rest and comfort. The Church daily presents for our consideration such heroic souls, not only that we may worthily honor them, but that we may be excited to imitate them.

Consider, too, the greatness of courage, the heroism, displayed by the martyrs. There is no kind of torture or suffering which they did not endure. Some were burned alive; others were torn to pieces by wild beasts; many had their flesh torn from their bodies with red-hot pincers; some were cast into caldrons of boiling oil; others were compelled to walk barefoot on burning coals, or were tied to the tails of wild horses and dragged through thickets and briars or over sharp stones. It would be almost impossible to enumerate all the tortures invented by the malice of devils to conquer the courage of the servants of God. We read of a martyr in Nicodemia who was scourged so cruelly that every blow brought away a piece of the flesh, leaving the bones exposed to view, and into these cruel wounds the executioner poured salt and vinegar; and, finding that life was not yet extinct, they laid the mangled body upon a slow fire, turning it from side to side with iron hooks until the soul took its flight to God. Read the lives of those brave soldiers of Christ, and your courage will be reanimated; you will grow ashamed of the little you have done for God or your soul.

They were human as well as we are. Their bodies were as

sensitive as ours to sufferings. They had the same God to assist them; they hoped for the same reward to which we aspire. If eternal life cost them so much, shall we refuse to mortify the irregular desires of the flesh to attain this blessed end? Shall we not have the courage to fast one day, when we see them almost dying of hunger? Shall we refuse to remain for a short time on our knees in prayer, when they continued to pray for their enemies during long hours of agony, even when nailed to the cross? Shall we refuse to resist our inclinations and passions, when they unhesitantly abandoned their bodies to the tortures of the executioner? They endured without murmuring the solitude and suffering of dark prisons, and shall we refuse our soul a few moments solitude in prayer each day to amend the past and to prepare for the future. If they submitted their bodies to the rack, to the wheel, to fire and the sword, shall we refuse to chastise ours for the love of Christ?

If these examples do not move you, lift your eyes to the cross and contemplate Him who hangs there in torments for love of you. "Think diligently," says the Apostle, "upon him that endured such opposition, that you be not wearied, fainting in your minds." (*Heb.* 12:3).

It is a marvelous example in every respect. For if we consider His sufferings, none could be greater; if we consider the Victim, none could be more noble; if we consider the motive, it was the highest degree of love; for He who was Innocence itself suffered and died to redeem us from our iniquities. The heavens were filled with awe at the spectacle; the earth trembled; the rocks were rent; all nature was moved.

Will man alone be insensible and refuse to imitate the example which God came on earth to give? Shall we be so ungrateful, so slothful, so presumptuous as to wish to win Heaven by a life of luxurious ease when suffering and labor were the portion of God on earth and of all His followers?

Hear the words in which St. Paul describes the sufferings of those faithful servants of Christ, the prophets, the Apostles, the martyrs, the confessors, the virgins, and all the saints: "Others had trial of mockeries and stripes, moreover also of bands and prisons. They were stoned; they were cut asunder; they were tempted; they were put to death by the sword; they wandered about in sheepskins, in goatskins, being in want, distressed, afflicted: of whom the world was not worthy; wandering in deserts, in mountains, and in dens, and in caves of the earth." (*Heb.* 11:36-38). If such were the lives of the saints and of Him who was the Saint of saints, what reason have you to think that you can reach Heaven by the way of pleasure and amusement? If you would share their glory, you must participate in their labors. If you would reign with them in Heaven, you must suffer with them on earth.

May these considerations reanimate your courage, dear Christian, and stimulate you to follow, as far as your grace will enable you, such bright examples.

We cannot, therefore, better conclude this work than in the words of Our Saviour: "If any man will come after me, let him deny himself, and take up his cross daily and follow me." (*Lk.* 9:23). In this brief counsel you will find a summary of His divine doctrine, and the secret of attaining the perfection taught in the Gospel. Thus, while the body may be a prey to hardships and labors, the soul will enjoy a paradise of peace, and this interior sweetness will enable you cheerfully to embrace all the sufferings of the exterior life.